Yorkshire VCs

Yorkshire VCs

Alan Whitworth

With additional material by
Max Arthur

Pen & Sword
MILITARY

First published in Great Britain in 2012 by
PEN & SWORD MILITARY
An imprint of
Pen & Sword Books Ltd
47 Church Street
Barnsley
South Yorkshire
S70 2AS

ISBN 978-1-84884-778-1

Typeset by Concept, Huddersfield, West Yorkshire.
Printed and bound in England by CPI Group (UK) Ltd, Croydon, CR0 4YY.

Pen & Sword Books Ltd incorporates the imprints of Pen & Sword Aviation,
Pen & Sword Family History, Pen & Sword Maritime, Pen & Sword Military,
Pen & Sword Discovery, Wharncliffe Local History, Wharncliffe True Crime,
Wharncliffe Transport, Pen & Sword Select, Pen & Sword Military Classics,
Leo Cooper, The Praetorian Press, Remember When, Seaforth Publishing and
Frontline Publishing.

For a complete list of Pen & Sword titles please contact
PEN & SWORD BOOKS LIMITED
47 Church Street, Barnsley, South Yorkshire, S70 2AS, England
E-mail: enquiries@pen-and-sword.co.uk
Website: www.pen-and-sword.co.uk

Contents

Dedicated to my late father
Sgt Peter G. Whitworth
who proudly served with the
92nd Argyll & Sutherland Highlanders Regiment

Foreword

By Brian Best, Editor,
Journal of the Victoria Cross Society

It has become increasingly popular for local historians to write about the men with local connections who have been awarded the Victoria Cross. This is a most laudable undertaking, for it reflects a pride in recognising this elite group of heroes in the context of a particular region. This book covers those heroes with a connection with Yorkshire: a total that is approximately 8 per cent of all the Victoria Crosses awarded – a truly significant number and one well worth acknowledging.

It is more than 150 years since the first group of VCs was announced in the *London Gazette* of 24 February 1857. The first investiture took place in Hyde Park on 26 June 1857, the largest royal event to that date to have been staged, when sixty-two men received their Crosses from Queen Victoria. The very first local recipient was fourteenth in line, Bombardier Thomas Wilkinson, born and bred in York. The most recent VC, Corporal Bryan Budd, also has Yorkshire associations, but sadly his award was posthumous. In between, there is an impressive roll-call of gallantry, and the author is to be congratulated for his work in highlighting this select band of regional heroes.

THE VICTORIA CROSS SOCIETY

Kintons, Harlequin Place, Crowborough, East Sussex TN6 1HZ
Tel: 01892 664234 e-mail: secretary@victoriacrosssociety.com

Preface

The year 2006 witnessed the 150th anniversary of the instigation of the Victoria Cross, by royal warrant dated 29 January 1856, 'the most democratic and at the same time the most exclusive of all' military honours awarded for courage in the face of the enemy, regardless of class, race or creed. The following year saw the 150th anniversary of the first investiture of the Victoria Cross, when sixty-two men received their medals from Queen Victoria in Hyde Park on 26 June 1857. Sailor Charles David Lucas, First Mate of HMS *Hecla*, was the very first Victoria Cross winner in the three centuries of its existence. Interestingly, the year 2012 recognises 100 years of British naval heritage, a century since the modern Royal Navy was formally established.

The Victoria Cross was originally conceived as an award for all ranks of the Navy and Army who, in the presence of an enemy, had performed some signal act of valour or devotion to their country,[2] but over time the conditions of award and scope for receipt have been extended to include virtually every citizen, including civilians and women. From its inception, the actual decoration was deliberately intended to be intrinsically 'worthless', simply a scrap of bronze without rich gems or precious metals. Its true worth lay in its associations, and it was an honour so rare that it was impossible to 'buy' or 'earn' it in the way several other high awards could be acquired. Though no specific comment on the medal's intrinsic lack of value was made in the inauguration warrant, this was the theory behind its creation, exemplified in spirit by a clause which stated that 'neither rank, nor long service, nor wounds, nor any other circumstance or condition whatsoever, save the merit of conspicuous bravery' should 'establish a sufficient claim to the honour'. This condition thereby placed 'all persons on a perfectly equal footing in relation to eligibility for the decoration' – the nearest thing to a completely democratic award ever created within the annals of military and naval history. This aspect was confirmed by the elective procedure laid down in those cases where a number of 'equally brave and distinguished persons' had been thought worthy of the honour. The names submitted to the sovereign were to be chosen by their fellow men taking part in the action concerned.

Its recipients were to bear no special privilege of knighthood, companionage, banners or robes, and the award contains no ranks within itself. It is not an 'order of chivalry', such as the Garter or the Bath, as it was once erroneously described by King Edward VII – a point that its founder, Queen Victoria, was at pains to draw attention to; it was simply a decoration 'to be highly prized and eagerly sought after by the officers and men of Our naval and military services'.

Pensions were granted to all holders of the Victoria Cross below commissioned rank. Initially a pension of £10 per year was made payable to all non-commissioned ranks. In July 1898 it was decided this amount might be increased in times of need, at discretion, to £50 and later to £75. It was not until 1959 that the pension was allowed irrespective of rank and increased to £100. In 1995 it was increased to £1,300, at which time there were thirty-three recipients still alive.

The 1856 warrant also provided for the expulsion of a holder if 'convicted of Treason, Cowardice, Felony or of any infamous Crime, or if he be accused of any such offence and doth not after a reasonable time surrender himself to be tried for the same'. Liability to expulsion lasted for life, not just for the period of service, but the sovereign retained the right to restore the award. It has been forfeited on eight occasions.

The first man to forfeit the Victoria Cross was Edward St John Daniel, who took to drink and became dissolute. He was arrested on 21 June for sodomy with four subordinate officers. The Admiralty stated that he was 'accused of a disgraceful offence' and had deserted to evade inquiry. The alleged desertion appears to have been engineered by his captain and the Admiral of the Mediterranean Fleet to avoid unwelcome revelations at a court martial. Daniel fled to New Zealand, where he served with the Armed Constabulary Field Force; he died in 1868 during Fenian disturbances among the Irish gold miners.

Others were erased from the register of holders after convictions ranging from the theft of ten bushels of oats to bigamy. Colour Sergeant Edmund Fowler of the Royal Irish Regiment faced forfeiture after conviction for embezzlement in 1887. He had been awarded his VC for his actions while serving as a private with the Cameronians in March 1879, after storming and clearing a cave sheltering armed Zulus who had just shot dead his officer. When the Secretary of State sought the Queen's permission to erase Fowler's name from the register, her secretary replied that she could not bring herself to approve it. Fowler had distinguished himself in earning the Cross and, as his sole punishment was reduction to the ranks, it appeared that his offence could not have been so serious: 'He is still considered fit to serve the Queen, and Her Majesty thinks he should retain his VC.' And so he did.

Those who forfeited the VC were also required to surrender the decoration itself. The Treasury Solicitor cautioned the War Office in 1908 that this was illegal, as the medal remained the property of the recipient. The War Office response was a catch-22 solution. It would return forfeited Crosses if the recipients applied for them, but it would not inform them that they could do so. King George V ended the affair. His secretary wrote in 1920, 'The King feels so strongly that, no matter the crime ... the decoration should not be forfeited. Even were a VC to be sentenced to be hanged for murder, he should be allowed to wear the VC on the scaffold.'

This came much too late for Private Valentine Bambrick of the 60th Rifles. Having taken his discharge from the Army at Aldershot in 1863, he was celebrating his new freedom in a local pub when he discovered Commissariat Sergeant Russell hitting a woman in an upstairs room; Bambrick intervened and gave him a thorough beating. Russell brought a charge of assault against Bambrick and accused him of stealing his medals. The woman, the only witness, disappeared. Russell and his cronies testified convincingly, and Bambrick was sentenced to three years in Pentonville. Mortified by this injustice and by the erasure of his name from the VC register, Bambrick was distraught at having to forfeit his Cross, unlawful though the measure was. He was found hanged in his cell on 1 April 1864, three months after his jailing. A note expressed his despair at the loss of his award. Private Bambrick was buried in an unmarked felon's grave.

There were no further erasures after 1908, and the names of the eight men who forfeited their awards have been restored to the register of holders. The present warrant still provides for the cancellation and annulment of an award and the removal of the recipient's name, but it seems unlikely that this will ever happen.

Exploitation of the VC for gain, while not technically misconduct, was considered discreditable and remains virtually unheard of. Piper George Findlater of the Gordon Highlanders was awarded his VC for gallantry in the 1897 Tirah Campaign in India. Although shot in both feet during the charge on 20 October and in great pain, he sat erect under heavy fire and continued playing *Cock o' the North*. He was decorated by the Queen at Netley Hospital. His deed became renowned, and he was engaged to play the march on stage at London's Alhambra Theatre for £30 a week – an amount far in excess of his army pay. Some disapproving officers clubbed together to stop the performances, and General Sir Evelyn Wood, in full dress uniform, visited Dundas Slater, the theatre manager, and offered to pay Findlater's salary if the act were cancelled. Slater laughingly refused, saying he had already spent £300 on advertising.

Since the original warrant of 1856, several other warrants have been issued modifying or extending its provisions. In 1858, for instance, Queen Victoria decreed that the Cross could be awarded to those who performed 'acts of conspicuous courage and bravery . . . in circumstances of extreme danger, such as the occurrence of a fire on board ship, or of the foundering of a vessel at sea, or under any other circumstances in which . . . life or public property may be saved'. In 1881 a new Victoria Cross Warrant was signed that stated, 'Our Will and Pleasure is that the qualification [for the award] shall be conspicuous bravery or devotion to the country *in the presence of the enemy*' – but for this stipulation, there would have been no need for the institution of the George Cross.

In 1902 Edward VII approved the important principle of awarding the VC posthumously. In 1911 King George V admitted native officers and men of the Indian Army to eligibility and by a lengthy warrant dated 22 May 1920 it was further extended to include the Royal Air Force, and 'matrons, sisters, nurses . . . serving regularly or temporarily under the orders, direction or supervision of the military authorities', emphasising, however, that it 'shall only be awarded for most conspicuous bravery or some daring or pre-eminent act of valour or self-sacrifice or extreme devotion to duty in the presence of the enemy'.

Queen Victoria herself chose the design for the new decoration: a cross patée in bronze, bearing the royal crest in its centre surmounting a scroll bearing the inscription 'For Valour'. It is connected by a V-shaped link to a bar engraved on the face with laurel leaves, and having a space on the reverse for the recipient's name. The date of the deed for which the honour is bestowed is engraved on the back of the Cross itself. It is worn on the left breast suspended from a 1½-inch wide ribbon. Initially, the medal was suspended on a royal blue ribbon for naval personnel and a red ribbon for army recipients, but by royal warrant dated 22 May 1920 it was decreed that henceforth all Victoria Crosses would be hung from a plain crimson ribbon, irrespective of the recipient's parent service.

The Cross itself measures little more than 1 inch square (35mm) and weighs nearly 1 ounce (27 grams),[3] calculated so that twelve finished medals together weigh 10–11 ounces.[4] All Victoria Crosses are cast in bronze from metal melted down from the cascabels of cannon captured from the Russians at Sebastopol in the Crimean War. (The cascabel is a large knob at the rear of the cannon to which ropes were tied in order to manhandle the gun.) They are fashioned by the London firm of Messrs Hancock, who made the very first Victoria Cross and have continued to do so. The last remaining cascabel is tended by 15 Regiment, Royal Logistic Corps at Donnington. Because they are cast and chased, no two Victoria Cross medals are exactly alike, and it seems fitting that each uniquely gallant act should be honoured by a decoration that itself remains unique.

Although the royal warrant instituting the Victoria Cross was not issued until January 1856, the earliest deed to merit the award was performed nineteen months earlier, on 21 June 1854, by Irishman Charles Davis Lucas, the twenty-year-old mate of HMS *Hecla*, during an attack on the fortress of Bomarsund in the Baltic. A live shell with its fuse still hissing landed on the deck of the *Hecla* from a Russian battery. Despite orders to take cover, Lucas calmly picked up the shell with his bare hands and threw it overboard; it exploded as it entered the sea, but the ship and crew were saved from certain destruction. Lucas was promoted to lieutenant on the spot by his commanding officer and eventually rose to the rank of rear admiral. Lucas was awarded the very first Victoria Cross, but he left it on a train with his other medals and it was never recovered; a replacement had to be made but was never inscribed.

On the morning of 26 June 1857 Queen Victoria held the first investiture ceremony for the newly instituted decoration that bore her name. Some sixty-two recipients who had been 'gazetted' – their names and deeds cited in the *London Gazette* – were present in Hyde Park, London, for the occasion. In keeping with the democratic spirit of the award, all the recipients stood shoulder to shoulder, regardless of rank, while the Queen, on horseback, presented the decoration to each man.

Today the Victoria Cross remains the supreme British award, taking absolute precedence over all other awards and decorations. In the 160 years of the medal's existence, the British sovereign has made 1,357 awards. Of these, 633 were won in the First World War, and 182 in the Second World War. These totals include three awards of a Bar to the VC – in effect, 'double VCs'. At the time of writing (2011), just twelve holders of the Victoria Cross are still alive, including one 'northern' recipient. It is an exclusive company, whose only membership criteria is courage.

On that register of brave men the reader will find listed the names, dates and deeds of fewer than one hundred men from Yorkshire. Some were born in this county, others lived or died there, or played a significant role in northern life. Within this group of Yorkshire Victoria Cross recipients are a number of 'firsts': for instance, a northern soldier was among the party credited with capturing the original Russian cannon from which all the early Victoria Crosses were cast; Second Lieutenant Richard Annand gained the first VC of the Second World War; and Colour Sergeant Major Stanley Hollis was the only man to be awarded a VC during the D-Day landings on 6 June 1944. Temporary Second Lieutenant Donald Bell was the only English professional football player to receive the VC; likewise, Temporary Second Lieutenant John Harrison was the only professional Rugby League player to gain the award.

Notes

1. This figure is made up of the following: 1,357 individuals; three double VCs; one VC to an unknown American soldier.
2. At this time there was no Royal Air Force (or indeed aeroplanes!).
3. Information supplied by Brian Best, Victoria Cross Society.
4. J. Glanfield, *Bravest of the Brave: The Story of the Victoria Cross* (Sutton Publishing, 2005).

Acknowledgements

I should like to record here the generous assistance I have received from various people and organisations in the preparation of this book, in particular John Blake for allowing the extensive use of text from *Heroes; The True Story Behind Every VC Winner Since World War Two* by Nigel Cawthorne (2007); Roger Dowson of Beck Isle Museum, Pickering; Mr Brian Best of the Victoria Cross Society for his invaluable help; the Victoria Cross and George Cross Association; Rupert Harding and Sarah Cook for their editorial guidance in the preparation of this book; and lastly to the staff at Pen & Sword Books for their excellent production skills.

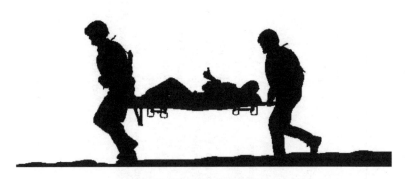

AUTHOR'S APPEAL

FROM THE SALE OF THIS BOOK I SHALL MAKE A DONATION
TO THE CHARITY **HELP FOR HEROES** PERHAPS YOU
TOO WOULD LIKE TO SUPPORT THE WORK OF THE
CHARITY **HELP FOR HEROES** IF SO PLEASE SEND YOUR
DONATIONS DIRECT BY TELEPHONE TO **01725 514 130**
OR TEXT 'HERO' TO **70900** TO DONATE £5* (+ Standard Network Charge)
Registered Charity No. 1120920
Help for Heroes, Unit 14, Downton Business Centre, Salisbury, Wilts SP5 3RB

British Army Campaigns 1660–2001

Dates	War	Campaigns	Medals awarded
1660–84	Against the Moors	Tangier	
1685	Monmouth Rebellion		
1689	Scottish		
1689–91	Against James II	Ireland	
1690–97	War of the Grand Alliance	Low Countries	
1701–13	War of Spanish Succession	Low Countries, Spain	
1715	Against the Old Pretender	Scotland	
1739–42	War of Jenkins' Ear	South America	
1741–48	War of Austrian Succession	Flanders, Germany, India, North America	
1745–46	Against the Young Pretender	England, Scotland	
1756–63	Seven Years War	Germany, Canada, West Indies, India, Mediterranean	
1771–1819	Maharatta Wars	India	1st India Medal (17 bars)
1776–83	American War of Independence	North America, West Indies, Gibraltar	
1793–1815	Napoleonic Wars	Low Countries, Mediterranean, Egypt, South America, Portugal–Spain, India, South Africa, Waterloo	Gold Medals and West Indies Cross (officers only) Seringapatam Medal Military General Service Medal (GSM 23 bars – sanctioned 1847) Waterloo Medal
1812–14	American War	North America	Military GSM (3 bars)
1814–16	Nepalese War		1st India Medal (bar)
1824–26	First Burma War		1st Burma Medal
1824–31	Ashanti War	West Africa	
1834–35	Kaffir War	South Africa	Medal for South Africa

Years	Campaign	Location	Medal
1839–42	First Afghan War		Medal for Capture of Guznee
			Jellalabad Medal
			Kandahar, Guhznee & Cabu Medal
			Medal for Defence of Kelat-I-Ghilzie
1841–42	First China War		China Medal
1843	Subjugation of Sinde	India	Sinde Medal
1843	Gwalior Campaign	India	Star for Gwalior Campaign
1845–46	First Sikh War	India	Medal for Sutlej Campaign (4 bars)
1846–47	First Maori War	New Zealand	New Zealand Medal
1846–47	Kaffir War	South Africa	Medal for South Africa
1848–49	Second Sikh War	India	Punjab Medal (3 bars)
1850–53	Kaffir War	South Africa	Medal for South Africa
1852–52	2nd Burmese War		India GSM (1854) (1 bar)
1854–56	Crimean War		Crimea Medal (4 bars)
1856–57	Persian War		India GSM (1854) (1 bar)
1857–58	Indian Mutiny		Indian Mutiny Medal (5 bars)
1857–60	Second China War		China Medal
1860–70	2nd/3rd Maori Wars		New Zealand Medal
1863	Umbeyla Expedition	India	India GSM (1854) (1 bar)
1866	Fenian Raid	Canada	Canada GSM (1899) (1 bar)
1867–68	Abyssinian Expedition		Abyssinian Medal
1870	Red River	Canada	Canada GSM (1899) (2 bars)
1870–80	Minor Expeditions	Bhutan, Looshai, Jowaki, Nagaland	Each a Bar to India GSM (1854)
1873–74	Ashanti War	West Africa	Ashanti Medal
1877–79	Zulu War	South Africa	Medal for South Africa (6 bars)
1878–80	2nd Afghan War		Medal for Afghanistan (6 bars)
			Kabul to Kandahar Star
1880–81	Basutoland/Transkei		Cape of Good Hope GSM (2 bars)
1881	First Boer War		
1882	Egyptian Campaign		Egyptian Medal (2 bars), Khedive's Star
1884–89	Sudan Campaign		Egyptian Medal (11 bars)

Dates	War	Campaigns	Medals awarded
1882–92	Operations NE Frontier of India and Burma	Burma (1887–89), Hazara (1888), Chin-Lushai (1889–90), Burma (1889–92), Lushai (1889–92), Samana (1891), Hazara (1891), Hunza (1891), NE Frontier (1891), Chin Hills (1892–93), Kachin Hills (1892–93)	Each a bar to India GSM (1854)
1885	Van Riel's Rebellion	Canada	North-West Canada Medal (1 bar)
1885–87	2nd Burmese War	India	India GSM (1854) (1 bar)
1888	Sikkim Campaign		India GSM (1854) (1 bar)
1891–98	Central Africa		Central Africa Medal (1 bar)
1893	Matabele War	East Africa	Chartered Company of South Africa Medal (2 bars)
1894–95	Waziristan Campaign	India	India GSM (1854) (1 bar)
1895	Chitral Campaign	India	India GSM (1854) (2 bars)
1895–96	3rd Ashanti War	West Africa	Ashanti Star
1896–97	Rhodesia		Chartered Company of South Africa Medal (2 bars)
1896–97	Expeditions in Nigeria	West Africa	Royal Niger Company's Medal (1 bar)
1896–98	Sudan		Sudan Medal
1897–98	Indian Frontier Expeditions	Malakand (1897), Samana (1897), Punjab (1895), Frontier (1897–98), Tirah (1897–98)	Each a bar to India Medal (1895)
1897–98	Operations in Uganda & Somaliland		East & Central Africa Medal (3 bars)
1899–1902	Second Boer War	South Africa	South Africa Medal (Queen's) (28 bars) King Edward's South Africa Medal (2 bars)
1900	Boxer Rebellion	China	China Medal (3 bars)
1900–20	Numerous small Expeditions in East and West Africa		Africa GSM (1902) (43 bars)

1901	Ashanti Rebellion	West Africa	Ashanti Medal (1 bar)
1901–02	Waziristan	India	India Medal (1895) (1 bar)
1903–04	Tibetan Expedition		Tibet Medal (1 bar)
1906	Zulu Rising	South Africa	Medal for Zulu Rising in Natal (1 bar)
1908	NW Frontier of India		India GSM (1908) (1 bar)
1911–12	Abor Expedition	NE Frontier of India	India GSM (1908) (1 bar)
1914–18	First World War	France/Flanders, S West Africa, S East Africa, China, Dardanelles, Egypt, Palestine, Mesopotamia, Salonika, Italy, Russia, NW Frontier India	1914 Star 1914–15 Star British War Medal Victory Medal India GSM (1908) (1 bar)
1919	3rd Afghan War		India GSM (1908) (1 bar) GSM (1919) (5 bars)
1919–20	Russia		
1919–20	Mahsud Expedition		
1919–21	Arab Insurrection	Mesopotamia	
1919–21	Ireland		
1919–21	Waziristan		India GSM (1908) (1 bar)
1921–22	Malabar Rebellion		India GSM (1908) (1 bar)
1930–31	Waziristan		India GSM (1908) (1 bar)
1930–32	Burma		India GSM (1908) (1 bar)
1933	Mohmand Expedition		India GSM (1908) (1 bar)
1935	NW Frontier of India		India GSM (1908) (1 bar)
1936–39	Arab Rebellion	Palestine	GSM (1918) (1 bars)
1936–39	NW Frontier of India		India GSM (1936) (2 bars)
1939–45	Second World War	Norway, France, Flanders (1939–40), East Africa (1940–41), North Africa (1940–43), Greece/Crete (1941), Hong Kong (1941), Iraq/Syria (1941), Malaya/Singapore (1941–42), Burma (1942–45), Sicily/Italy (1943–45), NW Europe (1944–45)	1939–45 Star, Africa Star, Italy Star, Pacific Star, Burma Star, France & Germany Star, Atlantic Star, Defence Medal, Victory Medal

Dates	War	Campaigns	Medals awarded
1945–46	South-East Asia	Indo-China, Dutch East Indies	GSM (1918) (1 bar)
1945–48	Palestine		GSM (1918) (1 bar)
1948–60	Malaya		GSM (1918) (1 bar)
1950–53	Korean War		Korean Medal, UN Service Medal
1952–56	Mau Mau Rebellion	Kenya	Africa GSM (1 bar)
1954–60	Cyprus		GSM (1918) (1 bar)
1956	Suez Expedition		GSM (1918) (1 bar)
1957–59	Muscat & Oman		GSM (1918) (1 bar)
1962	Brunei Revolt		GSM (1918) (1 bar)
1963–66	Borneo Campaign		GSM (1962) (3 bars)
1964–65	Cyprus	UN Peacekeeping Duty	UN Peacekeeping Medal
1964–67	Aden/Radfan		GSM (1962) (2 bars)
1969–2007	Northern Ireland		GSM (1962) (1 bar)
1979	Zimbabwe		Zimbabwe Medal
1982	Falklands War		South Atlantic Medal
1983–84	Lebanon	Multi-national Force	GSM (1962) (1 bar)
1990–91	Gulf War		Gulf War Medal
1992–95	Bosnia & Herzegovina		UN & NATO Medal
1994	Rwanda		UN Medal
1999	Sierra Leone		
2001–	Afghanistan		UN Medal

Complete List of Yorkshire Victoria Cross Holders

AARON, Arthur Louis
ALLEN, William Barnsley
ANDERSON, Eric
ATKINSON, Alfred
BELL, Donald Simpson
BEST-DUNKLEY, Bertram
BRYAN, Thomas
BUTLER, William Boynton
CALVERT, Laurence
CHAFER, George William
COOPER, Edward
COVERDALE, Charles Henry
CUNNINGHAM, John
DANIELS, Harry
DRESSER, Tom
EDWARDS, Wilfred
ESMONDE, Eugene Kingsmill
FIRTH, James
GLENN, J.A., see SMITH, James
GRANT, Robert
HACKETT, William
HARPER, John William
HARRISON, John
HEDGES, Frederick William
HILL-WALKER, Alan Richard
HIRSCH, David Philip
HOLLIS, Stanley Elton
HOLMES, Joel
HUGHES, Matthew
HULL, Charles

INGHAM, Samuel, see
  MEEKOSHA, Samuel
INSALL, Gilbert Stuart Martin
JACKSON, Thomas Norman
LAMBERT, George
LOOSEMORE, Arnold
McKAY, Ian John
McKENNA, Edward
McNESS, Frederick
MAGENNIS, James Joseph
MAUFE, Thomas Harold
  Broadbent
MEEKOSHA, Samuel
MORRELL, T., see YOUNG,
  Thomas
MOUNTAIN, Albert
MOYNIHAN, Andrew
NAPIER, William
NICHOLLS, Henry
ORMSBY, John William
PEARSON, John
POULTER, Arthur
PROCTER, Arthur Herbert
RAYNES, John Crawshaw
RIDGEWAY, Richard Kirby
SANDERS, George
SANDFORD, Richard Douglas
SHEPHERD, Albert Edward
SHEPHERD (SHEPPARD), John
SHORT, William Henry

SMITH, James Alexander Glenn
SYKES, Ernest
SYMONS, George
TRAYNOR, William Bernard
WALLER, Horace
WARD, Charles Burley

WHITE, Archie Cecil Thomas
WHITE, Jack
WILKINSON, Thomas
WOOD, Harry Blanshard
WYATT, George Harry

A Brief History of Modern British Campaigns

By Max Arthur

The Crimean War, 1854–1856

During Queen Victoria's long reign (1837–1901), Britain fought only one war against an established European power. In March 1854, standing alongside her traditional enemy France, she declared war on Russia. Although the war ostensibly arose out of a dispute between the Catholic Church and the Russian Orthodox Church over precedence at the holy places of Jerusalem and Nazareth, the real causes lay deeper. Tsar Nicholas I wanted to increase Russia's power and his most obvious area of expansion was south towards the Turkish Dardanelles, which would give the Russian fleet access to the Mediterranean and a port that would not freeze up in the winter. Britain, intent on maintaining her own domination of the Mediterranean, feared that the Russians might take control of Constantinople. France was equally wary of Russia and keen to make her own territorial gains. Turkey, the 'sick man of Europe', merely wanted to keep hold of her existing territory.

At the time the Ottoman Empire controlled Palestine, Egypt and a large portion of the Middle East. Sultan Abdul Medjid I, the Muslim ruler of Turkey, was thus able to grant privileges to the rival Christian churches, allowing them to protect the holy places under his jurisdiction, and he now came under pressure from France and Russia to allocate them. The French threatened military action against him if he did not offer them rights over the Church of the Holy Sepulchre in Jerusalem, while the Russians threatened to occupy Moldavia and Wallachia if he did. With nowhere to turn, the Sultan foolishly gave his word to both the French and the Russians. When his deception was discovered, the French sent a warship to Constantinople and ships to the Bay of Tripoli, causing the Sultan to accede to their demands in December 1852. The Tsar reacted angrily, mobilising two army corps and sending his ambassador, Prince Menshikov, to Constantinople to demand concessions from Turkey, including a recognition of the Tsar's right to the protectorate of all Orthodox laymen under Turkish rule. The Sultan rejected the Russian demands in May; on 22 June Russia duly invaded Moldavia and Wallachia.

Britain, which viewed Turkey as a buffer against Russian expansion, now felt it necessary to send her Mediterranean Fleet to the Dardanelles, followed by the French, to support her own proposed solution, a promise by the Sultan to protect the Christian religion; this was rejected by Turkey, not least because it did nothing about the occupied territories. The drift towards war had become an irresistible flow. On 4 October the Ottoman Empire demanded that Russia withdraw her troops by the 18th, and then made a formal alliance with Britain and France. Tsar Nicholas was convinced that Britain wanted to avoid war, but he was proved wrong after the Russian fleet defeated the Turkish fleet off the coast of Sinope on 30 November. On 3 January 1854 Britain and France moved their fleets into the Black Sea, and on 27 March declared war on Russia. At first the Allies planned to fight the war in two distinct theatres. A British Expeditionary Force of 27,000 men (four, eventually five, infantry divisions and one cavalry) was sent to the Balkans under the Commander-in-Chief Lord Raglan, an experienced administrator who had lost his right arm at Waterloo, along with the French *Armée de l'Orient* under Marshal de Saint-Arnaud, and at the same time an Allied fleet set sail for the Baltic under the command of Sir Charles Napier, a prickly Scot notorious for his refusal to wear naval uniform.

War in the Baltic, 1854
As Napier's fleet sailed towards the Baltic, its most obvious targets were Sveaborg, the fort protecting Helsingfors (now Helsinki), Bomarsund, a fortress on an island in the middle of the Baltic, and Kronstadt, an island protecting the approaches to St Petersburg. The fleet reached Kronstadt in June, but the Russian navy stayed in port and refused to confront the Allies. There was little that Napier could do. His small force could not effect a landing, and although his naval guns could do no damage at long range, he could not risk his ships approaching any closer and coming under fire themselves. After three days Napier was forced to report to London that an assault was impossible. All his fleet could do was implement a blockade to prevent the Russian fleet from sailing to the Balkans.

On 21 June Bomarsund was bombarded by the steam frigate *Hecla*, under the command of Captain Hall. His action angered Napier, who complained: 'If every Captain when detached chose to throw away all his shot against stone walls, the fleet would soon be inefficient.' The action was notable, however, for the conduct of First Mate Charles Lucas, who picked up a live shell and heaved it overboard. This was the first action for which the Victoria Cross was awarded, and Lucas was immediately promoted to lieutenant.

In August, his fleet reinforced by the arrival of 10,000 French soldiers and marines, and under considerable pressure to achieve some kind of result,

Napier decided to launch a full-scale attack on Bomarsund. The plan was for the fleet to surround the island to prevent the Russian navy from intervening while Allied troops besieged the fortress, which consisted of three round towers and a Great Fort built in a semi-circle. The first landings took place on 8 August, and on the following day two Victoria Crosses were earned by men involved in daring intelligence work on nearby Waldo Island. Within eight days the Russian garrison of 2,000 men had surrendered and the fortress had been reduced, in Napier's words, to 'a heap of ruins'. This first victory excited the British public into believing that the war might be over by Christmas. Napier now set his sights on the fortress of Sveaborg and a plan was formulated for a landing by 5,000 men, but almost at once Napier himself began to have doubts about its feasibility and the French, now suffering from a severe outbreak of cholera, refused to commit so many men to another landing. As the plan dissolved into confusion, Napier's offensive campaign effectively came to an end, although the Baltic blockade continued until October.

Despite having conducted a prudent and reasonably successful campaign, Napier paid the price for not delivering the quick and glorious knock-out blow expected by the British public. On his return to Portsmouth at the end of the year, he was asked to resign his commission.

War in the Balkans, 1854

As the British Expeditionary Force settled down in Constantinople and Scutari in the spring of 1854, the Russians began to suffer a series of defeats at the hands of the Turks and were soon in retreat to the north. By June they had abandoned Moldavia and Wallachia and were retreating towards Bucharest. On the 27th the British Cabinet authorised Lord Raglan to launch an assault on the Russian naval base at Sebastopol. The troops moved to Varna, where they were struck by an epidemic of cholera. Nevertheless, on 7 September they sailed for the ominously named landing point of Calamita Bay, 30 miles north of Sebastopol. Although the men were weakened by the cholera outbreak, the landings, from the 14th to the 18th, were unopposed and together with the French army the British began to march south. The French were on the right of the line, protected by the sea on one flank and the British on the other. At the River Alma they encountered the Russian army led by Prince Menshikov, who had massed his army with ninety-six guns on the high ground above the river. Menshikov, who had been castrated by Turkish gunfire during a previous encounter, was an understandably highly motivated opponent.

The Battle of Alma, 1854

On the morning of 20 September 1854 the Allies advanced along the Causeway, a track that led up a slope towards the heights. The Russians had built a telegraph station (known as Telegraph Hill) on high ground to the west of the Causeway, while to the east stood Kourgane Hill, a key strategic point on which Prince Menshikov had placed his headquarters. The Russians had built two earthworks on the slopes of Kourgane Hill, the Greater and the Lesser Redoubts. The Russian forces were massed across the Causeway. In all, some 36,000 Russian infantry, 3,400 cavalry and 2,500 artillerymen stood against the Allies. Russian batteries covered the hills and the valley between them. Such was the strength of the Russian position that Menshikov informed the Tsar that he would be able to hold it for three weeks.

The Allies decided to launch a pincer movement. The French were to advance along the seashore on the right flank before scaling the cliffs and capturing the heights, while the British were to advance on the centre and left flank. The French made good initial headway, General Bosquet's division duly scaling the cliffs and driving the Russian infantry back, but reinforcements failed to appear and the advance was soon halted, the troops being forced to take shelter near the village of Bourliouk. In the meantime the British were coming under heavy fire. Lord Raglan and his staff moved freely and fearlessly among the men in full view of the enemy. At 3.00pm Raglan gave the order for the infantry to advance. The British troops deployed into a long line, two deep, across a 2-mile front. A Russian captain later wrote, 'We did not think it possible for men to be found with such firmness of morale to be able to attack in this apparently weak formation our massive columns.'

The British crossed the river under heavy fire. On the far side they en-countered steep rocky ground but pressed on. As they approached the Greater Redoubt, the Russian guns, which had been pounding them, were pulled clear to safety, allowing the Light Division to capture the redoubt. It remained vulnerable without reinforcements, so the Scots Fusiliers, the Grenadier Guards and the Coldstream Guards marched forward to relieve the position, while the Highland Brigade pushed forward on their left. The Guards were met by 3,000 Russian troops, whom they mistook for their French allies. The British ceased firing and then, hearing a rogue bugle call, began to retire. As they retreated down the slope, they collided with their advancing comrades. In the chaos, Raglan called up two 9-pounder guns, which opened fire on the Russian positions. The second shot hit an ammunition wagon, which blew up, and the Russian artillerymen retreated, believing themselves to be in more danger than was the case. In the meantime the Highlanders began to regroup on Kourgane Hill, and by 4.00pm the hill had been comprehensively captured and the Russians were in retreat to Sebastopol. The Allied victory was com-plete. Six Victoria Crosses were won during the battle, including four by men of the Scots Fusiliers. For two whole days the Allies tended their wounded and buried their dead. On 23 September they pushed on towards Sebastopol.

The Siege of Sebastopol, 1854

The Allies now had to decide how to attack Sebastopol. Raglan was in favour of an immediate assault on the city (a move that senior Russian officers greatly feared), but the Allies finally settled on a plan submitted by Sir John Burgoyne, the Inspector General of Fortifications, for a formal siege from the south, using Balaklava and Kamiesch as supply bases, and wearing down the defences by prolonged heavy artillery. Sir George Cathcart, commander of the 4th Division and Raglan's proposed successor in the event of his death, felt that an ideal opportunity to take Sebastopol quickly was being wasted. 'I am sure I could walk into it with scarcely the loss of a man at night or an hour before day break,' he wrote to Raglan. Nevertheless, the Allies spent three weeks hauling their guns into position and building breastworks, while on the Russian side two men organised the preparations for the defence of the city: Admiral Kornilov, the naval commander and governor of the city, and Colonel Totleben, an engineering officer. Kornilov oversaw the scuttling of seven Russian warships to form a barrier across the entrance to Sebastopol harbour, while Totleben put together a series of earthwork defences fortified by the guns from the scuttled ships. He began to construct two forts, the Redan and the Malakoff Tower, on separate eastern hills but connected by a system of trenches. Within only thirty-six hours a hundred defensive guns were in position. In the meantime the Russian army was being led into the heart of the Crimea to protect the supply lines to Sebastopol.

The Allied guns finally opened up on Sebastopol on 17 October. British troops believed that within a few days the city would be overrun but this proved to be hopelessly over-optimistic. As the shelling continued apace, Admiral Kornilov was killed, but little permanent impact was made on the Russian defences. Five Victoria Crosses were won in October during the early part of the siege.

The Battle of Balaklava, 1854

As Sebastopol held firm, Menshikov saw an opportunity to attack Balaklava, the base supplying the besieging British army. Balaklava was defended by Royal Marine artillery on the heights outside the town, by six redoubts manned by 4,400 Turkish troops on the Causeway Heights and by a force of Lord Lucan's cavalry and Sir Colin Campbell's 93rd Highlanders overlooking the South Valley. The Causeway Heights looked down on to the North Valley, which was to be the scene of the infamous Charge of the Light Brigade.

At 5.00am on 25 October a large force of Russian troops attacked the Turkish redoubts on the Causeway Heights, taking four of them by 7.30am. The advance guard of Major General Rijov's 6th Hussar Brigade was now closing on Balaklava, with only the Highlanders barring their way. Sir Colin Campbell (a carpenter's son from Glasgow who would doubtless have risen higher than brigadier general had he been of 'better stock') cautioned his men: 'Remember there is no retreat from here. You must die where you stand.' Heeding their commander's words, the Highlanders stood firm against three lusty attacks by the Russian cavalry. *The Times* correspondent William Russell, watching from the heights, described the conduct of the Highlanders:

> The Russians on their left drew breath for a moment, and then in one grand line dashed at the Highlanders. The ground flies beneath their horses' feet; gathering speed at every stride, they dash on towards that thin red streak tipped with a line of steel ... With breathless suspense everyone waits the bursting of the wave upon the line of Gaelic rock; but ere they come within 150 yards, another deadly volley flashed from the leveled rifle, and carries death and terror into the Russians. They wheel about, open files right and left, and fly back faster than they came.

The 'thin red streak tipped with a line of steel' (a phrase coined by Russell and adapted by Tennyson for his 'thin red line') paints a vivid picture of the Highlanders' exploits.

Meanwhile, to the west the Heavy Brigade was neutralising the remainder of Rijov's force in a brief and frantic engagement. Considerable casualties were inflicted by the Heavy Brigade's swords, blunted and weather-rusted though they were, but a great deal more damage was caused by the 24-pounder howitzers brought to bear by the Royal Horse Artillery.

Throughout these actions the Light Brigade had not been called on. Among the lancers themselves, there was a feeling that they ought to have been sent in pursuit of the fleeing hussars. But unbeknownst to them, they were about to be sent on a mission of breathtaking futility.

The Charge of the Light Brigade, 1854
Watching the battle unfold, Lord Raglan was vexed to discover that the Russians were removing abandoned British guns from the redoubts captured from the Turks. He sent Captain Nolan to deliver the following order to Lord Lucan, the commander of the cavalry: 'Lord Raglan wishes the cavalry to advance rapidly to the front, follow the enemy and try to prevent the enemy carrying away the guns. Troop Horse Artillery may accompany. French

cavalry is on y[our] left. Immediate.' Unfortunately, from his position Lucan could not see the redoubts. The only guns that he could see were the twelve guns of the mighty Don Battery, which had earlier been trained on the Turks. An attack on these guns was quite clearly suicidal.

'Attack, sir? Attack what? What guns, sir?' asked Lucan, on receiving the order, to which Nolan flung out his arms in the general direction of the Don Battery and replied: 'There, my lord, is your enemy. There are your guns.' When Lucan passed the order on to his brother-in-law, Lord Cardigan, the commander of the Light Brigade, Cardigan also queried it. 'Allow me to point out that the Russians have a battery in the valley on our front and batteries and riflemen on both sides,' he said. 'I know it,' replied Lucan, 'but Lord Raglan will have it. We have no choice but to obey.'

Cardigan thus carried out what he believed were his orders and led the 632 men of the Light Brigade against the mighty Russian guns. As they moved forward, Captain Nolan, who had received permission to charge with the 17th Lancers in the first line, suddenly rode ahead motioning wildly with his arms. It may be that the true nature of the order had occurred to him and he was attempting to call off the charge. If this were his intention, he had no chance to share it, as he was immediately struck in the chest by a shell splinter and killed. The Heavy Brigade, which had been following the Light Brigade into the charge, was suddenly halted on Lucan's orders, leaving the Light Brigade to continue alone towards the guns. The Russians were astonished at the sight of the cavalry hurtling towards them. A captured British lancer was later asked by a Russian general what he had been given to drink to encourage him to charge in so reckless a fashion. General Bosquet, watching on the heights, remarked, '*C'est magnifique, mais ce n'est pas la guerre.*' In spite of the artillery fire, some of the cavalry did indeed reach the guns, cutting down the Russian gunners with their sabres as they passed them, before confronting the Russian cavalry, positioned to the rear of the artillery. So astonished were these Russian horsemen to be confronted by the Light Brigade that many of them fled, as did a number of the gunners. Before long, however, the Russians returned to their guns, and the remains of the Light Brigade wheeled round and rode back up the valley, pounded by the artillery as they went. The entire event lasted twenty-five minutes, during which time 110 men were killed, 130 were wounded and 58 taken prisoner, with 475 horses lost. The fact that 375 men returned unharmed was considered remarkable, an extraordinary testament to the bravery of the men involved. Nine of the survivors were awarded the Victoria Cross.

The charge marked the end of the Battle of Balaklava. The town itself had not been captured, but the Russians viewed the battle as a significant victory.

Winter was approaching and the Allied supply route had been cut with the loss of the Woronzoff Road. Yet an action described by William Russell in *The Times* as a 'hideous blunder' came to be remembered as a glorious, fearless act of obedience which represented the finest qualities of the British soldier. As Tennyson wrote:

> *When can their glory fade?*
> *O, the wild charge they made!*
> *All the world wonder'd.*
> *Honour the charge they made!*
> *Honour the Light Brigade,*
> *Noble six hundred.*

The Battle of Inkerman, 1854

As the siege of Sebastopol continued, six battalions of Russian infantry supported by four artillery pieces launched an attack on 28 October, which was halted by a unit of the Coldstream Guards led by Major Goodlake, who was subsequently awarded the Victoria Cross. This was merely a prelude to a much larger Russian attack on several fronts, intended to break the siege and rid the Crimea of the Allies before the winter descended. An assault was to be made on the 3,300 men of the 2nd Division and the Guards at Home Ridge; General Soimonov was to lead 19,000 infantry from Sebastopol towards Shell Hill, where he would be joined by 40,000 infantry commanded by General Dannenberg; covering fire would be provided by two Russian warships and by the artillery inside Sebastopol.

The conditions on the morning of 5 November were abysmal. Heavy rain had created a thick layer of mud, and worse still – for both armies – a thick fog lay over the area, restricting visibility to just a few metres. The soldiers involved in hand-to-hand fighting at Shell Hill were oblivious to the larger battle unfolding around them.

The focus of the battle soon settled on the Sandbag Battery, an unimportant earth wall to the right of the British on Home Ridge. This was seized by the Russians, who mistakenly thought it to be an important British position. It soon gained a psychological importance out of all proportion to its worth, and was taken and retaken several times by both sides. The Grenadier Guards captured it at one point (during this fighting three men, including Sir Charles Russell, earned the Victoria Cross), only to abandon it as worthless, yet as soon as the Okhotsk Regiment had walked back into it, the Scots Fusiliers launched an attack to take it back. Allied reinforcements arrived in the form of the formidable North African Zouaves, who succeeded in taking the right flank and putting an end to the fighting for the battery. They were assisted by two British 18-pounder guns, which caused confusion in the Russian positions. The battle wore on for three more hours until eventually the 21st and 88th Foot made a successful attack on the Russian artillery positions, after which General Dannenberg ordered the Russians to retreat. During the battle the Russians had suffered 10,729 casualties, the British 2,457 and the French 763. Certainly, the Russians lost the battle: they failed to take their objectives and suffered enormous casualties. Nevertheless, it was no great victory for the Allies. Raglan was criticised for a lack of effective leadership and it was clear that the Allies were no closer to taking Sebastopol.

Ten days after the Battle of Inkerman hurricane-force winds struck the Crimea, sinking twenty-one British ships in Balaklava harbour. One of these ships, *The Prince*, was carrying a large supply of cold weather clothing and medical supplies, which were desperately needed as the bitter Russian winter began to take hold. The weather was, in fact, to take a terrible toll on the British soldiers, in large part due to the British Army's lamentable lack of facilities and organisation. In total eighteen Victoria Crosses were awarded during this period.

Winter, 1854

The winter of 1854/55 was the coldest in Sebastopol for many years. The Tsar was well aware of its value to the Russians, noting that he had three generals – January, February and March – any of whom could overcome the British Army. The British soldiers were living in appalling conditions even before the cold weather had set in. The wind had forced many to abandon their tents, the rain kept their inadequate uniforms constantly wet and the deep mud infiltrated everything they possessed.

When the freezing weather arrived, life became unbearable. Food was scarce, forcing British troops to go begging to their French counterparts, offering their boots in exchange for something to eat. Lightweight tents and uniforms did not keep out the cold. Frostbite became a deadly enemy as any uncovered piece of the body turned into a sheet of ice. Although thousands of men were dying, supplies were failing to reach the troops. One reason was that the supply line from the harbour at Balaklava was barely functioning: twenty days' forage had been lost in the hurricane, the baggage animals had starved, and provisions arriving at the harbour were left to rot by the quayside. The only route suitable for resupply, the well-built Woronzoff Road, had been lost at the Battle of Balaklava and the alternative tracks were choked with mud, ice, snow and dead animals, making them impassable. Matters were made worse by the stifling bureaucracy and lack of any organised system within the army, which prevented crucial decisions from being made. On 23 December 1854 *The Times* thundered that the army was governed by 'incompetence, lethargy, aristocratic hauteur, official indifference, favour, routine, perverseness and stupidity'. Lord Aberdeen resigned and was replaced as Prime Minister by Lord Palmerston.

Of more immediate concern to the troops were the improvements that were beginning to be made in terms of healthcare. Sidney Herbert, the Secretary of War, had decided to send female nurses into the military hospitals, placing in charge of the operation Florence Nightingale, the manager of 'the Establishment for Gentlewomen during Illness' in Harley Street. She and her charges set out for the Scutari Hospital, where they arrived on 3 November; they found the hospital struggling to cope with poor hygiene, undisciplined staff and limited supplies. Bed linen went unwashed, soap was a rarity and the patients only received a bath every eighty days. Florence Nightingale set about tackling these issues straightaway, instigating a new drainage system and paving the hospital floors, and she kept up an insistent correspondence with Herbert, urging him to treat the bureaucratic paralysis that she found everywhere within the army medical system. In February 1855 the *Illustrated London News* christened her 'The Lady with the Lamp'.

Improvements were made in other areas. Alexis Soyer, the flamboyant ex-chef of the Reform Club in London, came out to the Crimea in February 1855 and immediately set about improving army catering. He improved the preparation of meat, introduced salt and pepper, invented a new type of teapot that prevented tea from stewing, designed a portable cooking stove, and stopped the cooks from throwing away the water in which meat was boiled, turning it instead into a nutritious soup.

Such improvements were welcomed but they came too late. Many more British soldiers were killed by the weather and the lack of military organisation during the Crimean War than were killed by the enemy. Nevertheless five Victoria Crosses were awarded that winter.

Spring, 1855

As the spring thaw began, news arrived of the death of Tsar Nicholas I. He was succeeded by his son Alexander II, who adopted a more liberal approach to home affairs by abolishing serfdom but refused to compromise on his country's stance on the war, declaring that he would 'perish sooner than surrender' in the Crimea. A great deal of diplomatic chess had been played over the winter months but the result was still stalemate. The siege of Sebastopol was to continue but conditions on the ground for the British troops had improved beyond recognition. Huts and medical supplies had started to arrive, as had horses, mules, buffalo and camels, the water supply had been purified, and most positively of all a railway had been built from the harbour at Balaklava to the Allied camps around Sebastopol – in just seven weeks, some 7 miles of track were laid. A visitor to Balaklava in April was 'not prepared to find the harbour in so good a state. All dead animals were towed out to sea, and no pains seemed spared to keep it clean.'

Nevertheless, the Allies were still arguing about tactics. The Russians, under the capable leadership of Totleben, had never ceased fortifying Sebastopol. The batteries were strongly defended and capable of being swiftly repositioned, while a complex network of tunnels had been dug underneath the city. The Russian positions were described as one entrenched camp stretching from Sebastopol harbour towards Balaklava. In response, the Allies dug trenches of their own. Fighting took on a new aspect, in which men crept out of one trench with fixed bayonets to attack enemy soldiers in an adjacent trench. A form of warfare had been born that would reach its climax sixty years later during the First World War.

The first significant action of the New Year took place on 22 February on a hill known as the Mamelon Vert, several hundred metres from the Malakoff Tower, the large stone tower at the heart of the city's defences. Totleben ordered two new redoubts to be built overnight on the Mamelon Vert, merely for the purpose of luring the French into a trap. On the night of 24/25 February the French duly sent 1,400 men to attack the redoubts, only to find the Russians waiting for them. Some 200 French soldiers were killed. A French sap pushed forward towards the Mamelon was bloodily repulsed on the night of 23/24 March, and the Allies determined that no further attacks would be made on Sebastopol until a heavy artillery bombardment had been launched. For ten days, beginning on 9 April, 138 British and 362 French guns bombarded Sebastopol. Every night the Russians repaired the damage caused during the day. It was clear that Totleben's remarkable defences would not wither under an onslaught.

That spring thirteen Victoria Crosses were awarded between February and May.

The Sea of Azov, 1855

Enthusiasm for the war was on the wane in England. The British guns had been of insufficient calibre to make a real impact on the Sebastopol defences and the large numbers of well-trained British soldiers lost over the winter had not been adequately replaced. As a maritime nation, Britain saw sea power as the logical means of victory, and if the Allies could gain control of the Sea of Azov at Kertch, 120 miles away, the supply line into Sebastopol could be cut.

The first Kertch expedition, consisting of British, French and Turkish troops, was aborted as it approached its objective because the ships were needed to bring the French Army of the Reserve from Constantinople. A second attempt began on 22 May 1855. Two days later the Allied troops landed at Kertch and took the town with ease. Although this episode was marred by looting and pillaging, the victory promised much for the Allies. Control of the Sea of Azov meant that a great proportion of the supplies intended for Sebastopol could be destroyed or rerouted.

Six VCs were awarded during this period.

The Quarries, the Redan and the Malakoff Tower, 1855

With control of the supply route secured, the Allies focused once more on the siege. On 6 June 1855 a third great bombardment of Sebastopol by British and French guns began, followed the next day by an attack. Attackers and defenders alike were aware that the key to the Allies taking and holding the city was control of the Malakoff Tower. The plan was that the British would attack an area known as the Quarries, while the French launched another attack on the Mamelon Vert, control of which would place the Allies in prime position to move on the Malakoff Tower. The French captured the Mamelon quickly, and pushed on, believing that they could take the Malakoff Tower, but the Russians counter-attacked, forcing the French from the Mamelon. By the evening they had retaken the Mamelon but had suffered 5,443 casualties in the process. In the meantime the British took the Quarries, suffering 671 casualties.

Buoyed by this success, the Allies planned to capitalise immediately. Raglan and the French commander, General Ainlable Pélissier (who had replaced Canrobert on 16 May), agreed that the French should advance on the Malakoff Tower while the British attacked the Redan. Some 600 Allied guns, supported by naval guns lying offshore, opened fire on the Russian defences on 17 June. It was the fiercest bombardment so far. Yet for some reason Pelissier decided to bring the French attack forward from 8.00am to 3.00am. Raglan was left with no option but to bring the British attack forward to fall in line with the French plans. The night was clear and as the British troops moved into position they were plainly observed by the Russian defenders, who made appropriate preparations. As the French advanced in chaotic formation – one column had mistaken a signal and advanced at 2.00am – they were mowed down by the defenders of the Malakoff. As he watched the fiasco unfold, Raglan felt that he had no option but to send the British forces forward. He explained in a subsequent dispatch that if the British troops 'had remained in our trenches, the French would have attributed their non-success to our refusal to participate in the operation'.

The British attack on the Redan took place under the heaviest fire imaginable. Shell splinters and bullets rained down so heavily on the men that they ran forward over 400 yards of open ground with their heads down as if running into a storm. The attack on both positions was a disastrous failure: the French suffered 3,500 casualties, the British 1,500. Twelve men won the Victoria Cross during the assault on the Redan, many of them for rescuing wounded comrades.

The lack of success began to weigh heavily on Lord Raglan. His health declined rapidly and on 28 June he died, worn out by the pressures he was forced to endure. He was replaced by Lieutenant General Sir James Simpson, who, on receiving the promotion, is supposed to have remarked, 'They must indeed be hard up when they appoint an old man like me.'

The Battle of Tchernaya, 1855

The war was placing a considerable strain on the economies of all the countries involved, but the greatest financial pressure was undoubtedly felt by Russia. The blockades and the loss of imports from Britain and France had taken their toll, while huge loans supplied by European banks were looking increasingly insecure. Alexander II was having to compromise on his pugnacious stance. Yet while he could no longer think in terms of victory at any price, he refused to sanction the possibility of retiring from Sebastopol. Rather, he ordered a decisive attack that, if successful, would put Russia in the strongest possible negotiating position. His plan was to march across the River Tchernaya and capture the Fediukhin Heights, a position held by French and Sardinian troops. The Russian commander, Prince Gorchakov, who had very little faith in the likely success of the attack, produced only an outline plan, giving very general directions to his commanders. To make matters worse, Gorchakov's plan, such as it was, had become common knowledge in St Petersburg and was soon revealed to the Allies.

The attack began before dawn on 16 August and was defeated by 10.00am. Although the Russian troops gained their initial objectives and forced a gap to open between the French and Sardinian forces, this early momentum was quickly lost and the attack dissolved into confusion. Huge Russian casualties outnumbered those of the Allies. Indeed, the Sardinians (who had joined the Alliance in January in the hope of gaining support for a united Italy) lost only fourteen men.

The Second Baltic Expedition, 1855

Once the winter ice had thawed, a second expedition set sail for the Baltic. Led by Rear Admiral Sir Richard Dundas, it was intended to enforce the naval blockade and to mount attacks on the fortresses that Sir Charles Napier had failed to secure. The fleet hydrographer Captain Bartholomew Sulivan, who was undertaking a detailed reconnaissance of the area, advised Dundas firmly that he should not attempt to attack Kronstadt, so he turned his attention to Sveaborg. The Russians had fortified Sveaborg's defences in the year since the last expedition, and they now laid nearly a thousand mines, a recently developed weapon in use for the first time, around the area. On the morning of 9 August the Allied fleet lined up in battle formation 2 miles off shore. The bombardment of the fortress began at 7.00am and continued until the next day. Sveaborg was effectively destroyed as a base for the Russian navy yet throughout this time not a single Allied vessel was hit by Russian guns nor was a single Allied casualty recorded. Once the bombardment subsided, the people of Helsingfors, convinced that an Allied invasion was to follow, hurried to evacuate the city – but no invasion came. The Allies were content that the bombardment should stand as a lesson to the Russians that they could never hope to defeat the Allied navies and that Kronstadt and St Petersburg would be next.

The Fall of Sebastopol, 1855
Following the defeat of the Russian Army at the Battle of Tchernaya, Pélissier gave orders to recommence the bombardment, and eight hundred Allied guns and three hundred mortars began to rain fire on to Sebastopol. By now, the damage was too extensive to be repaired effectively, but Alexander II insisted that there was to be no retreat and Gorchakov was not willing to disobey. However, on 26 August a pontoon bridge linking the south side of Sebastopol to the north side was completed by the Russians, preparing the ground for an eventual evacuation. Pélissier's plan of attack, disclosed to the British on 7 September, once again concentrated its focus on the Malakoff Tower. Some 25,000 French troops were to attack it, while a general advance was to be made along the entire front. Once again the British were to attack the Great Redan, led by the 2nd and the Light Divisions, while the Guards and Highlanders were held in reserve. One lesson had been learnt from the disastrous assault of 18 June: the British were not to attack until they were sure that the French had taken the Malakoff Tower.

The attack began, unusually, at midday on 8 September. The French 1st Division stormed the Malakoff from their trenches only a few yards away. The Russians were taken completely by surprise, and within ten minutes the tower, the key to overall control of Sebastopol, had fallen to the French. Seeing the British white ensign raised above the tower, the 90th and 97th Foot of the British Army charged towards the Redan without even waiting for orders.

Although a very few fought their way into the Redan (including Captain Lumley of the 97th and Sergeant Moynihan of the 90th, who were both awarded the Victoria Cross for their efforts), the vast majority were quickly shot down by a murderous fire from the bastions. They were followed by the 23rd Foot, who were similarly cut down. Before long the British troops began to waver and troops in the salient even refused to advance. The indignity of the episode could have been prevented, many thought, had the Guards and Highlanders been used in the attack, rather than men who had spent so long in the trenches.

Another attack was quickly planned for the following morning, but it never took place. Despite the failure of the British troops, the French capture of the Malakoff Tower convinced Gorchakov that the day was lost. At 5.30pm he ordered a retreat across the pontoon bridge. Riflemen and some of the gun crews remained behind to cover the retreat while for six or seven hours a huge wave of carts, horses and people swarmed across the bridge. As they retreated, the Russians spiked their guns, mined their bastions and detonated their powder stores. The Redan was blown up. Anything that could prove useful to the Allies was destroyed. Finally, when all but the most seriously wounded had retreated, the bridge itself was destroyed. As the dust settled, the British were able to walk into the ruins of the Redan, despite never having captured it. Henry Clifford VC, a captain in the Rifle Brigade, recalled:

> If a few days before I had been told 'on the morning of the 9th September at five o'clock Sebastopol will be in the hands of the Allies and you will stand in the Redan held by the English', I should have said, 'Oh, that will be a proud and happy moment, that will repay us for all we have gone through, even the loss of so many lives, so much suffering and hardship will not have been thrown away in vain!' But no, I stood in the Redan more humble, more dejected and with a heavier heart than I have felt since I left home.

Fifteen Victoria Crosses were awarded for actions in that encounter.

The Garrison at Kars, 1855

On 18 June 1855 the Russian Caucasus Army began a siege of the Turkish garrisons at Kars and Erzerum in Asia Minor. These garrisons were tempting to the Russians, as their capture would give Russia free access to the east. Omar Pasha had spent much of July and August trying to get the Allies' permission to release Turkish troops from the Crimea so that they could be redeployed across the Black Sea. The Turkish Minister of Foreign Affairs stressed that these garrisons were 'the key of the frontiers of Asia' and Britain, ever alert to the threat of Russian expansion in the east, was sympathetic to the Turkish dilemma.

On the morning of 23 September the Russians launched a fierce assault on the defenders of Kars. A bloody contest followed, during which the garrison, led by General Williams and inspired by British officers, managed to repel the Russians, who did not retreat far. They simply returned to their positions and continued the siege. They intensified the blockade and began sending deserters from the garrison straight back in. On the same day a conference of Allied generals agreed to allow Omar Pasha's force to travel across the Black Sea to relieve the city, but he took an agonisingly long time to arrive. In the meantime disease, cold and lack of food all took their toll on the garrison. General Williams had no choice. On 25 November General Muraviev accepted his surrender, but allowed him to lead his men out bearing their arms.

Peace, 1856

The Allies still could not agree on how the war should be pursued. At a meeting in Paris in January 1856 no final strategy was agreed upon: the British argued for an attack on Russian territory on the east coast of the Black Sea, while the French favoured an attack on Kronstadt. Both of these plans came to nothing and the Allied armies sat out another winter in the Crimea. Fortunately it was a mild winter and this time the British, who were now well supplied and living in healthy conditions, fared far better than the French, who lost between 25,000 and 40,000 men from typhus and cholera between January and March 1856.

Despite the loss of Sebastopol, Tsar Alexander II was feeling reasonably confident. He had won a victory at Kars, albeit a minor one, and had begun making plans for a fresh campaign in the spring. The Allies' inertia and the Tsar's confidence were soon undermined, however, by Austria's entry into the fray as a 'broker'. She offered an ultimatum to the Russians, that they should either agree to the Allies' demands or she would enter the war. Boxed into a corner, the Russians agreed to the demands.

On 30 March 1856 the peace treaty that brought an end to the Crimean War was signed in Paris. Crimea was returned to Russia and Kars was returned to Turkey. Moldavia and Wallachia were granted independent national administrations while remaining under Turkish sovereignty. The Black Sea was neutralised and no Russian naval bases were to be maintained on its shores. The Danube was opened up to free navigation and the Turkish Sultan agreed to guarantee the rights of his Christian subjects. A war that had claimed the lives of 500,000 Russians, 100,000 Frenchmen, 100,000 Turks and 22,000 British soldiers came to a formal end with the ratification of the treaty on 27 April.

In January 1856 Queen Victoria had approved the design of the Victoria Cross. It was conceived as a medal that could be awarded to men of any rank within the army and navy who performed an act of conspicuous bravery in the presence of the enemy. The first medals were made from the bronze of two Russian cannon captured at Sebastopol, and the first investiture took place in Hyde Park on 26 June 1857. On that day sixty-two of the 111 men who earned their crosses in the Crimea received their medals in front of an assortment of dignitaries including the Earl of Cardigan (the man who had led the Charge of the Light Brigade) and Sir Colin Campbell (the man whom many thought should have succeeded Lord Raglan). The VC winners were drawn up in single file near a small table on which lay the medals. A royal salute fired from field batteries indicated that Queen Victoria was approaching. She rode forward on horseback, accompanied by Prince Albert, the Prince of Wales and (rather poignantly) the Crown Prince of Russia. One by one, led by Lieutenant Henry Raby RN, these brave men came forward to accept the Victoria Cross from Her Majesty. As the men filed past, she leant down from her charger and pinned a medal on to each proud breast.

The Indian Mutiny, 1857–1858

Although ultimately unsuccessful, the Indian (or Sepoy) Mutiny against colonial rule in India tested Britain's military resources to the limits. The ferocious and sustained uprisings across the north of India, which began in May 1857 and lasted until late 1858, afforded many situations in which British and native soldiers demonstrated extreme courage in the face of the enemy.

Since the establishment of British rule in India, there had been a steady process of Westernisation – a breaking-down of both Hindu and Muslim traditions – which struck at the very heart of Indian life until every aspect of Indian culture and religion was threatened. Lord Dalhousie, Governor and High Commissioner from 1847 to 1856, wanted the way cleared to allow Hindu widows to remarry (the Hindu tradition was for widows to commit suttee [suicide] on their husband's death), and the whole caste system was being systematically dismantled. Feelings were running very high in northern India long before the sepoys (native Indian soldiers) in the Bengal Army found cause to rebel. Throughout British-ruled India there was unrest and a sense of outrage at the British destruction of the national culture, but it was only in the military sector that the Indians were organised enough to take action. It only needed one trigger to set off a full-scale rebellion, and that trigger appeared in the form of a religious taboo. In order to load the newly supplied Enfield rifles, the sepoys had to bite the ends off paper cartridges, which they believed –

rightly or not – were lubricated with pig and cow lard. To touch this with their mouths would be an affront to both Muslim and Hindu alike.

The first trouble arose on 27 February, when the 19th Bengal Infantry refused their new cartridges; the regiment was disbanded and British troops were sent for from Burma. On 24 April eighty-five troopers at Meerut garrison likewise refused to use the cartridges. Their punishment was ten years' hard labour, and on Saturday 9 May they were stripped of their uniforms and clapped in irons. Their comrades were outraged, but waited to strike until the following evening, when most of the British soldiers of the garrison were in their quarters some distance away and their officers were attending church parade, unarmed. Seizing the moment, they massacred most of the British at the garrison, including the women and children. The mutineers were joined by the two native infantry regiments at Meerut, and soon more men hurried to join them, until some 2,000 sepoys advanced on Delhi, leaving a trail of murder, arson, looting and rape in their wake. In an act of defiance against British rule, the ageing Moghul Emperor Bahadur Shah II, who lived in Delhi's Red Fort as a pensioner of the Honourable East India Company, was nominally restored to power.

As the mutineers neared Delhi on 11 May, their ranks were further swelled by sepoys of the city's garrison and some of the civilian population, and there ensued a horrific massacre of British and European men, women and children, and widespread looting and burning of their property and any Christian places of worship. As the mutineers swept through the city, the nine British officers remaining in the arsenal within the Red Fort realised that it would be a prime target for the rebels and made a courageous stand to prevent the arms and ammunition from falling into enemy hands.

The Delhi sepoys deserted as the mutineers assaulted the walls of the fort. Inside, Lieutenant Willoughby had all available guns set up to fire grapeshot at any breach of the courtyard walls, and in consultation with the other officers, decided to blow up the whole arsenal with themselves inside rather than let it be taken. Powder trails were laid ready for firing should the enemy break through into the courtyard. Met first with devastating grapeshot and then with individual rifle fire, the mutineers swarmed over the arsenal walls; after five hours' fierce fighting, Willoughby ordered the powder trails to be fired. Despite there being no real hope of surviving, Conductor Scully volunteered to fire the gunpowder; the resulting massive explosion was heard from 40 miles away, and the forty-foot walls around the arsenal collapsed, burying hundreds in rubble. Scully was killed in the explosion, but Willoughby, along with Lieutenants Raynor and Forrest and Deputy Assistant Commissary John Buckley, miraculously survived and struggled out to the city gates. Sadly Willoughby was killed shortly after their escape by insurgents in a nearby village. Raynor, Forrest and Buckley were all awarded the VC but, since it was not awarded posthumously at this time, the bravery of Scully and Willoughby went un-recognised.

Although deprived of the contents of the arsenal, the mutineers now con-trolled Delhi, and it was around the city that the first major operations of the mutiny were centred. It was a backs-to-the-wall struggle with no help from reinforcements, and unprecedented numbers of the hard-pressed defenders behaved with extraordinary courage.

The Siege of Delhi (1), 1857
Control of Delhi was the key to putting down the rebellion, so all available troops were called in. The Delhi Field Force of 4,000 British, Sikh and Pathan troops, including the loyal remnants of the Meerut garrison, approached the city under command of General Sir Harry Barnard. Sent out to meet them was a force of 30,000 mutineers with thirty guns. They met in battle on 8 June at Badle-ke-Serai. Despite the enemy's vastly superior numbers, good military tactics and leadership, solid discipline and great individual courage prevailed, and the Delhi Field Force was able to occupy the strategically important area of the ridge to the north-west of the city walls. Five Victoria Crosses were awarded for this encounter.

The Spread of Mutiny, 1857
Once the news of the Meerut mutiny reached other garrison towns, insur-rection spread across northern India. In Benares, in the south-east of the Oudh region, Colonel Gordon believed that his Sikh soldiers would stay loyal, but he had misgivings about the native infantry. A disarmament parade was hurriedly planned for the afternoon of 4 June and was under way when a shout came from among the sepoys that they were being disarmed so that the Europeans could shoot them down unopposed. Chaos broke out as the sepoys rearmed themselves, opened fire on the European troops and rampaged through the town, looting, killing and setting fire to buildings. Three VCs were awarded during this action. The mutiny was quashed in a day, but the backlash lasted much longer, and anyone even suspected of mutiny or inciting rebellion was publicly hanged.

The Siege of Delhi (2), 1857
At the ridge the Delhi Field Force, 600 cavalry and 2,300 infantry strong, with just twenty-two field guns, was now led by Colonel Archdale Wilson. Con-stantly attacked by the mutineers in repeated attempts to clear the ridge, the

men of the Field Force held on, despite cholera and battle injuries seriously depleting their strength. Although reinforcements arrived, the Field Force still numbered only 6,600 men by the end of July. Wilson and Nicholson, seeing that disease and injuries would only deplete their numbers further if they did not strike fast, decided to storm the breaches around Delhi on 13 September. During the period while the Field Force held the ridge, an extraordinary sixteen VC awards were made, mostly for the rescue of comrades, with some being decided by ballot.

Rebellions in the South, 1857
Mutiny flared up in Indore on 1 July, when the Maharaja's troops attacked the Residency. Here Colonel James Travers led a five-man charge to drive the rebels from a gun battery, earning the VC. In the far north, in the largely peaceful Punjab region, mutiny broke out at Jhelum on 7 July, in Kolapore in the far south on the 10th and at Oonao on the 29th. These rebellions were quickly suppressed, but the fighting was vicious and five VCs were earned in the three uprisings.

Arrah, 1857
On 25 July the garrison commander at Dinapore in the north-east attempted to disarm the sepoys, but over 2,000 of them escaped to nearby Arrah and besieged the garrison there. Three men of a small force sent to relieve this siege were awarded the VC when their party of just 400 was ambushed outside the town and forced into retreat; only half survived the encounter.

Oudh, 1857
In late July Brigadier General Sir Henry Havelock marched into Oudh with just 1,700 men and twelve field guns. Rebel resistance was spirited, so that, despite initial victories, by the 31st he had lost one-sixth of his original force through battle casualties and disease, ammunition was running low and there was insufficient transport to deal with the wounded. On that day he received the unwelcome news that the much-needed reinforcements he had been expecting had been held up dealing with the rebellion at Bihar. The planned advance to retake Lucknow now seemed unlikely, despite successful actions at Busherut-Gunge on 5 and 12 August (the latter against an enemy force of some 4,000), and Havelock moved back to Cawnpore.

On 14 August Havelock learned that some 2,000 Indians, mutineers from Sagar and some of the Nana's forces had assembled at Bithoor. His troops found the rebels well dug in in front of the Nana's Palace; despite concentrated pounding with heavy guns, the rebels held firm and victory was achieved only after several bayonet charges, during which sixty British soldiers were killed or wounded and twelve died from sunstroke.

Neemuch and Chota Behar, 1857
In mid-August, the garrison of European officers at Neemuch (the most southerly point to which the mutiny extended) remained under siege by a local rebel force which had moved in after the native Bengal troops had abandoned the fort for Delhi.

During September and early October widespread fighting continued to relieve various besieged British strongholds, including Chota Behar, where two Victoria Cross awards were made.

Assault on Delhi, 1857
Chief Commissioner Sir John Lawrence dispatched a mainly Sikh force under the command of Brigadier General John Nicholson, from the relative calm of the Punjab. A dour but ruthlessly effective soldier, Nicholson led from the front and, despite admitting personally to hating the Indians as a nation, he earned the respect and loyalty of all his men through his own example. In the past he had not been averse to blowing mutineers from the mouths of his cannon, and his Mobile Column had been responsible for quashing any potential uprising in the Punjab region. Deemed the ideal man for the job, he set out with three cavalry regiments, seven infantry battalions and a heavy siege engine to strengthen the Delhi Field Force and retake the city.

For Nicholson, contemplating an assault with just 5,000 men on a stronghold of more than 30,000, failure was not an option. The attack was to be launched in five columns, his own being directed to storm the main breach at the Kashmir Bastion. The operation would leave just a handful of troops and the sick to operate the guns and defend the ridge.

On 7 September the chief engineer, Lieutenant Colonel Richard Baird-Smith, began building four powerful batteries to the north of the city. The rebels, who had been expecting a British attack from the west, were taken by surprise, but very soon began raining fire on the unarmed Indian workmen constructing the siege batteries. By 12 September fifty guns and mortars were in place and they opened fire on the walls, causing the rebels to retire from the ruined bastions and take up positions in the open. Nicholson's five columns approached the city walls under cover of darkness on the morning of 14 September. As dawn broke, it became apparent that the mutineers had sandbagged the breaches, so time was lost as the siege guns shot these down. Now in daylight, the parties tasked with storming the walls found that the ladders were too short, and casualties mounted as mounds of anything available, including bodies, were stacked up to support the ladders. A 'forlorn hope' party sent to blow the Kashmir Gate came under heavy fire as the men led by Lieutenant Home moved in to position the gunpowder sacks at the gates, and a second party, led by Lieutenant Salkeld, then followed to tamp down the charges. Several men from these parties were killed, but Sergeant John Smith managed to light the fuses and the right-hand gate was blown off its hinges. With most of the sepoys inside killed or stunned by the blast, the column stormed the entrance and continued, according to plan, to clear the narrow streets of the city.

Fierce hand-to-hand fighting ensued, but the column led by Colonel George Campbell made good progress – so good, in fact, that he feared he had advanced so far as to be in danger of being cut off. He decided to make a tactical withdrawal, which was seen by the mutineers as an opportunity to give chase, and casualties mounted as the retiring troops came under attack. Any wounded men left to be taken by the enemy would be killed with terrible savagery, so every attempt was made to carry out fallen comrades – the heroic rescue by Lance Corporal Smith of a wounded man while under heavy fire earned him the VC. Later in the day Surgeon Reade also received the VC for saving the wounded at a dressing station from certain slaughter as the mutineers stormed the area; two more awards were made, to Sergeant McGuire and Drummer Ryan, who picked up and disposed of two burning cases of ammunition, so averting a massive explosion.

In an error of judgement, the Kashmiri contingent made a premature and unsupported assault, and as they turned and fled, followed by a horde of mutineers, No. 4 column, which was to have entered the city via the Kabul Gate, came under attack from the pursuing enemy. Chaos ensued as the column was driven back towards the ridge, and disaster was only prevented by the cool thinking and decisive action of Lieutenant Robert Shebbeare (later awarded the VC) in rallying a rearguard to cover the withdrawal. Even then, the mutineers surged on and were held off only by the fire of one troop of guns and a thin line of cavalry. British casualties were heavy, as the cavalry, holding their position in defence of the guns but unable to charge due to tangled undergrowth in front of them, were trapped under musket and gunfire.

By the afternoon Nicholson himself was mortally wounded, shot by a sepoy sniper, and about a quarter of the Delhi Field Force who had taken part in the assault were dead or injured, but a quarter of Delhi was back under British control. Wilson assumed command from a position holed up in St James's Church and, after much deliberation, decided to continue the attack. However, his troops had found the city's wine warehouses and soon anaesthetised themselves against the horror of that day and the preceding months by drinking themselves into a stupor. This delayed progress by some thirty-six hours, but the mutineers too seemed to have run out of steam and made no attempt at a counter-attack.

On 16 September the Delhi Field Force resumed the fight, this time with more sustained success. Siege guns supported the assault on the arsenal walls (repaired since the May explosion), and, as a group led by Surgeon Herbert Reade spiked the enemy guns, the Field Force stormed and took control of the arsenal.

The mutineers had now lost 171 guns and a huge supply of ammunition, but launched a final counter-attack, setting fire to a thatched building full of explosives. The actions of two men, Second Lieutenant Thackeray and Lieutenant Renny, in extinguishing the fire, then throwing grenades from the arsenal into the midst of the enemy turned the tide and quashed the attack. Delhi was effectively back under British control.

The reinstated king had fled the Red Fort with his family as the British approached and had taken refuge in a mausoleum outside the city. Wilson sent a party led by Major William Hodson to bring them back. This group was soon surrounded by armed rebels, but Hodson faced them down and persuaded the king and queen to accompany him back to Delhi. He then returned for the rest of the royal party and started to escort two of the king's sons and one grandson, all of whom had joined in the massacre of women and children in the initial assault; the same armed mob threatened to attempt a rescue, at which Hodson summarily shot all three, so removing the mutineers' only remaining figureheads.

The siege of Delhi and the operations to retake it had cost the Delhi Field Force 992 killed and 2,795 wounded, for the loss of a great many more enemy lives. Thirteen VCs were won that day.

The Delhi Field Force, 1857
Columns of troops from the Delhi Field Force were sent out to hound down the scattering groups of mutineers and resistance eventually petered out, despite a few more spirited attempts at defiance, as at Bolandshahr on 28 September, when seven VCs were awarded for what Home later described as 'tolerably sharp action'.

The Siege of Lucknow, 1857
To the east of Delhi lay the Oudh region, where the mutiny found some of its strongest support. Once an independent kingdom, Oudh had been so badly misruled that it was annexed by the Honourable East India Company, effectively wielding administrative power in India on behalf of the British

government. Many of the inhabitants were high-caste Hindus, fiercely pro-
tective of their traditions and way of life, who served in the Bengal Army.
Always resentful of this British intervention, these Hindus sided with the
mutineers and formed the strong core of the mutiny. The centre of activity in
Oudh was the capital, Lucknow, which lay between the River Goomtee to the
east and a canal to the south. The British Residency, like the other important
buildings in the city, was situated by the river and was contained within high
defensive walls.

The Chief Commissioner for Oudh, Brigadier General Sir Henry Lawrence
(brother of Sir John), had foreseen the likelihood of a local rebellion in the wake
of all the events in Meerut and Delhi. He accordingly stockpiled food and
ammunition in the grounds of the Residency against a siege, fortified the
perimeter (even setting up defensive gun positions), and laid plans for evacu-
ating all non-Indians in the city into the Residency in the event of an uprising.
Sure enough, on 30 May the garrison's Indian regiments joined the mutiny,
but they were driven out of the city. As all other British garrisons fell to the
mutineers during June 1857, only Lawrence's fortified Residency offered
resistance and a refuge for the city's European inhabitants.

On 29 June Lawrence received news of enemy forces approaching and sent
out troops to drive them back. The encounter was a disaster for the garrison.
The enemy numbers had been massively underestimated and the British,
hugely outnumbered, were driven into retreat, leaving behind some 200 dead
and losing five guns. The mutineers now closed in around the Residency and
kept it under constant attack. Lawrence himself was killed by a shell on 4 July
and was succeeded by Colonel J.E.W. Inglis, whose robust policy of frequent
aggressive forays kept the enemy's forward positions under pressure. Throughout July, August and September the forays continued, and many more individual acts of bravery were recognised, with Victoria Crosses being awarded to
nine men.

Cawnpore, 1857

In Britain the news of the atrocities against women and children in Meerut,
Delhi and the other fallen garrisons had hit hard, and the relief of the Lucknow
Residency was now paramount.

A mobile column was duly formed, commanded by Brigadier General Sir
Henry Havelock. Consisting of some 1,000 men and six guns, it set out from
Allahabad on 7 July, intending to relieve the besieged garrison at Cawnpore
before marching on Lucknow.

However, on 25 June, the garrison at Cawnpore, having run out of food and
ammunition, had finally sought terms for a surrender. It was agreed that the

British would march out on 27 June, under arms, with sixty rounds of ammunition; carriages would be provided to carry the women, children and infirm to a landing place on the Ganges about a mile from the city, where boats would be ready, and they would then be given safe conduct to Allahabad. A jittery peace prevailed as the embarkation went ahead, but suddenly a shot rang out. The British, on a knife-edge after the three-week siege, opened fire and the Nana's troops replied, so that the boats were set on fire. The sixty men who survived this attack were summarily killed, and the women and children were disembarked and imprisoned. There they remained until news was received on 15 July that the British were nearing the city – and the Nana gave the order for all the prisoners to be killed. The combined efforts of his sepoys and butchers with knives left only a few still alive by the following morning. These were thrown down a well and left to die. Havelock's men arrived outside Cawnpore to begin the assault on 17 July, hoping to free the women and children left in the city. Capturing the city, they found a scene of carnage. This atrocity, above all, was the spur for Havelock's men to exact a fierce and bloody revenge. Every captured rebel was made to go to the scene of the slaughter to assist in cleaning up – which was especially humiliating to high-caste Indians, as it was abhorrent to them to touch blood – and all were then hanged, whether guilty or not.

During the advance to Cawnpore, Havelock's small force had faced an enemy with around 13,000 Indian troops, but managed to proceed until confronted by a 24-pounder gun. Havelock sent his aide (who happened to be his son), Lieutenant Henry Havelock, to command the storming of this gun. Seeing no other officer, young Havelock led the 64th Regiment into the attack himself and successfully captured it. However, he had failed to notice Major Stifling of the 64th, whose horse had been shot from under him. Stirling should properly have led this attack and was galled at being upstaged by a younger officer – and his rancour was increased when Havelock senior recommended his son for the VC, one of five won that day. It was duly awarded, but was hotly opposed by the officers of the 64th and, on hearing their complaints, by the Commander-in-Chief, Lieutenant General Sir Colin Campbell. Lieutenant Havelock was evidently embarrassed, both by his father's nominating him and by the upset the award had caused, but he demonstrated extraordinary courage during the advance on Lucknow, following which he was recommended for the VC. He would have been the first man to receive a bar to his VC, but Campbell opposed it, arguing that he should not even have received the first award.

First Relief of Lucknow, September 1857
On 25 September Havelock's column arrived at Lucknow. By now it was about 3,000 strong and comprised a portion of the 1st Madras Fusiliers, the 64th and

78th Regiments, with some Sikhs, together with the 5th, from Mauritius, and the 90th, which had been en route to China. With Major General Sir James Outram, military commander of the Cawnpore and Dinapoor regions, acting in his capacity as Chief Commissioner of Oudh, the troops had fought their way through considerable opposition and searing heat. They were exhausted, with many sick or wounded – all they could do was get to the Residency and take refuge there, without any hope of breaking out without major reinforcements. To add to the woes of the garrison, disease was now rife in the Residency, with many dying of cholera, dysentery, smallpox and heatstroke. They could only sit tight and wait for much-needed support.

A total of nineteen VCs were awarded.

Second Relief of Lucknow: the Alum Bagh, 1857
Led by Brigadier General Hope Grant and Sir Colin Campbell, a united force, well equipped and with a greater strength of numbers, set out at the end of October and arrived on 12 November at the royal summer resort of Alum Bagh, a few miles from Lucknow, where Outram had left a small garrison before moving on to the city. In Alum Bagh, plans were laid to effect a breakout from within the Residency. Outram, still in the Residency, was anxious that the incoming forces should have a knowledgeable local guide to lead them through the labyrinth of narrow streets, cul-de-sacs and enclosed courts. One local Indian spy, Kanauji Lal, was prepared to leave the Residency and join Campbell's men, but Outram rightly feared that the relief commander would not trust him. So it was that a civilian volunteer, a 36-year-old clerk called Thomas Kavanagh, who was fluent in Hindustani, stained his skin, donned native Indian clothes and undertook the almost suicidal risky challenge of breaking out through the enemy lines with Lal, then guiding the relief column back through the city to the Residency. Kavanagh was one of eight men who received the VC in this enterprise.

Kavanagh's bravado and daring were rewarded as he led Campbell's men into Lucknow in an assault on 16 November, a day of ferocious close-quarters fighting. The plan was to take control of the strategically important fortified palaces along the troops' riverside line of advance; the first fortress to fall was the Secundra Bagh. Here Campbell's 93rd Highlanders expressed their fury at the earlier sepoy atrocities with a savage attack. Four VCs were won for the initial attack to open the gates, and a further seven as the 53rd Regiment's grenadier company surged through. As house-to-house fighting developed, Lieutenant Colonel Ewart personally killed eight of the enemy; when he was wounded, he was rescued by Private Grant (later awarded the VC), who killed five of the enemy using a captured sword.

Once the Secundra Bagh was cleared of mutineers, Campbell ordered his men on to the Shah Nujeff Mosque. This domed building lay in a walled enclosure, the entrance blocked with masonry, and a parapet on the roof allowed the defenders a panoramic vantage point from which to fire. In addition, a barracks or mess house to one side offered a further post from which to pour in crossfire. Campbell's battle plan was to bring heavy field guns up to close range for maximum effect, but this brought the gun crews within range of snipers and grenade throwers, causing heavy casualties. Fearing the imminent annihilation of the troops manning the guns, Lieutenant Salmon RN, Leading Seaman Harrison and an able seaman from the naval brigade climbed a tree whose branches abutted the mosque walls, and picked off the snipers and grenade throwers. In doing so they saved the gun crews and earned themselves VCs. (The third man, because he died in the attack, remained unrecognised.) As dusk fell, after three hours of fighting, the mosque walls were still intact, so Captain William Peel RN (who had been awarded the VC in the Crimea) brought his guns into action to great effect – especially in destroying enemy morale. Under the feint of a bugle sounding an advance, the defenders left through a breach in a rear wall. Sergeant Paton discovered this breach and, despite coming under heavy fire, led his regiment in to occupy the now deserted mosque – for which he earned a Victoria Cross. In total five VCs were awarded.

Further fierce fighting ensued the next day as Campbell's men stormed the Mess House and Moti Mahal buildings, while the Residency garrison sent out men to attack the now demoralised mutineers. The way was at last clear to evacuate the Residency.

Uprisings in the North, September 1857–February 1858
From September 1857 to February 1858 troops were called to put down uprisings throughout the north – at Bolandshahr, Agra, Mundisore, Dacca, Khodagunge, Rowa, Shunsabad, Choorpoorah, Sultanpore and Azamgarh – all of which saw fierce fighting and nine VC awards were made.

Lucknow Retaken, 1858
Campbell eventually returned his attention to Lucknow at the start of March 1858. Since occupying the city in November, the rebels had strengthened the surrounding defences and increased their numbers to over 100,000. The operation to retake the city began on 2 March and lasted until the 21st. The rebels fiercely contested every stronghold and a further thirteen VCs were awarded during the fighting.

On 29 March the army was reorganised into three all-arms forces, the Azamgarth Field Force under General Lugard, the Lucknow Field Force under

General Sir Hope Grant, and the Rohilcund Field Force under Brigadier General Walpole. All three saw action in mopping-up operations against fierce and often skilled resistance during the spring and summer of 1858. In total fourteen VCs were awarded during this period.

Major General Sir Hugh Rose's Campaign, 1858–1859

Most of the fighting in 1857–58 had been in the north, although there had been two rebellions in central India, at Gwalia and Jhansi; these were not put down until 1858, when Sir Hugh Rose, in command of the Central India Field Force (two brigades), advanced from Bombay in a campaign of unsurpassed speed and effectiveness. He set out on 6 January and on 3 February relieved Saugor, which had been besieged for eight months, then marched for Jhansi.

Mutiny had broken out among the Jhansi garrison to the south-west of Lucknow in June 1857. As at Cawnpore, when the beleaguered occupants of the besieged fort offered to turn it over to the rebels in exchange for their lives, the mutineers went back on their word and massacred them as they left. The fort remained in rebel hands, but now it had become imperative for the British to remove the threat posed by this major rebel stronghold, which had a garrison of 11,000 men. At the start of the rebellion it was questionable as to whether the Rani of Jhansi had condoned the massacre — her letter guaranteeing the safety of the evacuees either had been a sham, or perhaps had been ignored by the rebel troops. However, in February 1858 her stance was unequivocal – her troops insisted that she fight the approaching British force. Rose's column arrived and surrounded the town on the 21st, but the Rani had already made preparations for a long siege. An attempt to come to her aid and relieve the town was made by 20,000 men led by Tantia Topi but defeated at the Betwah River by 1,000 native troops and 500 British, and by 3 April the town was in British hands. Savage close-quarters fighting, spurred no doubt by a desire for vengeance for the earlier massacre, saw the award of seven Victoria Crosses.

The next objective was Kalpi, which controlled the road from Lucknow across the Yamuna River. It fell on 22 May, though the rebel force here was ten times the size of the British and Rose suffered his fifth bout of sunstroke during the action. Once Kalpi was secure, Rose was able to go on medical leave, but when Tantia Topi and the Rani of Jhansi joined forces, Gwalior went over to their side. Rose resumed his command, routed the rebels at the cantonments at the River Morar, and took Gwalior.

On 17 June the Rani assumed the red uniform of a sowar and led her troops against the British. Five VCs were awarded for a fierce charge against the enemy, during which the Rani was wounded. Although out of the action with her injury, she took aim at a British soldier, who, mistaking her for a rebel sepoy, shot her before she could fire. With her death, the rebels lost a major figurehead, and when Rose led his men to occupy the town on 19 June there was only scant resistance.

Effectively this was the last stand of the rebel forces and once these mutineers were put down, the Indian Mutiny came to an end.

Victorian Colonial Wars

The T'ai P'ing Rebellion, 1851–1864

In 1850, eight years after the Manchu Ch'ing Empire's defeat by the British in the Opium War, the popular leader Hung Hsiu-ch'an raised an army of T'ai P'ing rebels in Guangxi Province. His aim was to overthrow the weak Manchu Ch'ing emperor and declare a Utopian Christian 'Heavenly Kingdom of Great Peace'. Hung was a charismatic character and his philosophy – a mix of Chinese thinking and Protestant ethics – offered an end to the oppressive traditions of foot-binding, slavery, arranged marriages, concubinage, idol-worship and the destructive culture of opium-smoking. The rebels declared their new republic in 1851 and in March 1853 seized Nanking, establishing a new regime in which peasants owned the land in common.

An American adventurer named Frederick T. Ward became an unlikely ally for the Ch'ing Empire when he raised a small force of foreigners and led them against the T'ai P'ings. This motley mercenary group had the goal of plunder in mind, but they responded to discipline to achieve their own purposes and were very successful against the rebels. Ward led this 'Ever Victorious Army' to take back Shanghai, but he was killed in battle. His successor was an American called Burgevine, but he proved ineffectual and his place was taken, with the approval of the British authorities, by Major Charles Gordon (later killed at Khartoum). Britain saw how the T'ai P'ing regime had paralysed trade and wanted positive action to restore commerce. Under Gordon's leadership, the T'ai P'ings' strongholds were reduced until only Nanking remained to be retaken. During this campaign, at an engagement at Fung Wha, a VC was awarded to Able Seaman George Hinckley from HMS *Sphinx*. Imperial troops finally retook Nanking in July 1864, and after eleven years the rebellion was over. With the loss of an estimated 30,000,000 lives, it was the bloodiest civil war in history, and the second bloodiest war of any kind. Only the Second World War exacted a higher toll.

The Persian War, 1856–1857

In the days of British rule in India, a major influence on Britain's foreign policy was the threat of incursions into this part of the Empire by Russia or her minion states. Since Russia's victory over Persia in 1828, her influence over Persian policy had become increasingly evident and was now posing a latent threat to British India. It was with the Russian threat in mind that Britain had helped to create the buffer state of Afghanistan between India and Persia, and although the Afghan city of Herat had long been part of Persia, the British supported its incorporation into Afghanistan. So began a sporadic battle to hold the city. The Persian army invested Herat on 23 November 1838, but lifted the siege when Britain threatened to intervene. In 1851 the Shah in Herat allowed Persian troops to enter the city, but again British diplomatic pressure ousted them. Persia annexed Herat in October 1856; when diplomatic measures failed, Britain declared war on 1 November.

Within five days a British division from Bombay, under Major General Foster Stalker, launched an amphibious attack in the Persian Gulf, landing south of Bushire. Following the capture of the city's defensive forts, during which Captain John Wood of the 20th Bombay Native Infantry was awarded a VC, Bushire's governor surrendered under the heavy naval bombardment; soon after, 4,500 British troops from the 64th and 68th Regiments, under the overall command of Lieutenant General Sir James Outram, arrived as reinforcements. These men came under attack at Khooshab by a Persian force of 6,900 on 8 February and, for the loss of just ten killed and sixty-two wounded, routed the enemy, leaving some 700 Persians dead. This action saw the award of two VCs, to Lieutenant John Malcolmson and Lieutenant Arthur Moore of the 3rd Bombay Light Infantry. Outram crossed the Persian Gulf to Mohamrah on the Euphrates delta, where his men took the city easily after a fierce naval bombardment, sending the Persians into retreat. A small force under Commander Rennie pursued them up the Karoon River to Akwaz and captured the town on 1 April, but a peace treaty had already been signed on 4 March, resulting in the Persian withdrawal from Herat and the opening up of Persia for British trade.

The Taranaki Maori War, New Zealand, 1860–1861

As more immigrants from the northern hemisphere flooded into New Zealand's North Island in the 1850s, there was an increasing demand for land to accommodate them, and this had to be bought from the native Maoris by the British government. As a lever, the Governor announced a policy that the government would buy land from any individual, and that anyone obstructing this process would be committing treason against the crown. This was put to the test when a local Te Atiawa chief offered to sell an area of land in North Taranaki, known as the Pekapeka Block, to the British government. Not surprisingly, the 2,000 or more Te Atiawa Maoris living there were fiercely opposed to the sale, and their paramount chief, Wiremu Kingi, spoke for them; while they wanted no war, he could not let the sale go through. The local people obstructed attempts to survey the area, refused to move out and instead built up a fortified village or Pah at Te Kohia, just inside the Block.

On 17 March 1860 the British army attacked the Pah to begin the First Taranaki War. There followed more attacks, where the army, including the 40th Regiment and servicemen from HMS *Niger*, besieged Pahs at Pukete-kauere, Mahoetahi, Orongomai, Omata (at which action Leading Seaman William Odgers of HMS *Niger* was awarded the Victoria Cross). With the exception of the June attack on Pukete-kauere, where the Te Atiawa people put up spirited resistance to defeat the British forces, these actions were successful. In a skirmish near Huirangi Bush on 18 March 1861 Colour Sergeant John Lucas of the 40th Regiment earned a VC for bravery under heavy fire. However, weight of numbers and military muscle eventually prevailed. After the final attack on Te Arei Pah in March 1861, a truce was signed: although the disputed block of land became British-owned territory, the Maori people remained in possession of the area.

The Third China War, 1860

Chinese resentment of European traders and diplomats had already resulted in the First China War (or Opium War) of 1840–42, following which Hong Kong was ceded to Britain and five ports were opened up to European trade. An uneasy peace came to an end when the Chinese executed a French missionary and five Chinese sailors were taken off a British schooner and tried for piracy. The resulting conflict – the Second China War (1846–47) – was concluded after lengthy negotiations with the Treaty of Tientsin in June 1858, which opened eleven more ports to European trade, allowed European missions into Peking and guaranteed the safety of missionaries and travellers in China.

However, when the British and French commissioners set sail up the Pei-ho River to ratify the treaty, their vessels were fired on from the three Taku forts at the swampy mouth of the river. A combined Anglo-French expedition under Lieutenant General Sir James Hope Grant (who had served with distinction in the Indian Mutiny) and General de Montauban landed at Peh-Tang on 1 August 1860 to 'teach the Chinese a lesson' – so initiating the Third China War. The force, some 10,000 British (one cavalry regiment and six infantry battalions) and 7,000 French, advanced almost unopposed, but halted before the Taku Forts while engineers set about making roads across the surrounding swamps. The assault to take the forts was launched on 21 August, and during this action seven men earned VCs. After fierce fighting, the combined force took the forts and carried on towards Peking with the objective of ratifying the Tientsin Treaty, arriving in early October. The Chinese finally signed the Treaty of Peking on the 24th, ratifying the former treaty, adding Tientsin to the tally of open ports and ceding Kowloon to Britain on a ninety-nine year lease.

The Waikato–Hauhau Maori War, 1863–1866

The truce that concluded the Maori War in 1861 dealt only with the immediate territorial problem, and by 1863 the increasing flow of settlers to New Zealand's North Island and the consequent demand for land was once more the cause of fighting.

In July 1863 the 18th, 43rd, 57th, 65th and 68th Regiments and the 107th Bengal Infantry, the Royal Regiment of Artillery and detachments from HMS *Foretop* and the Auckland Militia launched a massive invasion of the Maori King Tawhiau's home area, the Waikato. They set about expelling the Maori people from their holdings and swept southwards, claiming land as they went, their route taking them through battles at Cameron Town, Pontoko, Rangiriri, Mangapiko River, Ohanpu, Tauranga and Nukumaru. The Waikato people and their allies were defeated at Orakau in 1864, after which Tawhiau fled west to the dense bushland where the Ngati people lived. The British pursued the king with an intention to 'repress the Maori', which they did ruthlessly. Major battles were fought at Gate Pa and Te Ranga. The Maoris put up spirited resistance defending their strongholds, taking full advantage of their local knowledge, but the British forces' superior organisation and fire-power finally forced the Maori to capitulate. In total thirteen VCs were awarded for bravery in this campaign.

The Umbeyla Expedition, 1863

During the late 1850s the Peshawar district of British-held India came under frequent attack by Hindustani Pathans based in the nearby Mahabun Mountains. The very warlike Pathans were vehemently opposed to British colonial rule. An expedition in 1858 under Sir Sydney Cotton drove the raiders from their base, but by 1863 they had regrouped around the mountain out-post of Malka. Without consulting the Commander-in-Chief, the Lieutenant Governor of the Punjab authorised an expedition to destroy Malka, and some 6,000 men under Brigadier General Sir Neville Chamberlain were taken out of the frontier defence for this mission. Chamberlain chose the Chamla Valley as his operational base, and, of the three points of access to it, he opted for the

Umbeyla Pass, under the impression that the local Bunerwal people were friendly. The vanguard of his 'Peshawar Column' reached the pass on 20 October, but it was a tough route and the rest of the column finally arrived two days later.

Unknown to Chamberlain, the Hindustanis had convinced the Bunerwals that the British would annexe their land if they failed to stand up to them, and on 22 October a reconnaissance party was attacked by Bunerwal tribesmen. Chamberlain fortified his position in the pass on two rocky outcrops – Eagle's Nest on Guru Mountain and Crag Piquet on the hills opposite – but these could only hold small numbers of men. In contrast, the Hindustanis had by now mustered the local tribesmen and moved in with a force of around 15,000 to trap Chamberlain and his men.

The two hill-top pickets were the focus of fierce action, as small companies of men defended them against massed swordsmen supported by accurate matchlock fire. On 30 October Crag Piquet was the centre of fierce hand-to-hand fighting, during which Lieutenant George Fosbery and Lieutenant Henry Pitcher earned VCs. Crag Piquet fell into Hindustani hands three times and was three times retaken in the next four weeks. On 20 November Chamberlain himself was seriously wounded, but gradually reinforcements were drafted in on the orders of the Commander-in-Chief, Sir Hugh Rose, and on 6 December Major General Garvock replaced Chamberlain. Nine days later Garvock broke out of the pass with a two-column attack by 4,800 men, supported by the 11th Bengal Cavalry led by Colonel Dighton Probyn VC. On 17 December a Bunerwal deputation surrendered to Garvock and a small party was sent out to burn Malka as originally planned. Peace was restored, but at the cost of around a thousand British casualties.

The Shimonoseki Expedition, 1864

The expansion of foreign trade into the Far East caused mounting resentment in Japan, and in 1863 the Daimyo (feudal landowner) of the Choshu clan began to take action to expel all foreigners from their land around the Straits of Shimonoseki. His forces launched attacks on European and American vessels, which, naturally, fired back. As the hostilities continued, so the European powers formed an international squadron, which quickly wiped out the Choshu clan's ships and forts. A British force, including the 20th and 67th Regiments, the Royal Artillery, Royal Engineers and Royal Marines, supported the united offensive. During these battles, fought mainly in the Shimonoseki Strait, Midshipman Duncan Boyes, Ordinary Seaman William Seeley and Captain of the After Guard Thomas Pride were awarded the VC. A treaty was subsequently signed with the Japanese government barring the fortification of the Straits of Shimonoseki and providing a large indemnity to the injured Europeans.

The Bhutan (or Duar) War, 1864–1865

The Indian state of Bhutan lies just to the east of Nepal. In 1864, following civil war in the region, Britain, protecting her interests in her Indian Empire, sent a peace mission to restore order in the state.

The leader of the victorious Punakha people had broken with the central administration and set up a rival government. The legitimate governor was deposed, so the British mission mediated, dealing alternately with the supporters of the deposed and the new governments. The latter, however, rejected all British attempts to broker peace, so in November 1864 Britain declared war on the new Bhutan regime. It was an ill-matched contest, as Bhutan had no regular army and such forces as it had were armed with matchlocks, bows and arrows, swords, knives and catapults. Wearing chain armour and carrying shields, these guards engaged the well-equipped British forces.

On 30 April 1865 a sharp engagement at Dewan Giri in the south-east of Bhutan drove the Bhutanese out of their positions. However, the resistance of a stubborn pocket of about 200 men prompted a courageous assault on their blockhouse by men of the Royal (later Bengal) Engineers; Lieutenant James Dundas and Major William Trevor were awarded VCs for their actions at this engagement.

Although the Bhutanese gained some battlefield victories, they were defeated in just five months. In the ensuing treaty Bhutan lost part of her sovereign territory and was forced to relinquish formerly occupied territories in the Assam and Bengal Duars, and the much-contested Dewan Giri area.

Canada – The Fenian Raids, 1866

Determined to liberate Ireland from British rule, the fiery Irish-American Fenian Brotherhood planned to spark a war between Britain and the United States – and to do so they decided to carry out attacks on the British dominion of Canada. Two raids were carried out across the US–Canadian border in early June 1866, but were repulsed by Canadian volunteers.

On 9 June Private Timothy O'Hea of the Rifle Brigade was awarded the VC for his actions in dealing with a fire in an ammunition van on a train; this action was responsible for the appending of a new royal warrant to the existing criteria of eligibility for receiving the VC. Previously awards were made only in recognition of deeds performed in action against the enemy, but henceforth awards would be made for acts of bravery carried out 'in circumstances of extreme danger'.

Although the US authorities took action to subdue the Fenians, they still launched further raids into Canada in late May 1870, from Vermont and New Hampshire – again unsuccessfully. Public pressure and a firm crackdown on Fenian activities in the US finally eliminated the threat.

The Gambia, 1866

In 1866 British forces were involved in trouble with a West African tribe in the Gambia. A punitive expedition was organised by Colonel D'Arcy, the Governor of Gambia, and duly invaded the kingdom of Barra, in which the tribe resided. One of the first actions in this campaign was an assault on the stockaded town of Tubabecolong. When the small force reached the town, D'Arcy called for volunteers to break down the stockade with axes. Private Hodge and another pioneer plied their axes in the face of intense fire until a breach was made. The regiment struggled through, but the tribesmen had been reinforced so strongly that they were able to beat the British off for a time.

D'Arcy recalled later that he found himself left alone in the breach with only Hodge by his side. He continued firing at the enemy while the big West Indian standing coolly by his side, conspicuous in his scarlet uniform with white facings, supplied him with loaded muskets. After a while the rest of the men reformed and came once more into the attack. Hodge then went ahead again, breaking a way for them through the bush-work defences.

To give his men a better chance of storming the place, Hodge ran round to the main entrance, drove off the enemy and forced open the two great gates which had been barricaded from within. Through these the West Indian Regiment charged with their bayonets fixed; when they emerged at the other side of the smoke-enveloped village, they left some hundreds of the enemy dead and dying in their wake.

The Andaman Islands Expedition, 1867

Britain needed a new penal settlement to accommodate prisoners from the Indian Mutiny (1857–1859) and in 1858 sent a small force to the former penal colony of the Andaman Islands in the Bay of Bengal to establish Fort Blair, despite concern over native cannibals' attacks on shipwrecked crews washed up on the islands.

The ship *Assam Valley* put in at the island of Little Andaman in 1867 and a small party of men went ashore, never to be seen again. Suspecting that they had been attacked by cannibal natives, part of the 24th Regiment – later the South Wales Borderers – was sent by steamer from Rangoon to investigate, arriving on 7 May. Attacked by natives shortly after landing, they retreated to the beach but were prevented from leaving by a sudden fierce storm. A party of five men from the steamer volunteered to rescue them, and all five were subsequently awarded the VC under the new clause added at the time of the Fenian raids into Canada in 1866, for extraordinary courage in the face of great danger.

The Abyssinian Expedition, 1867–1868

The Christian Emperor of Abyssinia (present-day Ethiopia) Theodor III (Tewodros) had consolidated his control in the mid-1850s and pursued an anti-Muslim crusade to reform the country. In February 1862 Captain Charles Cameron arrived as the new British consul, bearing a pair of pistols as a gift from Queen Victoria. He suggested that Theodor approach the Queen to negotiate a treaty of friendship, and a letter was duly sent, proposing an alliance with Britain to wipe out Islam. It seems that this letter went astray, and, receiving no response, the volatile Theodor imprisoned Cameron (who had angered him by visiting Muslim Sudan) and some British missionaries. Diplomatic means failed to resolve the problem, so Britain sent an ultimatum to Theodor, which he ignored. Plans were made for an attack on Theodor at his mountain capital of Magdala, to be led by Lieutenant General Sir Robert Napier, Commander-in-Chief of the Bombay Presidency Army in India since 1865. Napier arrived at Zula in Annesley Bay with a force of 13,000 fighting men and 36,000 pack animals (including forty-four elephants) to negotiate the mountainous route to Magdala, a journey of over forty days. Arriving at the plateau below the citadel, the British force repelled a charge by 6,500 tribesmen, shooting down 700 and wounding 1,200 for the loss of only two dead and eighteen wounded. In a panic, Theodor attempted suicide and then tried to escape, but had to return to Magdala with just a few hundred followers. That same day, 13 April 1868, Napier's troops assaulted the citadel gates – an action in which only fifteen men were wounded and two VCs were awarded. Theodor shot himself with one of Queen Victoria's pistols, Magdala was blown up and peace was restored.

The Lushai Expedition, 1872

Since 1850 Lushai tribesmen (later called the Mizo) had gradually migrated from the Chin Hills into Assam, subjugating the local people and imposing their own rule. They remained untouched by foreign political influence until Britain annexed Assam in north-eastern India in 1862. The Lushai were furious at this foreign intrusion and responded with raids into British territory, to which Britain replied with punitive expeditions. On one occasion in 1872 the Lushai kidnapped a girl, Mary Winchester, and a Field Force under General Brownlow set out to save her and punish her kidnappers. It was in the storming of the stockaded village of Lalgnoora that a Victoria Cross was awarded to Major Donald MacIntyre of the Bengal Staff Corps and 2nd Ghurkha Rifles.

The First Ashanti Expedition, 1873–1874

In 1872 the coastal fort of Elmina in Ashanti (present-day Ghana) came into British possession. This was the last trade outlet to the sea for the native Ashanti people and their king, Kofi Karikari, was ready to fight to protect it. Early in 1873 he mustered a 12,000-strong army, crossed the Pra River and invaded the coastal area but his forces were defeated by the British at Elmina. To emphasise their domination over the area, the British government appointed Major General Sir Garnet Wolseley as Governor and Commander-in-Chief, and instructed him to drive the Ashanti from the coastal region. In December several British units arrived to reinforce Wolseley's African levies, and in January 1874 Wolseley issued a warning to Karikari that he was ready to attack. He also offered an armistice if the Ashanti would retreat from the coast; when the negotiations failed, war became inevitable.

The battle at Amoaful on 31 January plainly demonstrated the imbalance of strength – the Ashanti fought bravely, using the tall undergrowth for camouflage, but superior British numbers and firepower prevailed. In this instance the Ashanti lost 150 men to just four on the British side. Wolseley's men captured the settlements of Abogu, Amoaful, Becquah and Ordashu, for which attacks four VCs were awarded. Wolseley went on to take and burn the capital, Kumasi, where stacks of human skulls pointed to a tradition of human sacrifice.

On 17 March 1874 the Treaty of Fomena brought the war to a close and hammered home the extent of the British victory. The Ashanti had to pay an indemnity of 50,000 ounces of gold, renounce all claims to Elmina and to any payment from Britain for use of the forts for trade. They also had to break off their alliances with nearby states. Thus weakened, they withdrew from the coast, leaving the trade routes open, and agreed to abandon their custom of human sacrifice.

Malaya, 1875–1876

Britain had occupied Singapore since 1819, but exercised a policy of not getting involved in local upheavals in the Malay states to the north. However, when civil war broke out in nearby Selangor in 1871 Britain did intervene, annexing the region. The next year trouble flared in Perak and threatened to spread to Singapore, so Perak too was annexed. These areas proved difficult to administer, with the British Resident James Birch's measures to keep law and order and stamp out slavery bringing him into direct conflict with the local Malay leaders.

In July 1875, seeing their power and revenue seriously threatened, the Malay tribal chiefs had Birch murdered. All Britain could muster in response was a scratch force of sixty men of the 1st and 10th Regiments, fifty Sikhs, twenty Penang police, fifteen Malay volunteers and four sailors, and this puny force was repulsed near Birch's former base on 4 November. Only when reinforcements arrived from Hong Kong and India was the tide turned. The 1st Ghurkhas captured the assassins' base of Kintra and nearby Kotah Lama, taking on the Malays in guerrilla-style fighting. The British force went on to take Perak on 20 December, in which action Captain George Channer of the Bengal Staff Corps earned the VC. After a major breakthrough at the Bukit Putus Pass, the dissident chiefs were arrested and the Sultan of Perak was deposed.

Baluchistan, 1877

During the Anglo-Indian War of 1838–1842 Britain had briefly occupied Baluchistan in the north-west of India to protect her lines of communication, but had been forced to leave in 1841. However, relations improved when treaties were signed in 1859 and 1876, strengthening Baluchistan's ties with the British Indian Empire, and in 1876 British forces set up a strongly garrisoned army station at Quetta in the west of Baluchistan, commanding the vital Bolan and Khojak passes through the mountains. On 26 July 1877 officers at this station were attacked by a group of coolies, and Captain Andrew Scott of the Bengal Staff Corps, serving with the 4th Sikh Infantry, earned a VC for his courage during the attack.

Five districts of Baluchistan were divided off later that year to become the British Province of Baluchistan.

The Ninth Cape Frontier War, 1877–1878

The Cape Frontier Wars spanned a century – a hundred years of intermittent warfare during which the African people, principally the pastoral Xhosa tribes of South Africa's Eastern Cape, struggled against the intrusion of the British and European settlers. In the so-called Ninth War the Ngika and Gaika sections of the Xhosa tribe took arms against the Fingoes, whom they felt to be favoured by the British colonists. But what started as a beer brawl between Gaikas and Fingoes near the old mission station at Butterworth suddenly blew up into a full-blown tribal conflict.

The ensuing war drew in British forces in support of colonial police helping the Fingoes against the Gaikas. It was an intermittent war of raids, ambushes, skirmishes and some small pitched battles around the Cape region, and was noteworthy for the first use of machine-guns in action by British troops. The first VC in South Africa was awarded to Major Hans Garrett Moore for an action at Draaibosch near Komgha on 29 December, when men of the 88th Regiment supported the police against a Gaika attack. This Ninth War concluded with Xhosa lands being incorporated into Cape Colony.

The Second and Third Afghan Wars, 1878–1880

Britain had been keeping a watchful eye on this important buffer zone to the north-west of British-ruled India as part of a policy of 'masterly inactivity'. In 1866 the Emir, Sher Ali, came to power. He was well disposed towards Britain and feared Russian encroachment in the region as much as Britain did, but, although prepared to support him with arms and funds, Britain would promise the Emir no other help. In 1872 Britain and Russia had signed an agreement under which Russia would respect Afghanistan's northern borders – there would be no need, the British government thought, to give any promises of support to Afghanistan.

However, in 1876 alarm bells sounded in the British corridors of power when Sher Ali reluctantly allowed a Russian mission to Kabul, and then, significantly, refused to admit Lord Lytton, sent out as Viceroy, to the country. This Russian encroachment into Central Asia was too close to British-ruled India to go unopposed. Lytton decided that Sher Ali must be removed; when his ultimatum demanding that a British envoy be admitted to Kabul was ignored, three columns of British troops moved into Afghanistan in November 1878.

One column, under Major General Sir Donald Stewart, advanced from Quetta over the Bolan Pass to Kandahar, while the second, under Lieutenant General Sir Samuel Browne, marched through the Khyber Pass, taking the fortress of Ali Masjid. The third, including the 5th Ghurkha Rifles, under Major General Frederick Roberts, set out along the Kurram Valley towards Kabul, but was met on 2 December at Peiwar Kotal by an Afghan force of about 18,000 men and eleven guns. After a careful reconnaissance, Roberts made a dummy attack under cover of darkness, leading his troops in a flanking movement to dislodge the Afghans, inflicting heavy casualties and capturing their guns.

Fighting in the harsh mountainous terrain continued into 1879: engagements on 31 January at the Bazar Valley, on 17 March and 21 April at the Khyber Pass and on 2 April at Futtehabad saw extraordinary acts of courage by men of the Royal Engineers and the Bengal Staff Corps rewarded by sixteen VC citations.

As the British advanced on Kabul, Sher Ali fled, leaving his son Yakub Khan to deal with the situation. He signed the Treaty of Gandamak on 26 May 1879, under which he relinquished control of foreign affairs to Britain in return for an annual subsidy and promises of support in the event of foreign aggression. He also had to accept a British envoy in Kabul, and was made to cede various frontier areas to Britain, and British control was extended as far as the Michni and Khyber Passes.

In 1879 the Afghan army mutinied, killing the British envoy and his escort. Roberts responded by occupying Kabul and deposing Yakub Khan on 6 October, after a sharp action to dislodge the Afghans from their hillside base at Charasiah, outside the city. In this action a VC was won by Major George White of the 92nd Regiment. Further punitive action on 24 October involved the 59th Regiment in an assault on an enemy stronghold on a hill at Shahjui. However, a popular uprising in December forced Roberts and his occupying troops to fall back to their base at Sherpur, just north of Kabul, where they were besieged for three weeks by a huge Afghan army. During this time men of the Gordon Highlanders, Seaforth Highlanders, the 5th Punjab Cavalry and the Bengal Staff Corps distinguished themselves by acts of extraordinary bravery. Roberts' men beat back a major attack on the night of 22/23 December, after which they returned to occupy Kabul again.

Abdur Rahman, Sher Ali's nephew, was installed as Emir in July 1880, but on 27 July Ayub Khan (Yakub Khan's brother) led a rebel force to defeat the British at Maiwand. They then laid siege to the occupying troops at Kandahar. Despite the severe pressure, the besieged force held out until, in a celebrated feat of endurance, Roberts marched from Kabul to Kandahar in just three weeks and defeated the rebels on 1 September.

In March 1887 British troops were finally withdrawn. Abdur Rahman remained in power until his death in 1907 and British troops had no occasion to re-enter Afghanistan until 1919.

The Zulu War, 1879

Imperial fervour was growing in Britain in the 1870s and in 1877, to secure the stability of lands in South Africa contested by both Britain and the Boers, Sir Bartle Frere was sent as British High Commissioner to create a federal dominion of British Colonies and Boer Republics. To achieve this, he needed control of the land bordering Natal and the Transvaal, which belonged to the Zulu tribesmen. The Zulu King Cetshwayo refused to give up his land, so on 11 January Lieutenant General Lord Chelmsford invaded Zululand with three columns of troops. The centre column, under Chelmsford himself, went in search of Cetshwayo and his army, heading across the Buffalo River towards Rorke's Drift.

Chelmsford, underestimating the Zulus' speed and military prowess, split his column in two. On 22 January his unprepared and under-strength camp at Isandlwana, including men of the 24th Regiment under the command of Lieutenant Colonel Henry Pulleine, was surprised by the main Zulu army, numbering some 14,000 warriors. The sheer weight of Zulu numbers swamped the camp, and 1,300 of the 1,700 defenders were massacred – it was a massive blow to British military prestige and confidence. The Zulus then moved straight on to Rorke's Drift, a small mission station consisting of two clay-brick thatched buildings, where B Company of the 2nd Battalion, 24th Regiment of Foot was stationed with elements of the Army Medical Department, the Commissariat and Transport Department and the Natal Native Contingent. In a masterly defensive action 139 men, mostly from the 24th Foot, held off the attack by about 4,000 Zulus armed with assegais for over twelve hours, during which time eleven men earned VCs – the most ever earned for a single action. When Chelmsford finally arrived with reinforcements, some 400–500 Zulus lay dead for the loss of just seventeen British lives.

The column to the east, under Colonel Charles Pearson, had driven east across the Tukela River to Eshowe, where they occupied the former Norwegian mission station. The defeat at Isandlwana left the flanking columns danger-ously exposed, and Pearson was faced with a choice: stay put and risk an attack from the full Zulu army or try to return south to the border with a view to returning in greater strength, but thereby risking being caught defenceless in the open. He opted to stay, despite the cramped and unhygienic conditions. As time passed, many lives were claimed by typhoid and other diseases. At last, after Pearson's men had endured three months under siege, Chelmsford broke through the Zulu cordon at Gingindlovu, arriving at Eshowe on 2 April.

In the wake of the defeat at Isandlwana only the left-hand (northern) column under Colonel Evelyn Wood remained operational, and it was left to his men to carry out diversionary attacks while Chelmsford went to Pearson's rescue. They fought a major action at the Ntombe River on 12 March, where one VC was earned, then met heavy opposition at Hlobane Mountain on the 28th; five VCs were won that day. The army had fallen back on Khambula, where they inflicted a major defeat on the Zulus: the concentrated British fire was deva-stating, and defeat was turned to a rout as a cavalry party pursued and dispatched the fleeing Zulu warriors.

With his troops consolidated and regrouped, Chelmsford planned his next attack. His first division, made up of relief troops and Pearson's men, would proceed under Pearson's command up the eastern coast; the second, under his own command, would advance through the centre of Zulu territory, via Rorke's Drift. This would enable his men to reclaim the military debris around

Isandlwana and bury their dead. By the end of June Chelmsford's men had fought through to the heart of Zulu territory, taking en route the surrender of many individual Zulu chiefs, who sensed imminent defeat.

On 3 July Lieutenant Colonel Redvers Buller, who had earned a VC at Hlobane with a supply train of the 80th Regiment, which was all but wiped out, led his 'Irregular Cavalry' on an ambush party and only narrowly escaped capture. The following day, however, there was no such uncertainty. Some 20,000 Zulus came face to face with a massive imperial army, and in an action which took just forty-five minutes the British routed the Zulus at their capital of Ulundi, which they put to the torch. This last battle left two British officers and ten men dead, compared with 1,500 Zulus lost. Cetshwayo escaped and remained on the run for two months, after which he was rounded up and sent into exile in Cape Town. The whole conflict had cost some 2,000 British lives and £5,000,000 – and the matter of the confederation of British colonies and Boer republics remained unsettled.

The Basuto War, 1879–1882

Basutoland, on the borders of Natal, had been a British Protectorate since 1868, but in 1871 the British Cape Colony annexed the Basutos' land, interfering with the chiefs' authority and the tribes' traditional laws. Resentment grew and in 1879 troops from Cape Colony were sent to quell the unrest. Following a severe defeat, the Basutos retreated into the hills and made a determined stand on a mountain named after their chief, Morosi. This almost impregnable natural stronghold was further defended by a series of stockade barriers on the only side that offered any access to attackers. In an action lasting from April to June men of the Cape Mounted Rifles carried out repeated attacks on the mountain, for which three VCs were awarded. In another significant attack, this time against the Bapedi stronghold of Sekukuni's Town, men of the 21st and 94th Regiments under Sir Garnet Wolseley reinforced the assault force on 27 November 1879. At first light the following morning a three-pronged attack was launched against the hillside stronghold, during which two men of the 94th Regiment earned VC citations. The campaign was concluded with Sekukuni's surrender on 2 December 1879.

In 1880 the Cape Colony authorities in Basutoland prepared to enforce the Cape Peace Preservation Act of 1878, which disarmed the natives; this gave rise to the Gun War. The Basutos rebelled against the act; taking up defensive positions in the rugged, mountainous terrain, they held the Cape Colony troops at bay with guerrilla-style attacks and sudden charges. On 14 January 1881 the Basutos charged a contingent of the 1st Cape Mounted Yeomanry, which action left thirty-seven dead or wounded, and it was here that the only doctor present earned a VC in recognition of his courage. Eventually the Cape government decided to seek a settlement. In the subsequent peace the Cape Colony administration was unable to reassert control, and on the appeal of the Basutos the British government in London took over responsibility for Basutoland in 1884.

The First Boer War, 1880–1881

After the end of the Zulu War in 1879 Britain's High Commissioner had failed to deliver the desired federal dominion of British colonies and Boer republics. Tension between the British and the Boer farmers was mounting: Gladstone's government was not prepared to give back the Boer territory of the Transvaal, which Britain had annexed, and Boer resentment was exacerbated further by the revenue-collecting activities of the Administrator of the Transvaal, Sir Owen Lanyon. This, combined with allegations of undisciplined behaviour by British troops in the Transvaal garrisons, pushed the Boers to boiling point, and on 16 December 1880 they declared a republic. Four days later a small column of 257 men of the 94th Regiment of Foot, en route to the garrison at Lydenburg, was ambushed at Bronkhorstspruit; caught unprepared, the British lost fifty-seven dead and over a hundred wounded and all the survivors were taken prisoner.

There were just seven British garrisons in the Transvaal, and the Boers were quick to surround them. On 16 January the 94th Regiment and Nourse's (Transvaal) Horse were engaged near the Boers' camp at Elandsfontein. The Boers' next strategic move was to cut off access to the Transvaal across the Orakensberg at Laing's Nek for the 2,000 British troops based in Natal. On 28 January 1881 Major General Sir George Pomeroy Coney, who had suc-ceeded Sir Garnet Wolseley as High Commissioner for South-East Africa on 24 April, ordered an assault on the Boer position at Laing's Nek, which was repulsed, leaving eighty-three dead and 111 wounded. Reinforcements under Brigadier General Sir Evelyn Wood – a veteran of the Zulu War – were due, but Coney had to keep communications open with the base at Newcastle. His small column of 300 men from the 60th Rifles was pinned down by just 250 Boers at Ingogo, where the British suffered 150 casualties.

These losses prompted Gladstone to try to open negotiations with the Boers. While waiting for a response to the proposed armistice, on 22 February forces at Wesselstroom including the 58th Regiment came under Boer attack and, there being no reply to Gladstone's overtures by the 26th, Coney went ahead with a move to outflank the Boers at Laing's Nek. His aim was to capture the high ground of Majuba Hill, 2,500 feet above the Boer camp; that night he sent 554 men to secure the summit, and it took them all night to scale the steep face of the extinct volcano. Reaching the top unopposed, Coney ignored recommendations to entrench; the following morning the Boers, taking advantage of their knowledge of the land and their mobility, scaled the hill under cover of fire from below. They easily overran the vulnerable British with a hail of rapid fire. Coney was killed at the start of the attack. In all, the British lost ninety-six officers and men, with 132 wounded and ninety-six taken prisoner, and one VC was awarded as a few men put up a spirited resistance to cover the retreat from the summit.

Wood, now in command of the army in Natal, arrived with reinforcements on 4 March, and was immediately ordered to seek an armistice. He confirmed the right to self-government for Transvaal, and on 23 March the Pretoria Convention was signed, granting the Boers independence under British sovereignty. With 390 British dead and 502 wounded, the British could only retire licking their wounds in the shame of defeat.

Sudan, 1881–1885

In 1881 the political situation in Sudan was disintegrating into chaos. The previous year General Charles Gordon had resigned as Governor-General, and his successor, receiving no direction from the British-run government in Cairo, soon lost control. Soon the illegal slave trade returned, the army on which the governor relied to keep order was woefully under-resourced, and the people were subjected to higher and higher taxes.

It was in this atmosphere of disorder and dissatisfaction that the self-styled Mahdi (or 'Guide') gathered the support of Islamic fanatics and started a full-scale revolt in 1881. By the end of 1882 the Mahdi's forces controlled much of the country. In occupying Egypt, Britain had also taken on responsibility for Egyptian Sudan, and it now became apparent that military action would have to be taken to suppress this revolt.

On 5 November 1883 at El Obeid the Mahdists wiped out an Egyptian force of 10,000 men sent to restore order under Colonel William Hicks; only the uncommitted reserve of 300 men survived. Egyptian forces suffered another defeat when the Beja tribesmen (dubbed 'fuzzy-wuzzies' by the British for their extravagant hair) rose up in support of the Mahdi and, under the leadership of Osman Digna, captured most of the Red Sea garrisons. At El Teb on 4 February 1884 they annihilated the forces under General Valentine Baker sent to prevent the capture of the Red Sea port of Suakim. Admiral Sir William Hewett VC landed there with a naval brigade of men from HMS *Decoy*, *Euryalus*, *Ranger* and *Sphinx* and defended the port fiercely, preventing it from being overrun. Reinforcements then began to arrive from Aden and Egypt, and on 29 February the Beja were defeated at El Teb by a force comprising

3,000 men under Major General Gerald Graham VC and a naval brigade under Commander E.N. Rolfe.

In a form of battle unfamiliar to the Mahdists, the naval brigade formed up in a huge square and advanced steadily upon the enemy, who sent small parties out to attack – but these found themselves shot down or bayoneted before they could strike. The attacks continued, however, the strongest being directed against the side of the square defended by Captain Wilson's men and their Gardner guns.

In a headlong rush the Mahdists managed to force a gap in the square, and were followed by further troops, hoping to capitalise on this breakthrough to infiltrate the formation. Undaunted, Captain Wilson took on the enemy single-handed, running the first man through with his sword; unfortunately it broke off at the hilt. Now unarmed and using just his fists, Wilson kept up a furious whirlwind of activity and managed to hold the enemy off until reinforcements came to his aid and the square was reformed. Amazingly, Wilson was only very slightly wounded during this furious onslaught. He was subsequently awarded a VC.

The Occupation of Egypt, 1882

By the late 1800s Egypt had suffered almost a century of misgovernment. In 1801, after Napoleon had been driven out, control had been returned to Turkey, so the country was part of the Ottoman Empire. The Sultan had forbidden the Khedive (the Viceroy) to impose taxes or contract loans in Egypt – a policy that spelled financial disaster – but with the opening of the Suez Canal in 1869 influence in Egypt took on a new significance and Disraeli's government was quick to buy up the Khedive's shares in the canal in 1875. By 1878 Egypt was virtually bankrupt and, to protect their interests in the canal, England and France took joint control of Egypt's finances, effectively running the country.

Nationalist feelings in Egypt ran high against the Khedive for allowing this to happen and in May 1882 Colonel Ahmed Arabi, the Egyptian Minister of War, led a revolt against this interference in the country's affairs. When the Khedive tried to dismiss Arabi in June, rioting broke out in Alexandria and more than fifty Europeans were killed. Despite British protests, Arabi continued to fortify the forts guarding the harbour at Alexandria, so Admiral Seymour, leading the British element of the joint Anglo-French squadron moored offshore, threatened to bombard the city and the harbour. At this point the French withdrew, relinquishing their interest in Egypt's affairs. On 11 July the British bombarded Alexandria for over ten hours (during which Gunner Israel Harding earned the VC), then withdrew. Overnight rioters set fire to the city and freed prisoners looted and murdered unchecked. By the following morning a white flag flew over Alexandria and a force of marines landed to accept the city's surrender. Arabi and his rebel army were still at large, however.

Skirmishes continued while the British waited for reinforcements. On 5 August Arabi's forces attacked a reconnaissance group at Kafr Dowar, resulting in a VC being awarded to Private Frederick Corbett of the King's Royal Rifle Corps. On 15 August Lieutenant General Sir Garnet Wolseley landed at Alexandria and immediately sent contingents to take control of Port Said and the canal itself. With access routes to Egypt secured, Wolseley sent troops to drive the rebels from Mukfar, where their sabotage activities threatened to cut the fresh-water supply between Ismailia and Cairo. These rebels were pursued to Kassassin, where they were defeated on 26 August by troops who then held the town, despite repeated heavy attacks.

During the night of 12/13 September Wolseley's force of 17,400 men attacked the fortifications at Tel-el-Kebir, held by 40,000 Egyptians with seventy guns. Two hours' fighting produced a resounding victory with only 469 British casualties, and a VC was earned by Lieutenant William Edwards. Wolseley went straight on to Cairo the next day to accept Arabi's surrender. The Khedive was restored to power but a British presence remained to oversee Egypt's return to financial stability.

The Chin Field Force, 1889 and the Karen-Ni Expedition, 1888–1889
Despite the British victory in the third Anglo–Burmese war, many native Burmese refused to accept the authority of the British army of occupation and resorted to guerrilla action. The guerrillas were led mainly by former officers of the disbanded Burmese Royal Army, village headmen and even royal princes. To the British they were not patriots but rebels and bandits, and the measures taken to suppress the rebel activity were severe and ruthless. Even those who aided the rebels were punished and British troops were responsible for many atrocities, including mass executions. The British adopted a punitive strategy: families of the village headmen were packed off to the secure territory of Lower Burma and their villages were burned, then new villages were established, led by strangers loyal to the British cause. The guerrilla troops targeted these new villages, and by 1890 more than 3,000 British troops were involved in the battle to maintain order and suppress the rebels' activities. On 1 January 1889 the Karene Field Force engaged the rebels at Lwekaw in the eastern Karen-Ni region, where the bravery of Surgeon John Crimmin was recognised with the award of the VC; likewise on 4 May, at the village of Tartan, Surgeon Ferdinand Le Quesne of the Chin Field Force also earned the VC. Action

against the Chin rebels continued when 3,500 men were sent to avenge raids in the Chin and Lushai areas on 15 November 1889, and eventually only sheer weight of numbers brought the military struggle to a close.

The Manipur Expedition, 1891

Tucked between Assam and Burma on India's north-east frontier lay the small hill state of Manipur, cut off from India by mountains, jungle and rivers. In September 1890 the Raja of Manipur was ousted in a palace coup, which the British government in India saw as a rebellion. In March 1891 the Chief Commissioner in Assam, James Wallace Quinton, was sent with a force of Ghurkhas, under the command of Lieutenant Colonel Charles Skene, to the capital Imphal to settle the uprising and banish the commander of the Manipuri army, the Sennaputti, who had engineered the coup. On 24 March, after refusing to be arrested, the Sennaputti drove off Skene's men, inflicting considerable casualties, and bombarded the British Residency. Along with Britain's political agent in Manipur, Frank St Clair Grimmond, Skene and Quinton went to the palace to parley – but on leaving were seized and beheaded.

Of Skene's men, 300 Ghurkhas remained to fight on, but fifty were taken prisoner and thirty-five broke out of Imphal. Some troops, and a few wounded, were led out through the jungle-clad mountains towards British territory in Assam by Grimmond's young widow, Ethel.

On 27 March Lieutenant Charles Grant, a young British officer serving with the 12th Madras Infantry in the Burmese village station of Tammu, heard of the rebellion in Manipur and set out across the mountains with a group of eighty Punjabi and Ghurkha troops to come to Skene's aid (news of his death having not yet reached the area). Only after a short but fierce engagement with Manipuri troops at Palel did Grant learn from prisoners that the three men had been killed. Believing Skene's troops to be under siege, he continued towards Imphal, and his men stormed and held Thobal near Manipur from 21 March to 9 April, when he was finally relieved. Grant was later awarded the VC for his action at Thobal.

At the end of April three columns under Major General Thomas Graham set out for Manipur, but only the Tammu column saw action. On arriving at the palace, Graham found it deserted. A thorough search found the Sennaputti disguised as a coolie, and he was duly tried and publicly hanged. Ethel Grimmond, dubbed 'the Heroine of Manipur', was awarded the Royal Red Cross and given a pension for life; the men who escaped with her, however, were court-martialled for desertion.

The Hunza-Naga Expedition, 1891

Late in 1891, following tribal unrest, an expedition was sent to the mountainous Hunza-Naga region in north-eastern India to storm the fort at Nilt and restore order. The 1,000-strong expedition, consisting mainly of Kashmir Imperial Service troops with sixteen British officers, arrived at the fort on 2 December and found it protected on three sides by precipices. The only approach to the gate was blocked by a rampart of felled trees. Since it was impossible to drag mountain guns up the surrounding cliffs, the storming party had to rely on rifle fire to cover their advance towards the gate in order to set explosive charges. Captain Fenton Aylmer and Lieutenant Guy Boisragon, who led the assault, were awarded VCs for their actions, which ensured the fort's capture. On 20 December Lieutenant John Smith was also awarded the VC for his bravery in storming an enemy position near the Nilt fort while under constant attack. Having achieved the capture of the enemy strongholds, the expedition effectively ended the localised unrest.

The Second Gambia Expedition, 1892

Early in 1891 a party from the Anglo-French Boundary Commission was attacked by tribesmen led by the local chief, Fodeh Cabbah, and several of the group were wounded. HMS *Alecto* was joined by a gunboat at Kansa on the Gambia River, and a landing party went ashore. The situation was defused when a local chief, hearing of the shore expedition, came to meet them and apologised for the attack. The men returned to their ships, but Fodeh Cabbah continued to cause trouble. Evading an expedition sent to capture him, he escaped on horseback into French territory. The naval brigade proceeded to burn down any towns and villages considered to be Fodeh Cabbah's strongholds and established a small entrenched post at Kaling, garrisoned by some sixty men of the West India Regiment.

The garrison remained into 1892, and in a number of engagements against Fodeh Cabbah's men more villages were destroyed. Most notably, at Toniatabe on 13 March, in an action to break down the town gates, Lance Corporal William Gordon of the West India Regiment earned the Victoria Cross.

As a punitive campaign, this was not a success, as Fodeh Cabbah's men retreated into French territory where the British were unable to follow them.

The Kachin Hills Expedition, Burma, 1892–1893

During the late 1880s British and Indian troops were deployed throughout the separate operational zones of Burma to control the rebellious border bandits or 'dacoits', who rose up against the British presence in their territory. By 1891 the northern area of Burma held by Britain was largely under control, but the Kachin tribe continued to cause trouble, plundering caravans travelling through the region and preying on travellers. On 28 December 1885 a British force moved in to occupy the Bhamo region in the Kachin Hills of Upper Burma. The Kachin people fiercely resisted the British annexation and the military police were constantly called on to quell uprisings and restore peace. In December 1892 the Kachins attacked a military police column en route to establish a post at Fort Sima and simultaneously launched a raid on the town of Myitkyna. An expedition of British and mixed forces was sent to put down the uprising, during which campaign Surgeon-Major Owen Lloyd earned the VC at Fort Sima on 6 January 1893. The Kachins were finally defeated at Palap after a short campaign during which three officers were killed and 102 sepoys and followers were killed or wounded.

The North-West Frontier, 1895
In 1889 the British entered the Chitral district of what is now northernmost Pakistan and established an agency, to which the local tribesmen remained very hostile. In January 1895 the Chitrali chief was overthrown and murdered, and this signalled the start of fighting among the local tribes. When Umrah Khan, ruler of the Narai district, invaded Chitral, Britain's political agent in Gilgit, Surgeon-Major George Robertson, arrived with 400 men to occupy the Chitral Fort. Umrah Khan joined forces with the Pathan chief Sher Afzal to drive the British out of Chitral.

The British garrison at the Chitral fort amounted to just 419 fighting men when Afzal arrived on 3 March with around 4,000 men and took up positions around the fort. A recce party went out from the fort and suffered heavy casualties before making a difficult retreat; during the sortie Surgeon-Captain Harry Whitchurch earned the VC. The garrison remained under siege until 19 April, when a small force under the command of Lieutenant Colonel James Kelly drove the Chitralis back, and the main relief party, 15,000 men led by Major General Sir Robert Low, seized Afzal. A new British-backed chief, Shuja-ul-Mulk, was confirmed as ruler and a British garrison was established at Chitral to keep the peace.

The Matabeleland Rebellion, 1896
In 1895 all the territories subject to the British South Africa Company were drawn together under the new name of Rhodesia, derived from the name of the company's leading spirit, Cecil Rhodes. By the end of March 1896 conditions for the Matabele people in the new Rhodesia drove them to rise up in rebellion. A VC was awarded to Trooper Herbert Henderson for his actions following an ambush by Matabele tribesmen at Campbell's Store. The uprising continued as

the Matabele were driven to desperation by the death of their cattle from disease, and enslaved by forced labour on the settlers' farms and in mines; when their witch doctors incited them to take action, they murdered all the men and women on the outlying farms. In a further Matabele attack on 22 April, during which a small group was surrounded near Bulawayo, a VC was awarded to Trooper Frank Baxter.

The BSAC could not keep control, so a relief force – the Bulawayo Field Force – was raised, comprising one group under Major Herbert Plumer, which entered the chief town of Bulawayo in May, and additional imperial troops under Sir Frederick Carrington, who joined Plumer's men in June. Notably, the chief of staff in Carrington's force was Robert Baden-Powell – who made a name for himself at Mafeking and later founded the Boy Scout movement; it was his prowess in scouting out and spying on the enemy that was responsible for much of his force's success. The Matabele tribesmen worked in small groups, using their knowledge of the terrain to set up mountain strongholds from which to carry out raids and ambushes. The campaign was one of small encounters, and it was finally brought to an end when Baden-Powell's chief native scout, Jan Grootboom, managed to get the Matabele chiefs to attend a parley with Cecil Rhodes. It took months to bring the whole region under control, and it was not until early 1897 that Baden-Powell was able to leave Africa to return home.

The Mashona Rebellion, Rhodesia, 1896–1897
Anti-colonial feeling among the tribal peoples of the newly created state of Rhodesia had long run high, but in June 1896 the Mashona tribesmen were fired to revolt by their spirit mediums, who convinced them that they would be impervious to bullets.

The main action of the revolt centred on the Alice Mine in the Mazoe Valley, where a group of Mashona surrounded the miners and their families. On 17 June the Chief Inspector of the Chartered Company's Telegraphs organised and led a party from Salisbury to rescue the miners, but it was on the 19th that a second party, led by Captain R.C. Nesbitt, joined the rescue mission to bring the miners and their families to safety, for which he was awarded the Victoria Cross.

The Sudan Campaign, 1896–1900
The defeat of General Gordon at Khartoum in 1885 was seen as a major British humiliation, and there were calls for revenge. No action was taken, however, until a new Conservative government under Lord Salisbury came to power in 1895. By then the government was also concerned about the Khalifa's regime in Sudan, which bordered British-held Egypt, and needed to restore the

perception of European strength in the region following Italy's thwarted attempt to expand her territories in Eritrea in March 1896.

In March 1896 the Egyptian army under Kitchener was ordered to retake Dongola Province in Sudan. On 7 June Kitchener led five Egyptian and five Sudanese battalions, one British engineer company and the machine-gun sections of the 1st North Staffords and the Connaught Rangers to defeat the dervish force at Firket. He then advanced, with reinforcements, to Hafir, where his men encountered the last organised resistance before reaching Dongola, which they occupied on 23 September.

In 1897 Kitchener planned a rail link between Wadi Halfa (at what is now the southern end of Lake Nasser) and Abu Hamed on the Nile to the south and east, so as not to have to rely on the looping course of the river for transport. Work began on 1 January 1897, with the route for the track being cleared of opposition by a force under Major General Sir Archibald Hunter, who reached Abu Hamed on 7 August and went on to occupy Berber, further south down the river, on 5 September. The Khalifa's army now threatened action, so Kitchener called in more British troops, who joined him in January 1898.

Kitchener attacked Emir Mahmoud's camp at Atbara on the Nile, to the south-east of Berber, routing the dervish defenders and capturing the Emir. Now with some 26,000 men, Kitchener advanced along the Nile towards the Khalifa's base at Omdurman, and by 1 September he had arrived within artillery range. In a grave tactical error, the Khalifa, instead of waiting for an attack in the hills around Omdurman, lined up his 40,000 men on the plain before the town. Early on the morning of 2 September the Khalifa's troops attacked, but the superior British artillery and awesome firepower repelled two attacks, inflicting massive losses – 11,000 killed, 16,000 wounded and 4,000 taken prisoner. Kitchener then marched out from his defended positions; in the following engagement Colonel Hector Macdonald's Sudanese Brigade and the 21st Lancers came under heavy attack, the latter carrying out one of the last major cavalry charges in history, during which VCs were earned by Private Thomas Byrne, Lieutenant the Honourable Raymond de Montmorency, Captain Paul Kenna and Captain Nevill Smyth. For the loss of just forty-eight dead, Kitchener advanced victorious into Omdurman and on 4 September British and Egyptian flags were raised over Omdurman. To avenge Gordon's death, his nephew blew up the tomb of the Mahdi who had defeated him.

Dervish resistance persisted, however, and on 7 September a small force under Colonel Parsons marched on Gedarif, south-east of Khartoum, and occupied the town on 22 September, during which action Captain the Honourable Alexander Hore-Ruthven earned the VC. It was not until November 1899 that British control was finally established in Sudan.

The North-West Frontier War, 1897–1898

In 1894 Colonel Sir Mortimer Durand's commission finalised the demarcation of new frontiers between India and Afghanistan, thereby bringing many frontier tribes into the British sphere of influence. These tribesmen were extremely hostile to this annexation and there was widespread unrest. Anti-British feeling was already running high when in 1897 the Amir of Afghanistan (only superficially pro-British) published a fiercely anti-Christian religious work in his assumed capacity as the King of Islam. This provoked a warlike spirit among the border Muslims, inciting uprisings against the British garrisons all along the frontier. Furthermore, since Britain had backed Greece in her recent war against Turkey, the Turkish Sultan took revenge by sending agents to Afghanistan to spread word that Britain's empire was crumbling and that there would be no troops available to contain an uprising in the frontier region. This coincided with the retirement of Colonel Robert Warburton as political officer in the Khyber Pass. The son of an Afghan mother, Warburton was fluent in Persian and Pushtu and was well respected by the tribesmen, and although he had set up the Khyber Rifles to man the forts along the pass, it was his personal influence which maintained the tenuous peace.

On 26 July 1897 the garrison at Malakand in the Swat Valley was alerted to an imminent attack across the border by Swati tribesmen led by the so-called 'Mad Mullah'. The garrison commander ordered a force to leave the garrison and secure the Amandra Pass 5 miles to the north, but the men were delayed and never left. Word soon came from the Chakandra Fort, near the pass, that the Mullah and his horde were approaching Malakand. Although there was a fort at Malakand, many men were based in a camp outside it; when the alarm sounded, Lieutenant Colonel McRae and Major Taylor led out a party of Sikhs to a narrow defile where, despite Taylor being killed, they prevented the enemy from surrounding the camp and cutting it off from the fort. For his bravery on the first day of the Malakand attack Lieutenant Edmond Costello was awarded the VC. The garrison held out against day and night attacks from 26 to 30 July, finally scattering the tribesmen with a bayonet charge on the night of the 30th. The Chakdara garrison also saw action: an estimated 2,000 tribesmen were killed there for the loss of five dead and ten wounded in fighting which lasted until 2 August. A punitive expedition of three brigades led by Brigadier General Sir Bindon Blood arrived to reinforce the garrisons on 31 July and remained in the region, quelling tribal unrest, until late October.

On 8 August 1897 Mohmand tribesmen raided Shabkadar near Peshawar, but the means to quash this uprising were already in the region. Two divisions of Sir Bindon Blood's expedition had advanced from Malakand to meet up at Bajour with another division under Major General Edmund Elles from Peshawar.

Blood's men reached Nawagai on 14 September, having detached a brigade to cross the Rambat Pass. These men were attacked in their camp the same night, but advanced the next day to deal with the rebel tribes in the Mohmand Valley. A further three columns under Brigadier General Jeffreys moved up the valley on 16 September, but met with fierce opposition. It was here that Lieutenant James Colvin, Corporal James Smith and Lieutenant Thomas Watson earned their VCs in an action to hold a small group of buildings at Bilot as Jeffreys retired.

At Nawagai Blood's troops came under heavy attack from 4,000 men led by Hadda Mullah; despite sustaining losses, Blood was able to link up with Elles, dispatching him to deal with the Upper Mohmands. Elles's well-conducted operation brought the Mohmand uprising to a close. It was one of a number of short campaigns fought in the frontier area.

In the spate of individual tribal uprisings by Afghans against the British, fighting broke out at Nawah Kill in the Swat Valley on 17 August. In rescuing a war correspondent here, Brevet Lieutenant Colonel Robert Adams, Lieutenant Alexander Fincastle and Lieutenant Hector MacLean all earned VCs. On 25 August 1897 Pathan Afridi tribesmen succeeded in taking control of the Khyber Pass. By the end of 1897 three field forces were needed to control the north-west frontier and the authorities in Simla issued an order at the end of September that the Khyber Pass must be retaken.

The Afridis were the most numerous and most aggressive of the frontier tribes – fine fighters who were well armed with long-range breech-loading rifles. Their neighbours in the Kohat and Khyber Passes and the Tirah area, to the south-west of the Peshawar Valley, were the less warlike Orakzais, who were nevertheless willing to join forces with the Afridis to regain their home-land. The Tirah was an oval-shaped plain of some 900 square miles that was jealously guarded by the Afridis, and never ventured into before by Europeans because of the almost impassable mountains that bordered it.

As Lieutenant General Sir William Lockhart's 35,000-strong Tirah Expeditionary Force set out, it was notionally the best-equipped yet in the frontier conflict. His plan was to enter the Tirah before the first snows, cross the Samana Range that bordered it to the south and subdue the Afridis and their allies by the end of December.

On 18 October Lockhart's men stormed the cliffs leading to the strategically important Dargai Heights, but lack of supplies forced them to withdraw. The Afridis reclaimed the position and it was not until 20 October, when supplies arrived, that another attack was made to regain the Heights. The well-armed Afridis fired at will on the exposed attackers, causing devastating casualties, but the heights were retaken – and in the process VCs were earned by Private Edward Lawson, Lieutenant Henry Pennell, Private Samuel Vickery and Piper George Findlater.

When the men of the Expeditionary Force eventually reached the Tirah plain, they found the villages deserted. Lockhart summoned the chiefs of the tribes to meet with him to discuss the terms of their surrender. No one appeared, and instead the Afridi warriors embarked on a guerrilla campaign of sniping and ambushing. In retaliation, Lockhart's men were ordered to raze the Tirah villages to the ground – only the mosques remained untouched. As the harsh winter approached, the Orakzais were driven to surrender but the Afridis remained defiant, their hatred of the British more intense than ever.

The Khyber was still not reclaimed and on 9 December, in order to avoid being trapped in the Tirah for the winter, Lockhart started a withdrawal in bitter weather. Without winter shelters, the columns had to bivouac by night around guttering camp fires and were subjected to constant night attacks over the five-day journey. However, despite heavy casualties, the columns eventually reached familiar territory and, carrying out a scorched-earth campaign, began to gain the upper hand. By the early spring of 1898 the Khyber Pass was retaken; the Afridis had had enough and gave up the fight for their homeland.

Although the Tirah campaign proper started with Lockhart's punitive expedition, an action at Nawah Kill on 17 August 1897 in which three VCs were earned is considered to be part of this overall campaign.

Crete, 1898

The Christian population of the Mediterranean island of Crete, with the support of the Greek government and the Greek military, rose up in revolt in 1857. Britain, France, Russia, Italy, Germany and Austria sent warships to restore peace, but no lasting political solution was reached: the Christians controlled the countryside while the Turks held the towns. Austria and Germany then withdrew, leaving Britain, France, Russia and Italy overseeing one district of the island each.

By 1898 the garrison in Candia, the British quarter, was down to a single regiment of the Highland Light Infantry. On 6 September the colonel of this regiment attempted to install a new collector of taxes to gather revenue from the export customs duties, at which a Muslim mob rose up in protest, killing nearly a hundred British soldiers and a thousand Christian inhabitants in the town of Candia. They went on to burn the British vice-consul in his home, set the town on fire and besiege the customs house. The beleaguered customs house garrison called on the British fleet under Admiral Noel, which bombarded the town. Two parties of fifty men from the torpedo boat HMS *Hazard* came ashore, and it was during their landing under fire that Surgeon William Maillard earned the Victoria Cross, the first naval medical officer to receive the medal. This was an unusual citation in that it was awarded in what was technically peacetime and therefore not against a declared 'enemy of the Crown'. The situation was eventually brought under control and the seven Muslim ringleaders were tried for the murder of two privates of the Highland Light Infantry, and hanged.

The Second Boer War, 1899–1902

Having subjugated the local southern African tribes to create the colonies of Natal and Cape Colony by the end of the nineteenth century, Britain now wanted to bring together her colonies and the Boer Republics – the Orange Free State and the Transvaal (the South African Republic) – in one British-dominated South African Federation.

The Boers, Dutch-speaking Calvinist farmers, had already suffered incursions from 'Uitlanders' ('outsiders', chiefly Britons, who now formed a majority in the population) after gold had been discovered in the Transvaal in 1886, and they had no wish to lose their independence. The war that resulted from this clash of wills lasted almost three years and cost Britain around £210 million and 52,156 casualties, including 20,721 dead. It was also a war in which, for the first time, technical innovations such as the electric telegraph, the field telephone and eventually steam traction engines were used, the latter to spare pack animals which, ill-suited to the harsh conditions and long distances covered, died in their thousands.

The High Commissioner in South Africa, Sir Alfred Milner, decided to use the representation of the Uitlanders in the Transvaal's government as the lever with which to remove Paul Kruger, President of the Transvaal. In August 1899 Kruger made the last of a series of concessions, offering to extend the franchise to the Uitlanders in return for Britain's agreement not to interfere in Boer affairs and to relinquish her claims to the Transvaal. Although conflict seemed inevitable, Britain did little to prepare for war. Only on 8 September were troops ordered from India to reinforce Natal, and mobilisation from Britain was not ordered until 7 October. Kruger mobilised on 27 September and on 9 October, with President Steyn of the Orange Free State, he presented an ultimatum, demanding that within forty-eight hours Britain should submit to arbitration on all points of difference, withdraw her troops from the Transvaal's borders and return all reinforcements that had arrived since 1 June.

The Boers, foreseeing no peaceful resolution, seized the initiative, struck first and invaded Cape Colony and Natal on 11 and 12 October 1899.

The Boers immediately cut off Mafeking, the northernmost town in Cape Colony, and surrounded Kimberley on 15 October. The Natal Field Force, under Lieutenant General Sir George White VC, set out towards Ladysmith and recorded initial successes on 20 and 21 October at Talana and Elandslaagte (at the latter four VCs were earned), but soon found itself driven into the town and under siege, with 13,500 troops and 7,500 civilians surrounded by 17,000 Boers. Well equipped with modern rapid-fire arms and heavy artillery, and tactically very cunning, they posed a very different sort of opposition from the South African tribesmen who had been relatively easily suppressed.

In the winter of 1899 Colonel Robert Baden-Powell and his men were besieged by the Boers in the small railway town of Mafeking on the north-west border of Cape Colony. His force, the Bechuanaland Protectorate Regiment, known disparagingly as 'the Loafers' had been recruited from local Rhodesians and consisted of frontier adventurers and not a few villains, but this formula had proved remarkably effective in the Zulu War, provided they were well trained and strongly led. To help him in his recruitment and training, Baden-Powell called on Captain Charles Fitzclarence of the Royal Fusiliers. His friends called him 'Fitz'; Baden-Powell referred to him as 'the Demon'.

B Squadron was drawn straight into the action two days after the Boer War began. On 14 October the Boers attacked an armoured train at Five Mile Bank outside Mafeking and the B Squadron troopers arrived to find themselves heavily outnumbered. Even though Fitzclarence had not had all the time he wanted to train his men, he led from the front and so inspired his men that they drove the Boers back, leaving fifty dead and many wounded. However, the following day the Boers regrouped and encircled the town. Mafeking was under siege, with Baden-Powell, Fitzclarence and their men inside; it was to remain so for the next eight months.

Baden-Powell was charged with keeping the Boers on their toes and tying up as many of them as possible in the siege. Outgunned by the Boer artillery, he opted for covert strikes. One such attack was planned for the night of 27 October. Fitzclarence led sixty of his own squadron and a few Cape Police in a charge against the Boer positions under cover of dark. Fitzclarence went in first, sword drawn, and accounted for four Boers killed in hand-to-hand fighting. The enemy retreated and in their panic fired on their own men. At the end of the attack 150 Boers lay dead or wounded for just six dead and nine wounded among Fitzclarence's men. Baden-Powell recorded that without Fitzclarence's 'extraordinary spirit and fearlessness, the attacks would have been failures and we should have suffered heavy losses in both men and prestige'.

To keep the Boers alert, Baden-Powell planned another raid on Boxing Day, this time on Game Tree Fort, some distance outside the town. The armoured train sent out to support the attack could not get through as the Boers had destroyed the rails, and any attack launched against the Boer stronghold was cut down in a hail of bullets. The Protectorate Regiment was called to storm the fort. Despite suffering casualties, they reached their objective – but were thwarted by heavy sandbagging and impenetrable iron roofing. It was left to Fitzclarence and B Squadron to break through in the second wave of the attack. The Boers fired constantly through loopholes, but, according to one reporter, 'Fitzclarence alone got inside and stabbed two or three. They shot him once, but he proceeded to bayonet another when they shot him a second time and he dropped down ... though not dead.' He had been shot in both legs, but recovered enough to play cricket within the beleaguered town.

For his bravery at Game Tree Fort, and previously on 27 October, Baden-Powell recommended Fitzclarence for the VC – the first of the Boer War.

Maintaining three major sieges (Mafeking, Ladysmith and Kimberley) seriously diluted the Boers' strength, but the British relief troops were similarly weakened. The newly arrived Commander-in-Chief Sir Redvers Buller split his force of some 47,000 men, directing his own efforts into relieving Ladysmith while Lieutenant General Lord Methuen was to reclaim Kimberley and Lieutenant General Sir William Gatacre was ordered to keep potential Boer reinforcements occupied. Disaster ensued. In what became known as 'Black Week', 10 to 17 December, Gatacre's force was defeated at Stormberg on the 10th, and two days later Methuen's men, weakened by an earlier battering in an ambush at Modder River just south of Kimberley, suffered a defeat at Magersfontein. Here, once again, the British walked into a well-laid trap as the Boers waited unseen in camouflaged trenches; three VCs were awarded for actions during the costly retreat. On Friday 15 December Buller attempted to cross the River Tugela at Colenso to the east, just 10 miles south of Ladysmith; despite commanding the largest British force amassed since the Battle of the Alma in the Crimea, he was no match for the Boers and their well-directed mobility, and was heavily defeated. During the rout seven VCs were earned.

In response to the defeats of Black Week, Field Marshal Lord Roberts was despatched to take supreme command, with Major General Kitchener as his Chief of Staff. He appreciated better than Buller the importance of public morale and the power of well-planned publicity for gains – and a light hand in reporting reverses. More materially, he addressed the problems of inadequate management and poor leadership, logistical shortcomings and lack of mobility.

The Boers surrounding Ladysmith now attempted to storm the town, but were thwarted by unsuccessful attacks on Caesar's Camp and Wagon Hill on 6 January; in these actions five VCs were earned, two of them awarded posthumously. Buller still drove on to lift the Ladysmith siege, but through naive military strategy and lack of foresight he suffered a costly defeat at Spion Kop on 23/24 January 1900, where nearly 1,200 men were killed or wounded in a bloody massacre. This disaster dented Buller's confidence. Even when the strategically vital Val Krantz to the south-east of Ladysmith had been secured he hesitated and failed to press home the attack to take the equally important Green Hill nearby; forty-eight hours later his men had withdrawn back across the Tugela. No ground had been gained, but thirty-four men had been killed and 335 wounded.

A week later, when his troops had had a much-needed respite, Buller led a successful attack which drove the Boers from south of the river. The same could not be said of the north side, however. Here the Boers were well dug in, and it took two days of fierce and costly fighting to dislodge them. There was a further setback at Hart's Hill on the Tugela on 23 February, as Major General Fitzroy Hart launched an ill-advised attack against unassailably strong Boer positions with further loss of life, but Buller finally moved in to relieve Ladysmith on 28 February – not a moment too soon for the starving inhabitants, who had been reduced to practically nil rations.

To the west, Roberts planned his advance on Kimberley, finally relieving the four-month siege on 15 February. Then, as Buller was finally lifting the siege at Ladysmith, the tide of war also turned in the west, as the Boers surrendered to Roberts at Paardeberg on 27 February. However, Roberts' progress was now held up for seven weeks by a serious outbreak of typhoid. During this period there was a setback at the Kom Spruit tributary of the Modder River on 31 March, where again there was needless loss of life in an ill-advised attack.

Soon Roberts resumed the drive eastward with a force of around 100,000 men, mustered from Kimberley, Pretoria and the north of Natal; the Boers, with no more than 30,000 men, were unable to sustain the 217-day siege at Mafeking, and were driven away on 17 May. The drive continued as Lieutenant General Sir Archibald Hunter crossed into the Transvaal at the start of May and Roberts pressed on to take Johannesburg, Pretoria and, to the far east, Koomati Poort. By June Britain had overrun the Orange Free State and annexed the gold-rich Transvaal.

However, despite jubilation in Britain, this was not the end of the war. The President of the Orange Free State, Marthinus Steyn, fled as Roberts' troops overran his capital and remained at large, inciting determined and skilled resistance, as did Kruger's deputy, Burgher. Boer commandos under the inspired command of Christiaan Rudolf de Wet and Jacobus Hercules de la Rey continued to harass the British troops for a further eighteen months after the so-called end of the war. Kitchener's response was to deprive the Boers of reinforcements, food, supplies and information by burning down their homesteads and gathering their families into concentration camps – a policy which was deplored at home and which backfired as fatal diseases spread through the camps. Without the distraction of dependents, the Boer guerrillas were free to fight single-mindedly. (Some 18,000 to 20,000 Boers – mainly women and children – died in the camps, along with around 14,000 black Africans in separate refugee camps.) Most effectively, however, Kitchener dealt with the Boers' mobility by building a network of blockhouses, linked by barbed wire, which also guarded the railway tracks, and by sending out frequent columns of mounted infantry, up to 2,000 strong, to sweep the veldt to seek out the enemy – if necessary in quick response to a telegraphed warning.

On 31 May 1902 the Boers had finally had enough and signed the Treaty of Vereeniging, surrendering their territories to British colonial rule, with a promise of self-government later.

During the course of the war seventy-eight VC awards were made. Much of the action was directed at lifting the sieges at Ladysmith, Kimberley and Mafeking, and VCs were earned in strategic battles to achieve these ends. However, the Boers' guerrilla ambush tactics following the notional end of the war proper also occasioned acts of great bravery and VCs were also awarded for actions during the policing of the region prior to the treaty being signed.

The Third Ashanti Expedition, 1900–1901
First suppressed in the cause of protecting trade routes and British nationals on the western coast of Africa in 1874, the Ashanti people of Gambia had again risen against British dominance in 1895. This rebellion had been quashed and a peace, albeit a grudging one, had continued until 1900, when the British decided to capture the symbolic 'Golden Stool', regarded by the Ashanti as a sign of authority.

In April 1900, on hearing of this, the Ashanti rebelled and besieged the fort of Kumassi, where the visiting governor, Sir Frederick Hodge, took refuge with his wife and some thousand others, and it was around this siege that the main action centred. Imperial troops were tied up in the Boer War in southern Africa and in the Boxer Rebellion in China, so few men were available to relieve the siege. An initial group of fifty men broke through on 15 April, and a further group on the 17th – but by the time 230 reinforcements arrived on 15 May, the situation in the fort was becoming desperate, without food or medical supplies. Not until 23 June was it possible to evacuate the 600 troops and around 1,000 civilians from Kumassi, leaving a garrison of about a hundred men.

In the meantime a relief party under Brigadier General James Willcocks was making its way to the fort, and in an engagement at Dompoassi on 6 June Sergeant John Mackenzie of the Seaforth Highlanders earned a VC. The column eventually relieved Kumassi on 23 July, but further fighting ensued as flying columns pursued the Ashanti, destroying their villages. Significantly, at Obassa, Willcocks' men inflicted a decisive defeat on 30 September, after which Captain Sir Charles Melliss was awarded the VC, and by November Ashanti opposition had been suppressed. In 1902 Ashanti was formally annexed as a crown colony.

The Boxer Rebellion, 1900

In the late nineteenth century a society was formed in China called the I-ho Chuan, or 'Society of Righteous and Harmonious Fists', known in the West as the 'Boxers'. Its objective was to rid China of foreigners and Christians, and the appointment of one of its founder members, Vu Hsien, as Governor of Shantung Province in March 1899 cleared the way for the Boxers to start their campaign. On 30 December a clergyman, the Reverend Brooks, was murdered in Shantung, and the Chinese Manchu regime's response on 11 January 1900 – that the Boxers should not be regarded as a criminal organisation – encouraged other fiercely xenophobic secret societies. By May the situation in Peking was so dangerous that the British Ambassador telegraphed the British Naval Commander-in-Chief, Vice Admiral Sir Edward Seymour, asking him to send guards to protect the legations. The Great Powers demanded that the Chinese Empress and her court take action to suppress these groups, but the request was ignored. On 2 June two missionaries were killed, and seven days later a royal edict was issued that openly encouraged the murder of foreigners.

Britain, America, Russia, France, Japan, Italy, Austria and Germany all had warships in Chinese ports to protect their nationals and their trade interests, and they all contributed to an allied force of 2,000 marines and sailors that was formed to relieve Peking. Seymour's column advanced by railway as far as Langfang, about 70 miles (110km) inland, but there the line was too damaged for it to advance further. Isolated and with 230 casualties, it was compelled to fall back towards Tientsin, about 35 miles (55km) inland; it took the arsenal near Hsiku, a few miles outside the city, on the 22nd, and then waited for reinforcements. The Taku Forts at the entrance to the Pei-Ho River had been captured on 17 June, an essential preliminary to any relief of Peking, but on 21 June war was declared on all foreigners; now able to act freely, the Boxers attacked the foreign settlements in Tientsin. Seymour's column was rescued by an international force of 2,000 men and Tientsin was captured on 14 July after fierce fighting, in which Midshipman Basil Guy was awarded the Victoria Cross.

Meanwhile in Peking, in compliance with an imperial order of 18 June, the Boxers had begun massacring Christians and foreigners and burning their buildings. The compound that held the foreign legations became a refuge for about 3,500 foreigners and Chinese Christians: besieged by about 300,000 Chinese, it was defended by 407 men. Fifty men of the Royal Marine Light Infantry from HMS *Orlando*, under the command of Captain Sir Lewis Halliday (who was awarded the Victoria Cross for his actions here), fought a fierce battle to protect the besieged British Legation.

Atrocities continued as a Roman Catholic bishop was burned alive in Mukden, and fifty-four missionaries were murdered in Shansi Province. With the arrival of British and allied troops in Shanghai in early August, fighting between the Chinese and Europeans began in earnest. An allied force of some 18,000 British and Americans advanced on Peking, reaching the outer city on the 14th, where men of the 14th Infantry scaled the Tartar Wall, raised the first foreign flag to fly there and opened up the way for British units to raise the siege of the compound. It had lasted fifty-five days.

The Manchu court fled the capital, but eventually had to accept the terms of the Boxer Protocol, which allowed the permanent stationing of fortified foreign legations in Peking, foreign garrisons along the Tientsin–Peking railway and the payment of a large indemnity.

Edwardian Colonial Wars
Somaliland, 1902–1905
Since the middle of the nineteenth century Britain had been securing her territory in Somaliland and defining its boundaries with those of French, Italian and Abyssinian Somaliland. The majority of local tribal chiefs accepted Britain's protection, but the most belligerent of the hostile chiefs was Mahommed bin Abdullah, a mullah of the Habr Suleiman Ogaden tribe. Claiming supernatural powers in support of his cause against the infidel, he gathered followers, mustering an army of some 15,000 dervishes. In 1899 bin Abdullah, dubbed the 'Mad Mullah', declared himself Mahdi and launched attacks against pro-British tribes. These tribes requested British protection and Colonel E.J. Swayne raised a body of about 2,000 mainly local troops – the Somali Levy – to take on the dervish rebels.

Starting in April 1901, Swayne carried out a number of cat-and-mouse attacks, but these were indecisive. In June, after several setbacks and suffering heavy casualties, the Mad Mullah retreated and regrouped, gathering more support in order to renew his campaign in October 1902. On 6 October Swayne's troops followed the dervishes into Italian territory (with permission) and were ambushed at Erego, where, despite heavy casualties, they drove off the enemy in an action where the only VC of the campaign was earned by Captain Alexander Cobbe of the King's African Rifles. Unfortunately, the Somali troops did not press home their victory and again the Mad Mullah withdrew to regroup. Despite a rout of the dervish troops by the Abyssinians on 31 May, the Mullah once again retreated unhindered and took refuge in the Nogal Valley.

The British government saw the Mullah's presence in Nogal as a continuing threat, and decided to destroy his power once and for all. Some 8,000 British troops led by Major General Sir Charles Egerton advanced on the Mullah's force of around 7,000 dervishes at Jidballi in British Somaliland in December 1903. During a reconnaissance foray a small mounted party was pursued by a large force of dervishes; for returning to save one of the party, Lieutenant Herbert Carter was awarded the VC. The second VC of the expedition was awarded to Lieutenant Clement Smith in the conclusive engagement against the Mullah's forces at Jidballi on 10 January. The British square withstood repeated attempts to charge it down, and superior firepower and discipline eventually broke up the Mullah's forces, which fled, pursued by the cavalry.

The Kano-Sokoto Expedition, 1903

In January 1900 Sir Frederick Lugard, the creator of the West African Frontier Force, arrived in Northern Nigeria as High Commissioner, with the temporary rank of brigadier general. The British government had recently terminated the Niger Company's charter and declared a protectorate over Northern and Southern Nigeria, and Lugard was tasked with building a new state in the un-developed region, where Muslim emirates drew their prosperity from trading in slaves taken from among their pagan neighbours. Lugard set about subjugating the emirs to bring them under the overall British protectorate, freeing the non-Muslim states from the threat of slavery and clearing the way for an infra-structure of transport routes and communications to support foreign trade.

In 1902 he ordered a series of raids against the Fulani emirates of Sokoto, Kano, Gando and Katsina, which were resisting his rule. A column of 700 men, a force quite disproportionate to the task, was sent to invade the ancient city of Kano. In February 1903 field guns delivered a devastating barrage, ripping through the mud-brick walls and causing massive casualties. The Emir's troops put up what resistance they could, but, inadequately armed, they were no match for the invaders' superior power. One group of just forty-five men under the command of Lieutenant Wallace Wright (later awarded the Victoria Cross for this action) held off cavalry and infantry charges by some 3,000 of the Emir's troops and eventually sent them into retreat in disarray.

Lugard then sent forces to the Fulani federation's capital of Sokoto, where the swords and spears of the Emir's men were useless against the heavy guns, and the city surrendered before it suffered the same damage as Kano. These two raids effectively quashed the Muslim emirates' opposition. The remaining cities surrendered, and Lugard was careful to appoint new emirs who were amenable to British control to avoid further opposition.

The Armed Mission to Tibet, 1903–1904

Although notionally under Chinese rule, Tibet had never subscribed to the trade regulations and border demarcations agreed by China with Britain in the late 1890s. This led to considerable unrest, but this alone was not the spur to military intervention. Word had reached the British government that China was engaged in secret negotiations to cede her interest in Tibet to Russia. This would provide a base from which Russia could threaten India's north-eastern frontiers, so in July 1903 a commercial mission with military escort under Colonel Francis Younghusband was sent to talk with the Chinese and Tibetans at Khamba Jong. The Tibetans refused to negotiate, so Britain sent him with a military mission to Lhasa to force the Tibetans to cooperate. Some 1,150 troops entered Tibet on 12 December but their commander, Brigadier General J.R.L. Macdonald, was not prepared to over-winter in Tibet and the advance was held up until March 1904. Macdonald's forces dispersed the opposition as they swept through Red Idol Gorge to Gyantse on 12 April. Although the 'jong' or fortress surrendered, it was not until 6 July, when the British stormed it, that its capture was consolidated. The sheer rock face of the approach offered no cover from fire, and after a day of artillery pounding, a breach was finally made to allow in the attacking forces. Lieutenant Grant led a company under heavy fire to make the first assault, for which action he was awarded the Victoria Cross.

The advance reached Lhasa on 3 August and it was left to Younghusband to reach an agreement with the Tibetans, which he concluded on 7 September. The expedition returned safely to India at the end of October.

Twentieth-Century Conflicts

First World War, 1914–1918

The history of the First World War is so well known and has been so extensively covered elsewhere that a summary is not included in this book for reasons of space.

The Inter-war Period

Following the Bolshevik Revolution in November 1917, which saw the overthrow of Tsar Nicholas II, Russia withdrew from the First World War, leaving the way clear for Germany to move troops unhindered to the Western Front.

Furthermore, under the terms of the Treaty of Brest-Litovsk, Germany was allowed to occupy large areas of European Russia. The Allies had substantial stockpiles of military equipment in these areas, especially in the northern ports of Murmansk and Archangel, and to prevent these supplies falling into German hands, in March 1918 an Allied force was sent to Russia, not just to secure the supplies but also to train Tsarist White Russian troops to reinforce a new Eastern Front. These forces were drawn into action against the Bolsheviks and were not withdrawn after the Armistice was signed in November 1918. Trapped and iced in by the Russian winter, the troops became increasingly discontented and there was a real threat of mutiny. The British government raised the North Russia Relief Force to oversee their safe withdrawal.

Although no Australian units were involved in this operation, a number of Australians who were awaiting repatriation after the war volunteered and enlisted in the British Army, joining the 45th Battalion, Royal Fusiliers and the 201st Battalion, Machine-Gun Corps, and went to Russia with the relief force, which arrived in June 1919.

The Bolsheviks made frequent attacks on the Allies during the evacuation. On 17 June British coastal motor-boats (CMBs) engaged and sank the cruiser *Olig*, during which action Lieutenant Augustine Agar earned the VC. In August an Australian, Corporal Arthur Sullivan, was awarded the VC for his bravery in a rearguard action in which the troops were retreating across the Sheika River. Agar was subsequently awarded the DSO on 17/18 August for an action in which eight coastal motor-boats, led by Commander Claude Dobson, carried out an attack on Bolshevik-held Kronstadt. Breaking into the inner harbour early on the morning of the 18th, the raiders sank the armoured cruiser *Pamiat Azova* and the dreadnought *Petropavlosk*, and seriously damaged the *Andrei Pervozvanni*. Three CMBs were sunk during the raid, for which Commander Claude Dobson and Lieutenant Gordon Steele were both awarded the VC.

On 29 August an assault was carried out to take a Bolshevik battery position north-west of Emtsa, which was achieved with only minor casualties owing to the action of Sergeant Samuel Pearse, whose self-sacrifice in taking out an enemy blockhouse earned him a posthumous VC. By September 1919 all British troops had been withdrawn.

North-West Frontier, 1919–1924
Since May 1919 British-occupied towns and military posts on India's north-western frontier had come under continual attack from Mahsud tribesmen. Following one such attack on a British convoy on 22 October that year, Captain Henry Adams set up an aid post to deal with the casualties and was awarded the

VC for his bravery under fire. A force of 63,000 men was mustered to put down the growing Mahsud insurrection, and it set out in November 1919 to invade the enemy's mountain territories. One column met no opposition from the Tochi Wazir tribesmen, who accepted British terms, but the Mahsuds refused to attend talks and a second column was sent to subjugate them by force. By 28 December, after heavy fighting, the column came within 4 miles of Kot Kai, at which point the Mahsuds agreed to British terms – only to break the agreement almost immediately. On 2 January 1920 a lightly manned advance position came under heavy Mahsud attack and the men's eventual safe withdrawal was accomplished with minimum loss of life due to the leadership of Lieutenant William Kenny, who was awarded the VC for this battle.

The column moved on to take the Mahsud capital of Kaniguram on 6 March 1920, and resistance had petered out by early May. However, in the wake of the uprising the Wana-Waziris in southern Waziristan refused to accept British terms, so another column was dispatched to set up permanent garrisons in the Wana region. These came under frequent attack and between November 1920 and March 1921 over 376 British lives were lost. In April, during a three-hour battle near Haidari Kach, Sepoy Ishar Singh became the first Sikh soldier to be awarded the VC. Raids became fewer and any uprisings were quickly put down by punitive expeditions over a period lasting until March 1924.

The Arab Revolt, Mesopotamia, 1920
After the First World War lands which had made up the German and Ottoman Empires were shared among the victors as 'mandate' territories by the League of Nations under the Sykes-Picot Agreement. Under this arrangement, the mandate lands – in Britain's case Iraq and Palestine – would remain under guidance until they were considered able to rule themselves.

There was immediate opposition to British rule in Iraq (Mesopotamia), and Sunni and Shia Muslim clerics cooperated to incite revolt. Exhausted and financially crippled by the war, Britain was obliged to draft in troops from India to deal with the rebellion; suppression was ruthless, with aerial bombardment of Iraqi villages carried out to quell the widespread unrest. On 24 July near Hillah, as his company was retiring, Captain George Henderson earned the VC for holding off repeated enemy charges and rallying his men until they could reach safety – prisoners taken by the Arab rebels were treated savagely, so capture was to be avoided at all costs.

The Second Mohmand Campaign, 1935
After years of unrest, as the tribes near India's north-western frontier battled against British colonial expansion, continued political pressure eventually

achieved the same rights and institutions for the people of the North-West Frontier Province as were enjoyed in British India. Meanwhile, across the border Afghanistan was developing into a stable state under the rule of Nadir Shah, who was anxious to stay on friendly terms with the British government in India. Unfortunately, this, and his willingness to accept Britain's frontier policies, caused violent antagonism within Afghanistan and there was an open conspiracy to oust him and restore a former ruler, Amanullah, to the throne. Shah had the leader of the conspiracy arrested and executed in 1932, but was himself assassinated in 1933 by the son of the executed rebel. Shah's 19-year-old son succeeded him and also maintained cordial relations with British India, but the hill tribes remained fiercely anti-British and embarked on a two-year rampage of robbery and murder which the Indian Army struggled to contain.

Eventually, in February 1935 the Nowshera Brigade was sent to deal with the powerful Mohmand military forces led by the Fakir of Alinger. Following a few minor skirmishes, the Mohmands launched a ferocious attack on the Kila Han position, held by a company of Sikh riflemen and a Ghurkha machine-gun platoon. After a night of fierce hand-to-hand fighting, the attackers were driven off, but this action prompted the British to mount a full-scale operation to quash the enemy forces to the west of Malakand and defeat the Fakir conclusively. This largely put an end to tribal revolt and order was reinforced by the presence of 30,000 Indian troops at the three main frontier forts. However, occasional feuds broke out, and it was at one such action on 29 September 1935 that Captain Godfrey Meynell earned the Victoria Cross. His medal was presented to his widow by King Edward VIII, the only VC to be awarded during his reign.

Second World War, 1939–1945
The history of the Second World War is so well known and has been so extensively covered elsewhere that a summary is not included in this book for reasons of space.

Palestine, 1945–1948
By the end of 1945 the British Army had two divisions in Palestine, 1st Infantry and 6th Airborne, whose primary role was to provide a strategic reserve in the Middle East. Jewish immigration had been restricted since 1939 so as to prevent Arab resentment erupting into another revolt, and this restriction was maintained after the war. Vast numbers of Jews from Europe, their lives shattered by the events of the past decade, were desperate to make a fresh start in their ancestral lands, but many of the refugee ships were turned back by

the British. This was too much for the Jews already in Palestine and at the end of October 1945 the Irgun, a Jewish underground army, launched a bombing campaign on economic targets in the country. There was a spate of rioting, followed by attacks on British troops. Reinforcements were rushed from Germany to fight what had now become a very unpleasant counter-insurgency campaign. Thousands of illegal weapons were found in cordon and search operations and many Jews were arrested on suspicion of terrorism, for this was what the Irgun forces were practising. Their worst atrocity was blowing up the King David Hotel in Jerusalem, which housed military and government offices, claiming the lives of ninety people.

Eventually, in November 1947 the United Nations (UN) stepped in and partitioned the country between Jews and Arabs. The result was an Arab back-lash, and by Christmas a virtual civil war was raging. The British government declared that its mandate would end in May 1948, and the British Army tried to achieve an orderly withdrawal. This was not easy, with both Jews and Arabs now attacking them. By the end of April 1948 the Jews had become confident enough to take their war against the Arabs into the few remaining British enclaves around Jaffa, Haifa and Jerusalem. Tanks and artillery were used against them, which at least demonstrated that it was not worth taking on the British Army in conventional warfare. The last two weeks were quiet, and the army withdrew to leave the newly created state of Israel to fight for its own survival.

India, 1947

A Labour government came to power in 1945 and pledged to grant independence to India, but this did not prevent continuing widespread unrest in the country. Lord Louis Mountbatten arrived as Viceroy in February 1947 with the pledge that the country would be split into two, reflecting the religious differences between Moslems and Hindus, and that independence would be granted to each by June 1948. This immediately created a wave of inter-religious strife, aggravated by the decision a little later to bring independence forward to August 1947. There were mass migrations across the borders of India into what was about to become Pakistan, and numerous massacres, often on board trains. Where British troops were present violence was generally pre-vented, but they were too few to have much effect. It was therefore with feelings of relief that the army finally left the country to end an association that had lasted over 200 years.

For the British officers in the old Indian Army it was, however, a time of tragedy. Many of them regarded India as home, and the prospect of beginning life afresh in the drabness of post-war Britain did not appeal. Nevertheless, while a few were able to stay on temporarily as advisers to the new Indian and Pakistani armies, the majority were faced with the stark choice of transferring to the British Army or retiring. Only one link with the old Indian Army was saved. In 1946 it had become apparent that the new Indian Army was prepared to take over only a proportion of the Ghurkha regiments, and Wavell suggested to the British government that the residue be transferred to the British Army. This was an attractive proposition, being the best way to retain political links with Nepal and also providing a solution to the problem of balancing Far East military commitments with the one-year conscription term. Consequently, after lengthy negotiations with the Nepalese and future Indian governments, it was agreed that four two-battalion regiments, the 2nd, 6th, 7th and 10th Ghurkha Rifles, would be transferred, and would be based in Malaya under 17th Division.

Malayan Emergency, 1948–1960
On 16 June 1948 young Chinese rebels killed three rubber-estate managers in various parts of Malaya; the attack marked the beginning of a counter-insurgency campaign that was to last for twelve years. The attacks had been instigated by the Chinese-run Malayan Communist Party, which believed that the time was ripe for revolution. The jungle, together with the mountainous landscape, provided the ideal terrain for the terrorist, and atrocities rapidly increased. By March 1950 the Communists had killed some 850 civilians, 325 policemen and 150 soldiers, and although 2,000 terrorists had been killed, captured or had surrendered, new recruits ensured that their strength was not reduced.

The 'Malayan Emergency' became a guerrilla war fought between Commonwealth armed forces and the Malayan National Liberation Army (MNLA), the military arm of the Malayan Communist Party. The title 'Malayan Emergency' was the colonial government's term for the conflict. The MNLA termed it the Anti-British National Liberation War. The rubber plantation and tin mining industries, however, pushed for the use of the term 'emergency', since their losses would not have been covered by Lloyd's insurers if it had been termed a 'war'.

In July 1948 Lieutenant General Sir Harold Briggs arrived as Director of Operations. He realised that the terrorists must be isolated by moving the thousands of Chinese supporters living in villages on the edge of the jungle. He also found a lack of worthwhile intelligence and instituted committees of military, police and government at every level. The administration of the country lacked the will, however, to coordinate the relevant agencies, and after the assassination of Sir Henry Gurney, the High Commissioner, in October

1951, General Sir Gerald Templer was appointed as High Commissioner and Director of Operations combined.

Some 45,000 troops were under Templer's command, including British, Ghurkhas, Australians, New Zealanders, Fijians, East Africans and the Malays themselves, whom Templer encouraged to take an increasing role. Security force and civilian casualties began to fall, while those of the terrorists, especially surrenders, increased. On 31 August 1957 the independence of Malaya, now to be called Malaysia, was declared amid popular rejoicing, removing any hope that the terrorists might achieve their long-term aim. Nevertheless it was three years before they were finally chased across the border with Thailand from where they continued from time to time to cause trouble.

While the Ghurkhas, whose permanent base the country now was, undoubtedly provided the backbone of the British Army's effort, many British battalions proved themselves expert jungle fighters. As in any counter-insurgency campaign, the need for constant alertness was paramount: a soldier might undergo days of 'jungle bashing' without seeing any sign of his enemy. Then suddenly there would be a burst of fire. To overcome the terrorist in this situation required superlative weapon handling and marksmanship, and training for these skills became one of Templer's priorities. Intelligence, too, was vital, and it was this that enabled the security forces to become increasingly successful in setting ambushes for the enemy. During twelve years in Malaysia some 11,000 terrorists were accounted for at a cost of 3,000 civilian lives and almost 2,000 of the security forces, including police; the army's share of the losses amounted to 350 British and 159 Ghurkha soldiers.

The Korean War, 1950–1953

After the Second World War Korea was divided up, by American and Soviet agreement, into the communist Democratic People's Republic of Korea in the north, which remained under Soviet influence, and the pro-Western Republic of Korea in the south.

On 25 June 1950 communist troops from North Korea invaded South Korea and the United Nations Security Council summoned the aid of all member nations in halting the attack. Britain's initial contribution was two battalions sent from Hong Kong, the 1st Argyll & Sutherland Highlanders and the 1st Middlesex, but numbers quickly grew to the equivalent of two brigades. In July 1951 these were combined with the Australian, British, Canadian, Indian and New Zealand troops to form the 1st Commonwealth Division under the command of General West. In total the conflict involved over 60,000 British troops, including many National Servicemen, mostly serving in independent brigades alongside the Commonwealth Division.

Despite early reverses, Allied reinforcements drove the North Koreans back, assisted by an amphibious landing by an American corps under the command of General Douglas MacArthur, which cut the communists' lines of supply north of the main battle ground.

China threatened to intervene if troops other than those of the Republic of Korea crossed into North Korea; nevertheless, US troops did so, with the approval of the UN, on 7 October. On the 21st Pyongyang fell and the US and Commonwealth troops headed for the Yalu River. The Chinese assembled an army of 330,000 men, and a massive attack began on 27 November. The Allied troops were then engaged in bitter fighting as they were forced south, and on 31 December the combined communist forces of China and North Korea again invaded South Korea.

In retaliation the Allies laid down a constant aerial bombardment, which halted the advance, and established a front line along the 38th Parallel, where fighting continued until July 1951, at which point truce negotiations started. There was a brief outbreak of fighting in June 1953, but by the end of July an armistice laid down the front line as the boundary between north and south.

Although the aerial bombardment played a major role, there was much close-quarter fighting. In an early action near Songiu in central South Korea, Major Kenneth Muir was awarded the VC for his initiative in carrying out attacks on enemy positions, and a further two VCs were awarded to Lieutenant Colonel James Came and Lieutenant Philip Curtis for their actions near the Imjin River against vastly superior enemy numbers. On 4 November 1951 Private William Speakman was also involved in close fighting as he made charging attacks with grenades, for which he too was awarded the Victoria Cross.

Mau Mau Rebellion, 1952–1956

In 1952 trouble erupted in East Africa when elements of the Kikuyu tribe in Kenya began agitating for the return of what they regarded as tribal lands. Two battalions of the King's African Rifles were all that were available at the time, so in October a British battalion, the Lancashire Fusiliers, was flown in from Britain. As the murders of loyal Kikuyu and European settlers mounted, more troops had to be brought in, until there were two British brigades, together with African troops. The Mau Mau, as the dissidents were known, operated from the forests, and large-scale sweep operations, very reminiscent of those used in the later stages of the Boer War, were initially employed against them. These, however, were relatively ineffective until the security forces concentrated on one area at a time. This concentration, together with harassment of Mau Mau supply lines and the integration of police and military intelligence staffs, as well as the setting up of a small War Cabinet – all lessons learnt in Malaya – enabled the rebellion to be put down by the spring of 1955. Thereafter the lead was taken by Special Forces, consisting of British officers and terrorists who had been 'turned', who tracked down and destroyed the remaining bands.

Cyprus, 1954–1960

This military campaign officially began on 1 April 1955, when a movement calling itself Ethniki Organosis Kuprion Agoniston (National Organisation of Cypriot Fighters, or EOKA for short), which was agitating for the union of Cyprus with Greece, launched simultaneous attacks on the British-controlled Cyprus Broadcasting Station in Nicosia (led by Markos Drakos), on the British Army's Wolseley barracks and on targets in Famagusta (led by Grigoris Afxentiou). Thereafter, unlike other anti-colonial movements, EOKA confined its acts to sabotaging military installations, ambushing military convoys and patrols, and assassinating British soldiers and local informers. It did not attempt to control any territory, a tactic that according to Grivas would not have suited the terrain and size of Cyprus or the imbalance of EOKA's conventional military capabilities with respect to the British Army.

The British garrison at the outset consisted of just two infantry battalions, an artillery and an engineer regiment, but as the violence increased this was clearly not enough. By January 1956 no fewer than four brigades were deployed, and Field Marshal Sir John Harding, who had commanded in Malaya during the early days, was appointed governor. He organised a number of large-scale operations in the Trudos Mountains, from where the EOKA bands, led by Colonel Grivas, were operating. A number of the bands were broken up but Grivas himself remained at large, although he had one or two narrow escapes.

After the interruption caused by Suez, the British Army concentrated once more on Cyprus, and by 1958 peace had been virtually restored to the island. Much negotiation with the Cypriots, Greeks and Turks was still required, however, before the violence was finally ended, and it was not until 1 August 1960 that the Republic of Cyprus came into being after eighty-two years of British rule. Britain, however, retained two sovereign base areas at Dhekelia and Akrotiri, as well as a number of radar and radio sites elsewhere on the island.

Suez Expedition, 1956

At the end of July 1956 Colonel Nasser, Egypt's Premier, declared that he was nationalising the Suez Canal. The last British troops had left Egypt in March 1956, and Nasser's declaration took the British and French governments by surprise. Prime Minister Eden believed that troops might well be required to make Nasser back down, and military planners considered that an entire corps would probably be required. The problem was that Britain lacked both the sea- and air-lift capability for such a force. In any event, because of the Cyprus emergency and the fact that King Idris of Libya refused to allow the 10th Armoured Division, then stationed in that country, to move across the border into Egypt, the troops had to be brought from Britain. In order to bring the regiments at home up to strength no fewer than 23,000 reservists were immediately called up and almost overnight a large number of military vehicles changed from their normal green to sand colour. A corps headquarters under General Sir Hugh Stockwell was brought across from Germany, but then there was another delay, caused mainly by US opposition. Eventually a plan was concocted in collusion with the Israelis, who would invade Sinai while the British and French landed in the Canal Zone masquerading as peace-keepers. The operation was finally launched at dawn on 5 November 1956 when French and British paratroops flying from Cyprus dropped on Port Said, to be followed by an amphibious landing by two Royal Marine Commandos with a third flown in by helicopter. It was the first British air-mobile operation. Fighting was sporadic and by midnight the following day a ceasefire had been imposed, largely thanks to international pressure. The British had lost eleven killed and ninety-two wounded, and the French ten killed and thirty-three wounded.

For the next two months British and French troops garrisoned the Canal until the UN took over. The enterprise had been politically unsatisfactory and had revealed severe military shortcomings. For the mobilised troops it had been a frustrating few months, and many of them never even got as far as Malta.

Muscat and Oman, 1957–1959

During this period various small forces, especially the SAS, which had been reactivated for Malaya, were helping the Sultans of Muscat and Oman to foil Saudi Arabian designs on their oilfields. The climax came in January 1959 when the SAS, supported by elements of the Life Guards, managed to capture the Saudi-backed rebel base in the Jebel Akhdar, a sheer limestone massif 40–50 miles in length and rising to 10,000ft, which was widely considered to be impregnable.

Jordan, 1958

In 1958 King Hussein of Jordan, who had been educated in England and had been an officer cadet at RMA Sandhurst, faced a revolt in his country and asked for British help. The 16th Parachute Brigade was flown to Amman and spent nearly four months there.

The Vietnam War, 1959–1975

The Vietnam War was essentially an American conflict, and British troops played no part in this protracted and politically messy war. However, Australian troops (to whom all four VCs of the war were awarded) became increasingly involved in the Vietnam War in the course of enforcing Australia's 'forward defence' planning policy. This complemented the United States' determination to contain the threat of communism in South-East Asia while also fulfilling Australia's obligations as a member of the South-East Asia Treaty Organization. In August 1962 Australian army advisers arrived to work with the US planners, assisting in training South Vietnamese troops for action – but without the mandate to take part in actual operations.

By early 1965 there were a hundred Australians working with the US advisory team, and when the first US combat troops arrived in Vietnam in March, the Australian premier, Robert Menzies, committed a force totalling 1,100 to the conflict, working in counter-insurgency operations. In March 1966 an Australian Task Force of 4,500 men was in action over an expanding area, but popular support for the war was falling in Australia and troops were finally withdrawn by June 1973.

The Australian Army Training Team Vietnam – known as 'The Team' – was the first and last Australian unit serving in Vietnam, and all four VC awards were made to 'Team' men. The unit was also honoured with the American US Presidential Meritorious Unit Citation and the Vietnamese Cross of Gallantry with Palm Unit Citation.

Kuwait, 1962

In June 1961 Iraq threatened Kuwait, which appealed to Britain for assistance, and a hastily made-up brigade sweltered there in the desert heat until October.

Brunei Revolution, 1962 and Borneo Campaign, 1963–1966

In December 1962 there was an Indonesian-inspired revolt against the Sultan of Brunei. It was quickly crushed by the Queen's Own Highlanders, 1/2nd Ghurkha Rifles and 42 Commando Royal Marines, which were quickly dispatched by Headquarters 17th Division in Malaya. President Sukarno retaliated by sending parties of irregulars across the border into Sarawak and Sabah (formerly North Borneo) to harry the authorities. Later in 1963, after Sarawak and Sabah had joined the Federation of Malaysia set up in September, Sukarno declared virtual open war and Indonesian troops began to make incursions. For the next three years the British Army found itself involved in another jungle campaign and the old skills of Malaya and Burma were quickly revived. General Walter Walker, himself widely experienced in jungle fighting in both Burma and Malaya as a Ghurkha battalion commander, was in command for most of the campaign and soon decided to take the war to the enemy's side of the border. Because Indonesia and Britain were not officially at war, this had to be done in great secrecy, and was given the codename Operation Claret. Patrols penetrated as much as 10 miles into Indonesian territory and laid often highly successful ambushes. The SAS, operating in four-man patrols, spent months at a time on Claret operations, befriending border villagers and sending back invaluable intelligence. On the home side of the border company base camps were built, complete with bunkers and trenches and 105mm pack howitzer guns.

The Malaysia–Indonesia Confrontation, 1963–1966
In September 1963 the Federation of Malaysia was officially recognised. It comprised the former British colonies of the Malay Peninsula, Singapore, Sabah and Sarawak in North Borneo, and was now governed by Prime Minister Tengku Abdul Rahman, who agreed to the continued presence of British armed forces in the country.

President Sukarno of Indonesia, to the south, regarded this military presence as a thinly disguised attempt to continue colonial rule and was concerned that the new federation would be used as a base from which troops could move to subvert the course of the revolution in his own country.

The so-called 'Confrontation' began with the aim of destabilising the Malaysian federations and raids were launched into Malaysian territory, even before its official recognition. At first, small parties of armed Indonesians crossed into Malaysia on propaganda and sabotage missions, but by 1964 regular units of the Indonesian army were involved. The British military presence had hitherto consisted of border-based companies tasked with protecting the local populace from Indonesian attack, but by 1965 Britain was prepared to take more aggressive measures. British troops now made offensive forays across the border, keeping the Indonesians on the defensive in their own territory, drastically reducing their incursions into Malaysia.

The only VC of the campaign was awarded to Lance Corporal Rambahadur Umbu, following an action in Sarawak on 21 November 1965. Eventually Indonesia ended hostilities on 11 August 1966, and rejoined the UN in September.

Cyprus, 1964–1965

This conflict on the Greek island of Cyprus began with the Turkish Army's invasion and occupation of Northern Cyprus in 1963. At the request of Archbishop Makarios, Britain was asked to provide a 'Peace Force' from its sovereign bases permanently stationed there, which was the forerunner of the later UN Force, charged with policing the 'Truce'. Major-General Peter Young took command, and by New Year's Day 1964 he had positioned his troops between the two sides in Nicosia and tried to impose a cease-fire. The general looked at a map of the capital and drew a line with a green chinagraph pencil. The Cypriot Turks were to stay to the north and the Greek Cypriots to the south. This became known as the 'Green Line'. The term is often misused to indicate the division of Cyprus today, but actually it only relates to Nicosia.

Members of the armed forces, with a Greek Cypriot policeman on board, patrolled the 'Green Line' in Nicosia. Other mobile patrols were provided to ensure the good behaviour and protection of UN personnel visiting the Nicosia bars and entertainment clubs. Later, the company was amalgamated with the United Nation's Peace-Keeping Force to become UNFICYP. Operation Tosca was the name given to the British contribution.

It was a bitter conflict, and there were even accusations against British Army personnel about inhuman treatment of both Greek and Turkish residents. Nevertheless, Cypriot Turks today still acknowledge individual acts of bravery by the British members of UNFICYP. They also talk about the soldiers who ignored the mandate and provided humanitarian help to starving villagers, against the wishes of senior non-British UN officers.

Aden, 1964

Aden was originally of interest to Britain as an anti-piracy station to protect shipping on the routes to British India. With the coming of the Suez Canal in 1869, it further served as a coaling station.

By 1963 anti-British guerrilla groups with varying political objectives had begun to coalesce into two larger, rival organizations: first, the Egyptian-supported National Liberation Front (NLF) and then the Front for the Liberation of Occupied South Yemen (FLOSY), which attacked each other as well as the British. Hostilities started with a grenade attack by the NLF against the British High Commissioner on 10 December 1963 at Aden airport, killing one person and injuring fifty. A state of emergency was then declared in the British Crown Colony of Aden and its hinterland, the Aden Protectorate.

By 1965 RAF Khormaksar was operating nine squadrons, including transport units with helicopters and a number of Hawker Hunter fighter-bomber aircraft. These were called in by the army for strikes against enemy positions, using 60-pounder high-explosive rockets and 30mm Aden cannon.

The emergency was further exacerbated by the Arab–Israeli War in June 1967. Nasser claimed that the British had helped Israel in the Six-Day War, and this led to a mutiny in the South Arabian Federation Army on 20 June, which also spread to the police. In July 1967 order was restored following the Battle of Crater. This battle, which was part of Operation Stirling Castle, brought to prominence Lieutenant Colonel Colin Campbell ('Mad Mitch') Mitchell of the 1st Battalion, Argyll & Sutherland Highlanders.

Nevertheless, deadly guerrilla attacks by the NLF soon resumed against British forces, with the British leaving Aden on 30 November 1967, earlier than had been planned by the British prime minister Harold Wilson, and without an agreement on the succeeding governance. The NLF seized power and established the People's Republic of South Yemen.

Northern Ireland, 1969–2007

The British Army was initially deployed as a peace-keeping force in the wake of Unionist attacks on Nationalist communities in Derry and Belfast, and to prevent further Loyalist attacks on Catholic communities. The army's presence in Northern Ireland was initially welcomed as a neutral force by the Catholic population, who had been under attack from Loyalists and the Royal Ulster Constabulary (RUC), but this largely changed following a three-day military clampdown (the 'Falls Curfew') on the Falls area of west Belfast in July 1970.

On 9 August 1971 the Unionist government of Northern Ireland introduced internment without trial (Operation Demetrius) and hundreds of Catholics were 'lifted' in pre-dawn raids. The operation was directed only at the IRA and no Loyalists were arrested. During the three days of violence and riots that followed, twenty-two people died and 7,000 Catholics were burned out of their homes.

However, the real turning point in the relationship between the Army and the Catholic community came on 30 January 1972, more commonly known as 'Bloody Sunday', when it was alleged that paratroopers killed fourteen civil-rights protesters in Derry. The deceased, along with seventeen injured and thousands of others, were taking part in an anti-internment march when the paratroopers opened fire. It is widely acknowledged that 'Bloody Sunday' was the beginning of the 'Troubles'.

The locally recruited Ulster Defence Regiment was formed, later becoming the Royal Irish Regiment in 1992. Over 700 soldiers were killed during the Troubles. Following the IRA ceasefires between 1994 and 1996 and since 1997, demilitarisation has taken place as part of the peace process, reducing the military presence from 30,000 to 5,000 troops. There was a steady reduction in the number of troops deployed there in the wake of the Good Friday Agreement signed in 1998.

In 2005, after the Provisional Irish Republican Army announced an end to its armed conflict in Northern Ireland, the British Army dismantled posts and withdrew many troops, and reduced troop levels to that of a peace-time garrison. Operation Banner (the operational name for the British armed forces' operation in Northern Ireland from August 1969) ended at midnight on 31 July 2007, bringing to an end some thirty-eight years of continuous deployment, making it the longest campaign in the British Army's history. An internal British Army document released in 2007 stated that although the British Army had failed to defeat the IRA, it had made it impossible for them to win through the use of violence. Operation Helvetica replaced Operation Banner in 2007, maintaining fewer servicemen in a much more benign environment. From 1971 to 1997 a total of 763 British military personnel were killed during the Troubles and 6,100 wounded. The British armed forces killed over 300 people. A total of 303 RUC officers were killed in the same time period. In March 2009 two soldiers and a police officer were killed in separate dissident republican attacks in Northern Ireland.

The Falklands War, 1982

On 2 April 1982 Argentina invaded the Falkland Islands – the Malvinas – to reclaim what it regarded as its own territory. The following day Argentinian troops invaded the British-held island of South Georgia, and on 6 April the Task Force set out from the UK to repel the invaders.

During the next two months concentrated air, sea and land operations were carried out in the harsh and inhospitable climate of the South Atlantic. May saw the sinking of the Argentinian ship *General Belgrano*, an Exocet attack on HMS *Sheffield* and the sinking of HMS *Ardent*, *Antelope* and *Coventry* and the container ship *Atlantic Conveyor*. British troops landed at San Carlos and were engaged in fierce fighting with well-entrenched Argentinian forces, 2nd Battalion, Parachute Regiment eventually retaking Goose Green on 28 May, during which attack at nearby Darwin Lieutenant Colonel Herbert 'H' Jones won the VC. The Argentinian troops were systematically removed from Mount Harriet, Two Sisters and Mount Longdon on the night of 11/12 June. The last VC of this conflict was awarded to Sergeant Ian McKay for his action on Mount Longdon. The following night 3rd Commando Brigade and 7th Infantry Brigade cleared Tumbledown, Wireless Ridge and Mount William, following which the Argentinian forces surrendered.

Gulf War in Iraq, 1990–1992
On 2 August 1990 Iraqi troops invaded Kuwait, over-running the small oil state in less than a day. Saudi Arabia to the immediate south came under threat and six days later, with United Nations backing, US forces began to deploy to the country, quickly followed by some from the Arab League. On 12 August the RAF began to deploy Tornado aircraft, and France sent the aircraft carrier *Clemenceau* to the region. Britain, too, agreed to send ground forces and initially offered either 3 Commando Brigade or 5 Airborne Brigade, both Falklands veterans and ear-marked for operations outside Europe. The Americans, however, declined both. Consequently, 7th Armoured Brigade, stationed on the North German Plain, was selected for what was codenamed Operation Granby. It consisted of two armoured regiments, the Royal Scots Dragoon Guards and the Queen's Royal Irish Hussars, both equipped with Challenger tanks, and the 1st Staffords with Warrior vehicles. The brigade was also reinforced by the 5/16th Queens Royal Lancers, an armoured reconnaissance regiment equipped with Scimitar tracked reconnaissance and Striker Swingfire ATGW vehicles. Besides its own direct-support artillery regiment, equipped with M109 155mm self-propelled guns, it was also given additional artillery, especially some US-produced Multiple Launched Rocket Systems (MLRS), which had recently come into service. Royal Engineers, armoured, field and support, were also deployed in force and, since the brigade would be operating far from home with Allies using different weapons systems and equipment, there was a large logistics element.

On arrival in the Gulf, 7th Armoured Brigade was placed under the command of the US Marines on the Kuwait–Saudi border and began desert training. A particular concern was the belief that Saddam Hussein (d. 2006) had a chemical warfare capability, and so much attention was paid to training in full NBC equipment – not easy in the heat, although the weather was getting cooler.

On 8 November President Bush, realising that there were now sufficient Coalition forces in-theatre to deter the Iraqis from invading Saudi Arabia, now turned his attention to evicting them from Kuwait. The sanctions imposed at the outset did not appear to be having much effect, and Saddam Hussein was as intransigent as ever. Evidence was also coming out of Kuwait about the maltreatment of the inhabitants, and it had become increasingly apparent that only force would achieve Kuwait's liberation. Bush therefore announced a massive reinforcement of the Coalition forces. Further forces would be sent from the United States and an armour-heavy corps from the US Seventh Army in Germany.

The additional British contribution was to be Headquarters 1st Armoured Division under Major General Rupert Smith, and 4th Armoured Brigade. This brigade had one Challenger regiment, the 14th/20th King's Hussars, and two mechanised infantry battalions, the Royal Scots and 3rd Battalion, Royal Regiment of Fusiliers, both equipped with Warriors. These reinforcements were deployed to the Gulf by mid-December. Concern that there might be heavy casualties, especially due to chemical warfare, prompted the unusual step of mobilising a TA General Hospital based at Glasgow for the Gulf, and its members responded willingly to the call.

President Bush had issued an ultimatum to Saddam Hussein to withdraw from Kuwait by 15 January, but as the date neared Iraqi forces were still firmly entrenched in Kuwait. Now Operation Desert Shield became Desert Storm when the Coalition air offensive against Iraq was launched. The objectives of this were to destroy the Iraqi Air Force, preferably on the ground, to cause maximum degradation to the Iraqis' ability to command, control and communicate with their forces on the ground, to disrupt their supply routes into Kuwait and, finally, to inflict maximum damage on the forces in Kuwait itself.

The air campaign was to last some six weeks and in the meantime planning and preparation for the ground offensive continued. General Norman Schwarzkopf, the Coalition's overall commander, hoped to make the Iraqis believe that he would strike directly into Kuwait from Saudi Arabia and would support this with amphibious landings on the Kuwait coast. In truth, the decisive blow was to be struck by the armour-heavy US VII Corps, which would cross the more weakly defended Saudi–Iraq border and then swing east into Kuwait.

The British 1st Armoured Division was still under US Marine command and a good relationship had been established. General Sir Peter de la Billière, the highly decorated ex-SAS British overall commander, considered that the division would be better employed with VII Corps because of the punch it was able to pack and that, since both the US corps and the British division were used to operating under NATO procedures, there would be better inter-operation. Schwarzkopf agreed to this and, while the air campaign continued, the whole division, complete with its large logistics tail, was shifted, in great secrecy, some 100 miles westwards.

While this was going on, the Iraqis launched their Scud offensive against Israel and Saudi Arabia. Men of the SAS and the Royal Marines' Special Boat Squadron (SBS) now performed an invaluable service. They had originally been deployed deep behind the Iraqi lines to disrupt communications and gather intelligence, but they were now tasked with locating the elusive mobile Scud launchers.

As the weeks wore on the Coalition forces began to soften up the Iraqi defences with fixed and rotary wing attacks and artillery barrages, notably by the Royal Artillery's three field and two heavy regiments, which became adept at quickly deploying, firing a few salvoes and then withdrawing – so-called 'shoot and scoot' tactics. Three further infantry battalions also arrived in the Gulf to cope with the expected large number of Iraqi prisoners of war.

The long wait finally came to an end on Sunday, 24 February when the ground offensive began. US Marines and Arabs breached the Iraqi defences on the Kuwait border, while US XVIII Corps did the same in the extreme west. To their immediate right US VII Corps also crossed into Iraq, with 1st Armoured Division on the right. There now began a four-day operation, which had all the hallmarks of a classic Blitzkrieg campaign. One result of this successful engagement was an enormous numbers of prisoners, most of them dazed from weeks of air attack and by the suddenness of the onslaught. British casualties were few, but there was one tragic incident when a US A-10 ground-attack aircraft knocked out two of the Fusiliers' Warrior tanks, killing nine men and wounding thirteen others. It was, of course, a genuine mistake, brought about by the 'fog of war' created by a fast-moving battle.

When the ceasefire came into effect on 28 February 1991 the 1st Armoured Division had just reached its final objective, the road running north from Kuwait City. It had advanced nearly 150 miles in less than ninety-six hours, fighting much of the way: an impressive performance.

Bosnia and Herzegovina, 1992–1995

The war here began in April 1992 and came about as a result of the break-up of Yugoslavia. It involved several factions, the main belligerents being the forces of the Republic of Bosnia and Herzegovina and those of the self-proclaimed Bosnian Serb and Bosnian Croat entities within Bosnia and Herzegovina, Republika Srpska and Herzeg-Bosnia, which were led and supplied by Serbia and Croatia respectively. Following the Slovenian and Croatian secessions from the Socialist Federal Republic of Yugoslavia in 1991, the multi-ethnic Socialist Republic of Bosnia and Herzegovina, inhabited by mainly Muslim Bosniaks (44 per cent), Orthodox Serbs (31 per cent) and Catholic Croats (17 per cent), passed a referendum for independence on 29 February 1992. This was rejected by Bosnian Serb political representatives, who had boycotted the referendum and established their own republic. Following the declaration of independence, Bosnian Serb forces, supported by the Serbian government of Slobodan Miloeviæ and the Yugoslav People's Army (JNA), attacked the Republic of Bosnia and Herzegovina in order to secure Serbian territory, and war soon broke out across Bosnia, accompanied by the ethnic cleansing of the Bosniak population, especially in Eastern Bosnia.

It was principally a territorial conflict, initially between the Serb forces mostly organized in the Army of Republika Srpska (VRS) on the one side, and the multi-ethnic Army of the Republic of Bosnia and Herzegovina (ARBiH), which was largely though not exclusively composed of Bosniaks, and the Croat forces in the Croatian Defence Council (HVO) on the other side. The Croats also aimed at securing parts of Bosnia and Herzegovina as Croatian. The Serb and Croat political leadership agreed on a partition of Bosnia with the Karađorđevo and Graz agreements, resulting in the Croat forces turning on the Army of the Republic of Bosnia and Herzegovina. The war was characterized by bitter fighting, indiscriminate shelling of cities and towns, ethnic cleansing, systematic mass rape and genocide. Events such as the 'Siege of Sarajevo' and the 'Srebrenica Massacre' became iconic of the conflict.

The Serbs, although initially superior owing to the vast quantities of weapons and resources provided by the JNA, eventually lost momentum as Bosniaks and Croats allied themselves against the Republika Srpska in 1994 with the creation of the Federation of Bosnia and Herzegovina following the Washington agreement. After the Srebrenica and Markale massacres, NATO intervened during 1995 with Operation Deliberate Force taking on the positions of the Army of Republika Srpska, which proved key in ending the war. The war was officially brought to an end after the signing of the General Framework Agreement for Peace in Bosnia and Herzegovina in Paris on 14 December 1995. Peace negotiations were held in Dayton, Ohio, and were finalized on 21 December 1995. The accords are known as the Dayton Agreement. A 1995 report by the American CIA found Serbian forces responsible for 90 per cent of the war crimes committed during the conflict. By early 2008 the International Criminal Tribunal for the former Yugoslavia had convicted forty-five Serbs, twelve Croats and four Bosniaks of war crimes in connection with the war in Bosnia. The most recent research places the number of dead at around 100,000–110,000 and the number displaced at over 2.2 million, making it the most devastating conflict in Europe since the end of the Second World War.

Initially, in support of the UN relief workers, the British sent a battalion group of 2,500 men, built around the 1st Battalion, Cheshire Regiment and an armoured reconnaissance squadron of the 9th/12th Royal Lancers. This force arrived in central Bosnia in November 1992 for a six-month tour. Later, in March 2002 the Welsh Guards were deployed from Bruneval Barracks, Aldershot on Operation Palatine. Their mission was to provide a safe and secure environment in which the country could progress towards normality. One of the main methods of facilitating this was to disarm the local population, a task that was conducted through a series of operations to remove weapons from the community. To ensure that this was a success the battalion deployed with over 850 men, including C Squadron, Household Cavalry Regiment. The battalion was responsible for an area of operations covering over 16,000 square kilometres. As a result the battalion was split in order to make sure that the whole area was covered. Companies lived and operated from an old shoe factory, an old bus depot and an old metal factory as well as smaller houses that were home to platoon-sized groups for much of the tour. Many operations to remove weapons from the community were carried out, resulting in the seizure of a staggering amount of illegally held weapons and ammunition. The tally by the end of the tour amounted to 400 small arms, 900 grenades and 80,000 rounds of ammunition.

The Battalion also carried out operations in support of organisations such as the International Criminal Tribunal for the former Yugoslavia in the search for war criminals or conducting training on the nearby Manjaca Ranges. The battalion went on a second tour in 2006.

Peacekeeping in Macedonia also saw high levels of British involvement, in the period of instability that almost broke out into full-scale war between the government and ethnic Albanian guerrillas, still armed from the Kosovo crisis, in 2001. In March 2003 NATO's peacekeeping mission in Macedonia was formally handed over to the European Union.

NATO brought the Stabilisation Force (SFOR) to a conclusion in December 2004 in light of the improved security situation in both Bosnia and Herzegovina (BiH) and the wider region. Peacekeeping responsibilities were assumed by the European Union force EUFOR. British troops served in the country under NATO, the UN and then EUFOR until 2007, when the situation was considered to be sufficiently stabilised for troop numbers to be reduced. In October 2008 Defence Secretary John Hutton announced that 'following a review of the security situation', Britain's contributions to the NATO/EU Balkans Operational Reserve Force would cease on 31 December 2008.

Between early 1993 and June 2010 seventy-two British military personnel died on operations in the former Yugoslavian countries of Bosnia, Kosovo and Macedonia.

Rwanda, 1994
In 1994 a contingent of the British Army found itself deployed to the African state of Rwanda, where a blood-bath had erupted when the ruling Hutus set about massacring their rivals, the Tutsis. They in turn overthrew the regime and most Hutus then fled to refugee camps across Rwanda's borders. The British Army contributed to a force sent to support UN relief efforts. Two

years later, with growing anarchy in eastern Zaire threatening the lives of the Rwandan refugees there, another UN force was put together in anticipation of mobilisation, but in the end they were stood down as the crisis melted away.

Sierra Leone, 1999

In 1999 the British Army was deployed to Sierra Leone, a former British colony, on Operation Palliser to aid the government in quelling violent uprisings by militiamen, under United Nations resolutions. Troops remain in the region to provide military support and training to the Sierra Leonean government.

Afghanistan War, 2001–

The Afghanistan War was provoked by a series of coordinated terrorist attacks against the United States on 11 September 2001 (now known universally as '9/11'). Terrorists hijacked four commercial passenger jet airliners and intentionally crashed two of the airliners into the Twin Towers of the World Trade Centre in New York City, killing everyone on board and many others working in the buildings. Both buildings collapsed within two hours, destroying nearby buildings and damaging others. The hijackers crashed a third airliner into the Pentagon in Arlington, Virginia, just outside Washington, DC. The fourth plane crashed into a field near Shanksville in rural Pennsylvania after some of its passengers and flight crew attempted to retake control of the plane, which the hijackers had redirected toward Washington, DC to target the White House or Capitol Hill. There were no survivors from any of the flights. Nearly 3,000 people and the nineteen hijackers died in the attacks. According to the New York State Health Department, 836 responders, including fire-fighters and police personnel, had also died by June 2009.

This atrocity resulted in the US-led war in Afghanistan, with the support of the United Kingdom and the Afghan United Front (Northern Alliance), which started on 7 October 2001 as Operation Enduring Freedom. It was designed to capture or kill Osama bin Laden and al-Qaeda militants, as well as replace the Taliban with a US-friendly government. The Bush Doctrine stated that, as a matter of policy, it would not distinguish between al-Qaeda and nations that harboured its activists.

Several Afghan leaders were invited to Germany in December 2001 for the UN-sponsored Bonn Agreement, which was intended to restore stability and governance in their country. In the first step the Afghan Transitional Administration was formed and was installed on 22 December 2001. Chaired by Hamid Karzai, it numbered thirty leaders and included a Supreme Court, an Interim Administration and a Special Independent Commission.

Simultaneously the UN Security Council established the International Security Assistance Force (ISAF) in December 2001 to provide basic security for the people of Afghanistan and assist the Karzai administration. Since 2002 the total number of ISAF and US military personnel has climbed from 15,000 to 150,000. The majority of them belong to various branches of the United States armed forces, who are not only fighting the Taliban insurgency but also training the military of Afghanistan and the Afghan National Police. They are scheduled to withdraw slowly until the end of 2014 but Vice-President Joe Biden has proposed to station an unknown number of US military personnel there after the 2014 deadline if the security situation requires it and the Afghan government and people desire it.

A *loya jirga* (grand assembly) was convened in June 2002 by former King Zahir Shah, who returned from exile after twenty-nine years. Hamid Karzai was elected President for the two years in the *jirga*, in which the Afghan Interim Authority was also replaced with the Transitional Islamic State of Afghanistan (TISA). A constitutional *loya jirga* was held in December 2003, adopting the new 2004 constitution, with a presidential form of government and a bicameral legislature. Karzai was elected in the 2004 presidential elections, followed by winning a second term in the 2009 presidential elections. Both the 2005 and the 2010 parliamentary elections were also successful.

In recent years NATO and Afghan troops have led many offensives against the Taliban, but have not been able to completely dislodge their presence. By 2009 a Taliban-led shadow government had begun to form, complete with its own version of the mediation court. In 2010 the American President Barack Obama deployed an additional 30,000 soldiers over a period of six months, but proposed that he will begin troop withdrawals by 2012.

At the end of July 2011 the Netherlands became the first NATO country to end its combat mission in Afghanistan after four years' deployment. The recall of the 1,900 Dutch troops was a politically significant act in response to rising casualties and growing doubts about the war. Canada will withdraw 2,700 troops in 2011 and Poland will pull out its 2,600 soldiers in 2012.

As part of Operation Enduring Freedom the 3rd Division was deployed in Kabul, to assist in the liberation of the troubled capital. The Royal Marines' 3 Commando Brigade (part of the Royal Navy but including a number of army units) also swept the mountains. The British Army is today concentrating on fighting Taliban forces and bringing security to Helmand province. Approximately 9,000 British troops (including Marines, airmen and sailors) are currently in Afghanistan, making it the second largest force after the USA. Around 500 extra British troops were deployed in 2009, bringing the British Army deployment total up to 9,500 (excluding Special Forces). Between 2001 and June 2011 a total of 362 British military personnel died on operations, mainly in Afghanistan.

Iraq War, 2003

The 2003 invasion of Iraq (19 March–1 May 2003) was the start of the conflict known as the Iraq War or Operation Iraqi Freedom, in which a combined force of troops from the United States, the United Kingdom and smaller contingents from Australia, Poland and Spain invaded Iraq and toppled the regime of Saddam Hussein in twenty-one days of major combat operations. This phase (March–April 2003) consisted of a conventionally fought war which concluded with the fall of the Iraq capital Baghdad.

This was considered a continuation of the Gulf War of 1991. After the Coalition Forces' success, Saddam Hussein had agreed to surrender and/or destroy several types of weapon, including SCUD missiles and weapons of mass destruction (WMD). Since then the USA and Britain had been keeping a tight rein on Saddam Hussein, effectively waging an undeclared war against Iraq for twelve years. American President Bill Clinton had maintained sanctions and ordered air strikes in the 'Iraqi no-fly zones' with Operation Desert Fox, in the hope that Saddam would be overthrown by his political enemies inside Iraq; he had also signed into law H.R. 4655, the Iraq Liberation Act, which appropriated funds to Iraqi opposition groups.

Four countries participated with troops during the initial invasion phase, which lasted from 19 March to 9 April 2003. These were the United States (148,000), the United Kingdom (45,000), Australia (2,000) and Poland (194). Thirty-six other countries were involved in its aftermath. In preparation for the invasion, 100,000 American troops were assembled in Kuwait by 18 February. The United States supplied the majority of the invading forces, but also received support from Kurdish irregulars in Iraqi Kurdistan.

The invasion was preceded by an air strike on the Presidential Palace in Baghdad on 19 March 2003. The following day coalition forces launched an incursion into Basra Province from their massing point close to the Iraqi–Kuwait border. While Special Forces launched an amphibious assault from the Persian Gulf to secure Basra and the surrounding petroleum fields, the main invasion army moved into southern Iraq, occupying the region and engaging in the Battle of Nasiriyah on 23 March. Massive air strikes across the country and against Iraqi command and control points threw the defending army into chaos and prevented any effective resistance. On 26 March the 173rd Airborne Brigade was air-dropped near the northern city of Kirkuk, where it joined forces with Kurdish rebels and fought several actions against the Iraqi army to secure the northern part of the country.

The main body of coalition forces continued to drive into the heart of Iraq and met with little resistance. Most of the Iraqi military was quickly defeated and Baghdad was occupied on 9 April. Other operations occurred against pockets of the Iraqi army, including the capture and occupation of Kirkuk on 10 April, and the attack and capture of Tikrit on 15 April. The Iraqi President Saddam Hussein and the central leadership went into hiding as the coalition forces completed their occupation of the country. On 1 May an end to major combat operations was declared, ending the invasion period and beginning the military occupation period.

Despite the Gulf War ending on 28 February 1991 with a cease-fire negotiated between the UN Coalition and Iraq, the USA and its allies tried to keep Saddam in check with military actions such as Operation Southern Watch, which was conducted by Joint Task Force Southwest Asia (JTF-SWA) with the mission of monitoring and controlling airspace south of the 32nd Parallel (extended to the 33rd Parallel in 1996), as well as using economic sanctions. Time revealed the extent of the biological weapons (BW) programme in Iraq, begun in the early 1980s with help from the United States and Britain, in violation of the Biological Weapons Convention (BWC) of 1972. Details of the BW programme – along with a chemical weapons programme – surfaced in the wake of the Gulf War (1990–91) following investigations conducted by the United Nations Special Commission (UNSCOM), which had been charged with the post-war disarmament of Saddam's Iraq. The investigation concluded that there was no evidence the programme had continued after the war. The USA and its allies then maintained a policy of 'containment' towards Iraq. This policy involved numerous economic sanctions by the UN Security Council, US and British enforcement of Iraqi no-fly zones declared by the USA and the UK to protect Kurds in Iraqi Kurdistan and Shias in the south from aerial attacks by Iraqi government forces during the 1991 uprisings, and ongoing inspections to prevent Iraqi development of chemical, biological and nuclear weapons. Iraqi military helicopters and planes regularly contested the no-fly zones.

An American Central Command, Combined Forces Air Component Commander Report indicated that as of 30 April 2003, there were a total of 466,985 US personnel deployed for Operation Iraqi Freedom, including 54,955 USAF; 2,084 USAF Reserve; 7,207 Air National Guard; 74,405 USMC; 9,501 USMC Reserve; 61,296 USN (681 are members of the US Coast Guard); 2,056 USN Reserve; 233,342 US Army; 10,683 US Army Reserve; and 8,866 Army National Guard. Members of the Coalition included Australia (2,000 invasion); Poland (200 invasion – 2,500); United Kingdom (46,000 invasion); and the United States (150,000 to 250,000 invasion).

British troops, in what was codenamed Operation Telic, participated in the 2003 invasion of Iraq. The 1st Armoured Division was deployed to the Gulf and commanded British forces in the area, securing areas in southern Iraq, including the city of Basra during the invasion. A total of 46,000 troops from all British services were committed to the operation at its start, including some 5,000 Royal Navy and Royal Fleet Auxiliary sailors and 4,000 Royal Marines, 26,000 British Army soldiers and 8,100 Royal Air Force airmen.

The invasion of Iraq was strongly opposed by some traditional American allies, including the governments of France, Germany, New Zealand and Canada, whose leaders argued that there was no evidence of weapons of mass destruction (WMD) in Iraq and that invading the country was not justified in the context of UNMOVIC's 12 February 2003 report. On 15 February 2003, a month before the invasion, there were worldwide protests against the Iraq war, including a rally of three million people in Rome, which is listed in the *Guinness Book of Records* as the largest ever anti-war rally. According to the French academic Dominique Reynié, between 3 January and 12 April 2003 some 36 million people across the globe took part in almost 3,000 protests against the Iraq war. In 2005 the CIA released a report saying that no weapons of mass destruction (WMD) had been found in Iraq.

The United Kingdom was a major contributor to the United States-led invasion of Iraq. In Britain this war proved unpopular, with many British citizens believing that the Iraq conflict had really nothing to do with Britain, which appeared to have been brought into the conflict through treaty and political alliances. However, the House of Commons voted for the conflict. The British Army controlled the southern regions of Iraq and maintained a peace-keeping presence in the city of Basra until its withdrawal on 30 April 2009. In total 179 British military personnel died on operations in Iraq. All British troops were withdrawn after the Iraqi government refused to extend their mandate.

As of mid-2011, the British Army employs 110,210 regular soldiers (including the 3,860-strong Brigade of Ghurkhas) and 33,100 Territorials, a combined component strength of 143,310 troops. In addition, there are 121,800 regular reserves of the British Army.

The full-time element of the British Army has also been referred to as the Regular Army since the creation of the reservist Territorial Force in 1908. The British Army is still deployed in many of the world's war zones as part of both Expeditionary Forces and in United Nations peacekeeping forces. The British Army is currently deployed in Kosovo, Cyprus, Germany and Afghanistan, among other places.

Yorkshire Victoria Cross Holders

AARON, Arthur Louis [1943]

Rank/Service: Flight Sergeant; 218 Squadron, RAF Volunteer Reserve
Other Decorations: DFM (Gazetted 19 October 1943)
VC Location: Leeds City Museum
Date of Gazette: 5 November 1943
Place/Date of Birth: Leeds, Yorkshire; 5 March 1922
Place/Date of Death: Bone, North Africa; 13 August 1943
Grave: Bone War Cemetery, Algeria
Memorial: St Mary's Church, Bexwell, Norfolk
Town/County Connections: Leeds, Yorkshire

Account of Deed: On 12/13 August 1943, during a raid on Turin, Italy, Flight Sergeant Aaron's Stirling bomber was attacked by a night-fighter* and very badly damaged, with one engine put out of action. The navigator was killed, and other members of the crew were wounded. Flight Sergeant Aaron's jaw was broken and part of his face was torn away; he had also been hit in the lung and his right arm was useless. As he fell forward over the control column, the aircraft dived several thousand feet; control was regained by the flight engineer at 3,000 feet. Unable to speak, Aaron gestured to the bomb aimer to take over the controls. A course was then set southwards in an endeavour to fly the crippled bomber to Sicily or North Africa. Aaron was assisted to the rear of the aircraft and treated with morphine. After resting for some time he rallied and, mindful of his responsibility as captain of the aircraft, insisted on returning to the pilot's cockpit, where he was lifted into his seat and had his feet placed on the rudder bar. Twice he made determined attempts to take control and hold the aircraft to its course but his weakness was evident and he was persuaded, with difficulty, to desist. Although in great pain and suffering from exhaustion, he continued to help by writing instructions with his left hand. Some five hours

* Officially the attack was credited to an enemy night-fighter, but in fact it was generally known that Aaron's aircraft had been shot at by another unidentified Stirling of the same squadron – what today we would term 'Friendly Fire'.

after leaving the target, and with the fuel tanks beginning to run low, the flare path at Bone airfield was sighted. Aaron summoned his failing strength to direct the bomb aimer in the hazardous task of landing the damaged aircraft in the darkness with its undercarriage retracted. Four aborted attempts were made under his direction; by the fifth attempt Aaron was so near to collapsing that he had to be restrained by the crew and the difficult landing was completed by the bomb aimer. Aaron died nine hours after the aircraft touched down.

Biographical Detail: Born in Leeds on 5 March 1922, Arthur 'Art' Aaron was the son of an Englishman, Benjamin Aaron, who had married a girl originally from Switzerland, who had come to Scotland before 1914 to work for the family of the Rector of Aberdeen University, Adam-Smith.

Educated at Roundhay School, Leeds, he won an art scholarship in 1939 and entered Leeds College of Architecture with a career as an architect in mind. Keen on both mountains and rock-climbing and flying, his first encounter with flight was as a boy with a short jaunt in one of Alan Cobham's travelling aerial circuses near Penrith. He joined the Leeds University Squadron of the Air Defence Cadet Corps (later renamed the Air Training Corps (ATC)), and eventually enlisted in the RAF for pilot training on 15 September 1941. In early December Aaron was sent to the USA and began flying instruction at No. 1 (British) FTS, Terrell, Texas, graduating as a sergeant pilot on 19 June 1942.

Returning to England, Aaron underwent further advanced instruction at No. 6 (P) AFU and No. 26 OUT, before being sent to No. 1657 Heavy Conversion Unit (HCU) to acquire experience in handling the giant four-engined Short Stirling bomber. Finally, on 17 April 1943, Aaron joined his first operational unit, 218 Gold Coast Squadron based at Downham Market in East Anglia.

Promoted to flight sergeant on 1 May 1943, his constant aim was crew efficiency during operations, and to that end he insisted that all the crew members gained some knowledge and experience of one another's jobs.

An early indication of Aaron's streak of determination came on the night his aircraft was partly crippled by flak on the approach to an enemy target. Undeterred by the damage, which resulted in his Stirling being only partially controllable, he continued his sortie, bombed the objective and then brought his aircraft safely home. His actions that night in October 1943 earned him a Distinguished Flying Medal (DFM).

Arthur Louis Aaron was buried with full military honours in Bone Military Cemetery. On 25 February 1944 his parents received their son's medals at an investiture at Buckingham Palace, and shortly afterwards Benjamin Aaron, his father, was present at a mass parade of ATC cadets in Wellington Barracks, London, where the ATC Commandant, Air Marshal Sir Leslie Gossage, read out the VC citation of their most distinguished ex-cadets.

Two years later, in August 1946, his parents' home was burgled and all Aaron's medals were stolen; after a police appeal, the medals were returned anonymously through the post. In December 1953 Benjamin Aaron presented his son's medals to Leeds City Museum for permanent public display.

ALLEN, William Barnsley [1916]

Rank/Service: Captain (later Major); Royal Army Medical Corps, attached
   246th (West Riding) Brigade, Royal Field Artillery
Other Decorations: DSO, MC and Bar
VC Location: Army Medical Services Museum, Mytchett
Date of Gazette: 26 October 1916
Place/Date of Birth: Sheffield, Yorkshire; 8 June 1892
Place/Date of Death: Bracklesham, Nr Chichester, Sussex; 27 October 1933
Grave: Earnley Cemetery, Bracklesham Bay, Sussex. 'In loving memory of
   Joe William Barnsley Allen, VC, DSO, MC, MB, Ch.B, RAMC died
   27th August 1933 aged 40 years. At Rest. Also of his dear wife Gertrude,
   died 28th July 1953, aged 59 years. In Peace'
Town/County Connections: Sheffield, Yorkshire; Hounslow, Middlesex

Account of Deed: On 13 September 1916, near Mesnil, France, when gun detachments were unloading high explosive ammunition, the enemy suddenly began to shell the battery position. The first shell fell on one of the limbers, exploded the ammunition and caused several casualties. Captain Allen at once ran across under heavy shell-fire and started attending to the wounded. He himself was hit four times by pieces of shrapnel, but he went on coolly with his work until the last man had been attended to and removed. He then went to tend a wounded officer and only then reported his own injuries.

Biographical Detail: William B. Allen was born in Sheffield on 8 June 1892 at 14 Botanical Road, Sheffield. His father Percy Edwin Allen was a successful commercial traveller, and his mother Edith was the daughter of Joseph Barnsley of Taptonville Crescent, Sheffield. His elder sister Edith was born on 27 July 1890 and his younger sister Barbara was born four years after him on 13 September 1896. The address for the family at the time of Barbara's birth is given as 42 Southgrove Road, Ecclesall, Sheffield; sometime after this date the family moved to Endcliffe Vale Road.

William was educated at what was then St Cuthbert's College, Worksop. In 1908, at the age of seventeen, he went to Sheffield University, graduating with an honours degree in June 1914. During his time at the University he was awarded the Gold Medal in Pathology (1913), the Kaye Scholarship for the highest marks in physiology and anatomy, and three bronze medals.

While at Sheffield University William was a member of the Officers' Training Corps, and he is still honoured today there. Just off the main mess in the Somme Barracks in West Street, Sheffield there is an ante-room named the 'Allen VC Room', which proudly displays on the wall a framed photograph of William, his VC citation, and a copy of his VC and several of his other medals.

He joined the Royal Hospital as an assistant house physician but within weeks had enlisted with the 3rd West Riding Field Ambulance. In fact his date of enlistment is given in the records as 8 August 1914, four days after the outbreak of war. He was soon in France.

In May 1916, while on leave, he married at Gainsborough, Lincolnshire, Mary 'Mollie' Young, the younger daughter of Mr W.Y. Mercer. In August 1916 he was awarded the Military Cross and ten months later, in June 1917, he was awarded a bar to the MC. He was invalided back to England the same month. In January 1918 he was appointed acting major but on 18 February 1918 he was transferred to the regular RAMC with the rank of captain, the rank he held at the conclusion of the war. In October 1918 he was wounded for the third time and sent back to England for the second time. This time he was awarded the DSO. Altogether he had served in France for three years and two months.

Hardly anything is known about William's life after 1918, beyond the fact that he stayed on in the army. There are suggestions that he divorced his first wife Mary and married Gertrude Craggs in 1925. However, a court case in July 1932 in Chichester revealed a number of personal problems that William had faced in the intervening years.

He was charged, as Major Allen, with driving a motor car while under the influence of drink. His defence stated that Major Allen had 'suffered as no other man in England had suffered'. He had been wounded in the chest and afterwards in the eyes. He was blind for a total of six months. In total he had been wounded seven times during the war. After the Armistice he went to India, where he contracted malaria and dysentery. On his return to England these diseases were exacerbated by bouts of sleeping sickness and pleurisy. He took to drugs and whisky to combat these ailments and by 1932, although he was no longer on drugs, he still took the whisky. Unfortunately, his defence had no effect whatsoever on the Bench; Major Allen was fined and had his licence suspended for five years.

William did not live to complete the ban. Thirteen months later Dr C.R. Sadler was called by phone at 7.15am to attend Major Allen. On arriving at the house he found him propped up in bed, unconscious, blue in the face and breathing very slowly. His pupils were dilated and he had an abnormal temperature. He died within half an hour of the doctor's arrival. In contradiction to the evidence given in the court case a year earlier, the doctor knew that William was still taking drugs.

An inquest was held in Chichester on 28 August 1933, presided over by the Deputy Coroner for Chichester, Mr F.B. Tompkins. Dr Sadler confirmed that William was taking drugs – Veronal, opium and morphine – but he had no idea of the quantities. It appeared that he had overdosed on opium. The doctor confirmed that he had never heard William threaten to take his life and in his opinion he was not likely to do so. The coroner stated that he was given to understand that the major was in the habit of taking drugs straight from the bottle, without measuring the amount. In such circumstances an overdose could easily occur, and he recorded a verdict of accidental death.

However, the court case in June 1932 and the inquest in 1933 do not tell the whole story. Dr John Lunn, who had recently retired from the department of community medicine, pointed out that far from being in decline after the war, William was fine. An army colleague had met him on Armistice Day in Sheffield in November 1918 and recalled that William was his usual intelligent cheery self. The following year he gave evidence in a murder case involving the colonel of his unit, who had shot and murdered a fellow officer. *The Times* reported that his testimony was clear and concise. It appeared that he served in the army up until 1923, and then left to go into medical practice in Hounslow, London.

Dr Lunn, firmly believed that what 'did' for William Allen was encephalitis lethargica, or the after-effects of sleeping sickness. This disease was first diagnosed in 1918 by Arthur J. Hall, who was Professor of Medicine at Sheffield University. The symptoms are variable, but the illness usually starts with a high fever, headache and sore throat. Double vision, disturbance of eye movements, weakness of the upper body, tremors and strange movements, neck stiffness, intense muscle pains, a slowing of physical and mental response, drowsiness and lethargy soon follow. Unusual brain and nerve symptoms may occur, and the person's behaviour and personality may change too. Occasionally they become psychotic, with extremely disturbed thinking. Sometimes the illness is mistaken for epilepsy, hysteria or even drug or alcohol abuse. As the body shuts down, patients become increasingly sleepy and some may lose consciousness, slipping into a coma that can last months or even years, which is why the disease is sometimes referred to as sleeping sickness.

William contracted the illness in 1924, but how he caught it is a mystery. The court case in 1932 refers to his service in India, where he certainly contracted malaria and dysentery, but even today the causes of the illness are not known. The condition is not curable and even now treatment is only targeted at supporting the person through their illness and dealing with symptoms as they occur.

William's obituary appeared in *The Times* on 29 August 1933. In January 1933, a few months before his death, the *London Gazette* announced: 'Major Allen, Royal Army Medical Corps, ceased to belong to the Reserve of Officers on account of ill-health.'

His parents Percy Edwin Allen and Edith Barnsley were married in the December quarter of 1889 (PRO REF Ecclesall Bierlow, vol. 9C, p. 477). Confirmation of his birth can be found in the PRO registers for the June quarter of 1892 (Allen, William Barnsley, Ecclesall Bierlow, vol. 9C, p. 455). William attended the Victoria Cross Reunion Dinner on Saturday, 9 November 1929 in the Royal Gallery, House of Lords, Palace of Westminster, London.

ANDERSON, Eric [1943]

Rank/Service: Private; 5th Battalion, East Yorkshire Regiment
VC Location: Prince of Wales's Own Regiment of Yorkshire, York
Date of Gazette: 29 July 1943
Place/Date of Birth: Fagley, Bradford, Yorkshire; 15 September 1915
Place/Date of Death: Akarit, Tunisia; 6 April 1943
Grave: Sfax War Cemetery, Tunisia
Memorials: Beverley Minster; St John's United Reformed Church, Bradford
Town/County Connections: Bradford, Yorkshire
Significant Remarks: First stretcher-bearer in the Second World War to win
   a VC

Account of Deed: On 6 April 1943 A Company of the East Yorkshire Regiment made a dawn attack on a strong position on the Wadi Akarit in Tunisia, but very heavy enemy fire forced the Yorkshiremen to withdraw temporarily behind the crest of a hill and take shelter. Despite the withering fire, Private Anderson, a stretcher-bearer, went forward alone to rescue wounded men trapped in no-man's-land. On three separate occasions Anderson brought in his wounded comrades, and was rendering first aid to a fourth when he was mortally wounded. Anderson's body was recovered from the battlefield a week later.

Biographical Detail: Eric Anderson was born in Fagley, near Bradford, West Yorkshire, the only son of George and Mary Anderson. Before joining the army in 1940, Eric was a driver for a firm of building contractors at Idle. It is also known that he sang in Eccleshill church choir. On 3 April 1993, almost fifty years to the day since Anderson earned his VC, a service of remembrance was held at Bradford Cathedral and a plaque unveiled there. Coincidentally the day he won his VC was also the date of his first wedding anniversary to his wife Irene, who later presented his medals to the Regimental Museum.

Over the past years several commemorative plaques have been unveiled in Bradford and another in Beverley Minster. In September 1987 another plaque was unveiled at Bradford Cathedral next to one unveiled nine months previously in memory of James Magennis, the Belfast-born naval VC, who lived in Bradford for most of his life after the war.

ATKINSON, Alfred [1902]

Rank/Service: 3264 Sergeant; 1st Battalion, Yorkshire Regiment (Alexandra, Princess of Wales's Own)
VC Location: Green Howards Regimental Museum, Richmond
Date of Gazette: 8 August 1902
Place/Date of Birth: Leeds, Yorkshire; 6 February 1874
Place/Date of Death: Nr Paardeberg, South Africa; 21 February 1900
Memorials: Green Howard Memorial close to battlefield; York – both erected in 1904
Town/County Connections: Leeds, Yorkshire

Account of Deed: On 18 February 1900, during the Battle of Paardeberg in South Africa, Sergeant Atkinson went out seven times under heavy and close fire to obtain water for the wounded. During the seventh attempt he was wounded in the head, and died three days afterwards.

Biographical Detail: Alfred Atkinson, the youngest of five children of James and Margaret Atkinson, was born in Armley, Leeds, on 6 February 1874. In October 1873 his father had been discharged from the Royal Artillery at Aldershot, where he had been a farrier-sergeant. Both his parents had been in the Crimean War and James Atkinson is thought to have been one of the small band of mounted artillerymen who captured the two bronze Russian cannon at Sebastopol from which the Victoria Crosses were subsequently cast.

Alfred enlisted in Leeds in November 1891 and was posted to the Green Howards in Richmond. After basic training he joined the 1st Battalion, Princess of Wales's Own Yorkshire Regiment (the full title of the Green Howards), at Portsmouth, where he was promoted to corporal in February 1892. He took his certificate of musketry with the new .303 Lee Enfield rifle at Fort Gomer, near Portsmouth, and on 16 November was promoted to lance sergeant.

The battalion sailed to Jersey to take up residence in Fort Regent and St Peter's near St Helier, where Atkinson was promoted to the full rank of sergeant in E Company. On 16 December 1897 Sergeant Atkinson completed his seven years' service with the colours and transferred to the Reserve.

Along with 450 other reservists, he joined the Green Howards in Albuera Barracks, Aldershot, on 22 November 1899 and sailed from Southampton two days later for Cape Town, South Africa, to take part in the Boer War.

Sergeant Alfred Atkinson was buried at Gruisbank near Paardeberg on 21 February 1900, and was subsequently awarded a posthumous Victoria Cross for his gallantry. The VC was sent by post to his parents on 28 April 1902 but it was not announced in the *London Gazette* until 8 August 1902. The medals of both Sergeant Atkinson and his father were sold at Sotheby's to Messrs Spinks & Company for £70 in November 1911. In 1959 they were purchased by the regiment from a collector for £650 and are now held by the Green Howards Regimental Museum.

BELL, Donald Simpson [1917]

Rank/Service: Temporary Second Lieutenant; 9th Battalion, Yorkshire Regiment (Alexandra, Princess of Wales's Own)

VC Location: Green Howards Regimental Museum, Richmond

Date of Gazette: 9 September 1917

Place/Date of Birth: Harrogate, Yorkshire; 3 December 1890

Place/Date of Death: Somme, France; 10 July 1916

Grave: Gordon's Dump Cemetery, France, Plot 6, Row A, Grave 8

Memorials: St Paul's Church, Harrogate; Starbeck War Memorial; stained glass window, Westminster College, London

Town/County Connections: Harrogate, Yorkshire

Significant Remarks: Bell was the first professional footballer to leave a playing career to enlist

Account of Deed: On 5 July 1916, at the Horseshoe Trench on the Somme, the attacking company came under heavy fire from a well-placed enemy machine-gun. Second Lieutenant Bell immediately, on his own initiative, crept up a communication trench, and then, followed by a corporal and a private, rushed across open ground under very heavy fire and attacked the machine-gun, shooting the gunner and destroying the gun and its personnel with bombs. He lost his life five days later performing a very similar act of bravery.

Biographical Detail: Donald 'Donny' Simpson Bell, the youngest son of Smith and Annie Bell (née Simpson), was born on 3 December 1890 and grew up in the comfortable surroundings of Milton Lodge, 87 East Parade, Harrogate. He had one elder brother, William (who served in the Army Service Corps in the First World War), and six sisters, one of whom died in infancy. His education began at St Peter's CoE School, and it was here that he began to excel at sport. Fortunately, he was able to concentrate on his schooling at the same time and gained a scholarship to attend the nearby Knaresborough Grammar School. At Knaresborough he won colours in rugby, swimming, cricket and hockey but his first love was football and as a keen amateur he turned out for Starbeck, Mirfield United and Bishop Auckland, the high standard at the latter club making the teenage Bell's achievements all the more remarkable. His father, however, pushed Donny to succeed academically, unconvinced that sport could provide the lifestyle he would wish for his youngest son. It was during this time that Bell met and became friends with Archie White, a fellow Yorkshire lad from Boroughbridge and another sporting pupil. He, like Donny, would earn a Victoria Cross on the Somme.

By the time he turned eighteen Bell was a strapping lad in excess of six foot tall with a powerful physique to match. He made the decision to venture to London, where he attended the Westminster Training College and embarked on a career in teaching. In his first year he was posted as one of the first division of trainee teachers, excelling at geography, English, maths and modern history. His love of sport continued and when not attending lectures he had trials with (and later turned out as an amateur for) Crystal Palace, then in the Southern League First Division and attracting crowds of over 15,000. That season ended with Palace finishing seventh in the table. Donald turned his attention to rugby a year later and, after lining up in the back row for Westminster College, caught the eye of a number of top amateur sides. His accommodation during this period was in a north London suburb and as such he was able to play for the Hertfordshire County XV, much to the envy of many of his college friends.

In 1911 Donald completed his education and returned to his home town of Harrogate, where he secured a position as assistant master at Starbeck Council School. In his first year he won the hearts of his pupils when he turned out as an amateur for Newcastle United, a top side of the day, which had lifted the league title three times and appeared in five FA Cup finals in seven years.

While at Newcastle Donny tried a move from defender to forward; perhaps his electrifying pace had caught the eye in training. The switch was a near-disaster as he squandered chance after chance; the trial ended at half-time and in a post-match interview with a local reporter Donald conceded, 'Until I returned to the defence we never looked like getting a goal, afterwards we got several.' His defensive performances for Newcastle were sound and during the summer he was approached by local side Bradford Park Avenue to join them for the 1912/13 season; he made his debut as full back on 13 April 1913. Despite being a Second Division side, they offered more 'boot money' (£2 10*s* a week) than Newcastle and in addition the switch enabled Donny to play local rugby and cricket while still teaching at Starbeck. With a monthly income of just £10, the sporting spin-offs were a welcome addition. It was a fairly successful season for Bradford as they finished mid-table but for Bell, however, the opportunities to play had proved limited. At a time when the club really decided to push for promotion to the 'big league', Donald, at the age of twenty-two, decided to leave his teaching position and turn professional.

Prior to the start of the 1913/14 season Donald seized the chance to improve his match fitness by touring Denmark as part of a Yorkshire representative side. On his return, however, he soon became understudy to the impressive Watson at right back but three months into the season he got his chance against Leicester Fosse on 3 November. Bradford ran out 3–2 winners and leapt to fourth in the table, Bell being particularly effective against Leicester forward Tommy Benfield. Benfield, an ex-soldier of the Leicestershire Regiment, signed for Derby County the following year and scored fifteen times in their Second Division championship side. He rejoined the colours in 1916 and was killed serving with 6/Leicestershire Regiment in September 1918.

Donald Bell retained his first-team place in a vital away game against Wolverhampton Wanderers a week later. Widely tipped for promotion, Wolves had built a side around a number of internationals. Although the Midlands side would finish a disappointing ninth, when Donny and his Bradford team-mates arrived they were facing the league leaders and it seemed they had little hope of success.

Only an undeserved 81st minute goal by the Wolves striker Sam Brookes separated the sides and again Donald's own performance caught the eye; the influential *Athletic News* reported: 'Mason was very solid in the visitors' goal, but his work was not of a most difficult character for he had in front of him two sterling backs in Bell and Watson, who kept their rivals so well at bay that most of the shots which came in were from a fairly lengthy range.'

Bell's appearances then tailed off as regular players recovered from injury. He played twice more for Bradford, who continued to push for a promotion place. Donald was then selected to play in a crucial away game to league leaders Notts County in January 1914. That game ended in a draw and in frustration for Donny as he picked up a serious injury in the closing stages that would force a premature end to his season. Ultimately, it proved to be a successful campaign for Bradford Park Avenue, despite Bell's injury, as they finished runners-up to Notts County but ahead of Woolwich Arsenal on points and thus secured promotion to the First Division. Bell's performance over the season was reported in a Bradford paper: 'Bell is one of the best types of the professional footballer, broadminded in outlook and scrupulously fair in his play. Had it not been for an accident he would probably have secured a regular place in the side. Indeed, some of his displays, particularly those in the matches with Notts County at Trent Bridge and Wolverhampton Wanderers at Molineux, were good enough for any team in the country.' (The reference to Trent Bridge is interesting. Notts County played at the county cricket ground for a spell before moving to Meadow Lane, and this may be an error on the reporter's behalf as the side had moved into their new ground in 1910, three seasons before the game under discussion was played.)

That summer a chance meeting with Rhoda Margaret Bonson would lead to Bell's marriage. When war became inevitable Donald had already reported back to Bradford for pre-season training; despite now having the opportunity to play against sides like Sheffield Wednesday, Aston Villa and Manchester United, his responsibility to do his duty for his country was always at the forefront of his mind. As early as late August he wrote to the club requesting they release him to serve with the colours: 'I have given the subject some very serious consideration and have now come to the conclusion I am duty bound to join the ranks. Will you therefore kindly ask the directors of the Bradford Football Club to release me from my engagement?'

Mr T.E. Maley responded with positive news: they would allow him to leave their employment to join up. Maley would later say of Bell: 'He was about six feet tall and when fit about 13st 8lbs. With it all, he was most gentle. He played many fine games for our team. At Nottingham against Notts County he played grandly but the best of games was against the Wolves, when he completely eclipsed Brooks and Company.'

On 24 October 1914, at the age of twenty-four, Lance Corporal 15722 D.S. Bell joined A Company, 9th Battalion, the West Yorkshire Regiment, and in so doing became the first professional footballer to leave their career and enlist. Initially life was dreary, with a routine of training and drill at his unit's base in Wisley, Surrey. Like the thousands of men who had answered Kitchener's call, he longed to get to France and teach the Hun a lesson. In May 1915 he bumped into his old school friend Archie White, then an officer in the Yorkshire Regiment (Green Howards). He was quite astonished to find Donny serving in the ranks and enquired as to why he hadn't been commissioned. Bell was said to have replied 'If only', and Archie introduced him to his own CO, Lieutenant Colonel E.H. Chapman. A good judge of character, within minutes Chapman recognised Bell's potential and agreed to support his application to become an officer in the Green Howards.

This was duly applied for on 10 May 1915 and Bell was commissioned into the 9th Battalion, the Yorkshire Regiment (Green Howards) in June of that year. His unit, now part of the 23rd Division, embarked for France two months later in August 1915. By now, he had proposed to Rhoda and they planned to marry on his first spell of home leave. After a period in France, Bell came home on leave and on 5 June 1916 he married his sweetheart Rhoda at the Wesleyan Chapel at Kirkby Stephen in Yorkshire. There was little time for a honeymoon but after a few days at home Donald returned to his unit, which had moved further south and was busy preparing for its part in the great Battle of the Somme.

On 7 July 1916 Second Lieutenant Bell wrote what was to be his last letter from a dugout near the village of Contalmaison on the Somme, in which he described an action that was to contribute to his gallantry award.

> When the battalion went over, I, with my team, crawled up a communication trench and attacked the gun and the trench and I hit the gun first shot from about 20 yards and knocked it over. The G.C.C. has been over to congratulate the battalion and he personally thanked me. I must confess it was the biggest fluke alive and I did nothing. I only chucked one bomb but it did the trick. The C.C. says I saved the situation for this gun was doing all the damage. I am glad I have been so fortunate for Pa's sake; for I know he likes his lads to be at the top of the tree. He used to be always on about too much play and too little work, but my athletics came in handy this trip. The only thing is I am sore at the elbows and knees with crawling over limestone flints. Please don't worry about me, I believe that God is watching over me and it rests with him whether I pull through or not ... There is talk of me getting a military cross or something of the sort, talk about luck! Fancy, just chucking one's bombs, even if it was a bull's eye.

Bell was killed on 10 July, shot in the head. The spot where his body was found became known as Bell's Redoubt and a rough wooden cross was erected at the time by members of the battalion, who carved on it the words, 'he gave his life for others'. The helmet Donald wore in the action that led to his death was pierced by a German bullet and is today on display in the Green Howards Museum.

On receiving the news that his son was to receive the Victoria Cross, Donny's father decided that his wife Rhoda should accept the award personally from the King at Buckingham Palace; she was at this time staying with relatives at Charlwood on the Altringham Road, Wilmslow, Cheshire. A first-class rail warrant enabled her to travel to London Euston and she was presented with the medal by King George V on 13 December 1916. With the medal came a widow's pension of £100 per annum and she also received a gratuity of £100 from the *Daily Mail* as she had been a registered reader with the newspaper.

Rhoda had been married for just over a month when her husband died, and for most of that month Donald had been on active service. She never re-married.

After the war Bell's body was removed to Gordon's Dump Cemetery, less than a mile from Contalmaison. A memorial was erected at Bells Redoubt and dedicated to Bell on 9 July 2000. His medals have been loaned since 1964 to the Green Howards Regimental Museum by his nephew, Donald Simpson Bell.

Bell's batman, Private John Baynes, wrote in a letter to Rhoda: 'I would to God that my late master and friend had still been with us, or, better still, been at home with you. The men worshipped him in their simple, wholehearted way and so they ought, he saved the lot of us from being completely wiped out by his heroic act.'

> *Harrogate Herald*, 30 June 1920, 'Wednesday Gossip'
> Among those present at the King's garden party to winners of the VC, were Mr and Mrs Smith Bell and Mrs Donald Bell. 'Don' Bell, as he was popularly known, made the great sacrifice shortly after the award, but had he lived the day would have been the happiest in his life. Mr Smith Bell was struck by the simplicity and humanity of the party, and speaks in high terms of the King's great interest in the men. Corporal Hull, who was also present with his parents, is now a policeman at Leeds. His mother was delighted that His Majesty should remember the circumstances under which her boy won his VC, and speaks highly of the welcome they received.

On 25 November 2004 Spinks auctioned the outstanding Somme VC group of medals belonging to Donald Bell, whose story was published in the October 2003 *Journal of the Victoria Cross Society*.

BEST-DUNKLEY, Bertram [1917]

Rank/Service: Temporary Lieutenant Colonel Commanding; 2/5th Battalion, Lancashire Fusiliers
VC Location: Lancashire Fusiliers Museum, Bury, Manchester
Date of Gazette: 6 September 1917
Place/Date of Birth: York; 3 August 1890

Place/Date of Death: Nr Ypres, Belgium; 5 August 1917
Grave: Mendingham Military Cemetery, Proven, Belgium. 'Lieutenant
    Colonel B. Best-Dunkley, VC Lancashire Fusiliers 5th August 1917'
Town/County Connections: York

Account of Deed: On 31 July 1917 at Wieltje, Belgium, when the leading waves
of an attack had become disorganised by rifle and machine-gun fire at very close
range from positions that were believed to be in British hands, Lieutenant
Colonel Best-Dunkley dashed forward, rallied his men and personally led them
to the assault of these positions, which, despite heavy losses, were carried. He
continued to lead his battalion until all their objectives had been gained. Later
in the day, when the British position was threatened, he collected his battalion
headquarters, led them to the attack and beat off the advancing enemy. He
subsequently died of his wounds.

BRYAN, Thomas [1917]

Rank/Service: Lance Corporal; 25th (S) Battalion, Northumberland Fusiliers
VC Location: Lord Ashcroft VC Collection
Date of Gazette: 8 June 1917
Place/Date of Birth: Stourbridge, Worcestershire; 21 January 1882
Place/Date of Death: Doncaster, Yorkshire; 13 October 1945
Grave: Arksey Cemetery, Doncaster
Memorial: Castleford Civic Centre
Town/County Connections: Stourbridge, Worcestershire; Doncaster and
    Castleford, Yorkshire

Account of Deed: During an attack on 9 April 1917 near Arras, France, Lance
Corporal Bryan, although wounded, went forward alone in order to silence a
machine-gun that was inflicting much damage; he worked his way along the
communication trench, approached the gun from behind, disabled it and killed
two of the team. The results of Bryan's action were very far-reaching.

Biographical Detail: Born in Stourbridge, Worcestershire, Bryan moved to the
West Riding town of Castleford and became a miner. He also played rugby
league for Castleford during the 1906/07 season. He enlisted in April 1915 and
was drafted into the Northumberland Fusiliers. He was presented with his
Victoria Cross in August 1917 by King George V at St James's Park football
ground, Newcastle, in front of a crowd of 40,000. After the war he returned to
the pits before becoming a greengrocer with his own shop in Bentley, near
Doncaster, where he died on 13 October 1945, aged sixty-three.

BUTLER, William Boynton [1917]

Rank/Service: Private; 17th Battalion, West Yorkshire Regiment (Prince of
  Wales's Own) and 106th Transport Motor Battery
VC Location: Private (Not on public display)
Date of Gazette: 17 October 1917
Place/Date of Birth: Leeds, Yorkshire; 20 November 1894
Place/Date of Death: Leeds, Yorkshire; 25 March 1972
Grave: Hunsley Cemetery, Leeds (erected 1994). 'William Boynton Butler,
  VC, Croix de Guerre, 17/1280 17th Bn. West Yorkshire (Bantams) born
  20th Nov 1894 died 25th Mar 1972'
Town/County Connections: Leeds, Yorkshire
Significant Remarks: Awarded the Croix de Guerre (France)

Account of Deed: On 6 August 1917, east of L'empire in France, Private Butler
was in charge of a Stokes gun in trenches that were being heavily shelled.
Suddenly one of the fly-off levers of a Stokes shell came off, firing the shell into
the emplacement. Private Butler picked up the shell and shouted a warning to a
party of infantry. He then turned and put himself between the party of men
and the live shell, holding it until they were out of danger; he then threw it
onto the parapet and took cover. The shell exploded, damaging the trench, but
only contusing Private Butler.

Biographical Detail: William Butler was born at 29 Back Stanley View, Armley,
Leeds, and died in Leeds General Infirmary on 25 March 1972. On the day
before his investiture, Butler went to see his mother and father in Leeds, but,
owing to a misunderstanding, they had already travelled up to London.
Consequently, he found himself locked out of the house and had to sit on the
doorstep until someone recognised him.

CALVERT, Laurence [1918]

Rank/Service: Sergeant; 5th Battalion, King's Own Yorkshire Light Infantry
Other Decorations: MM
VC Location: Lord Ashcroft VC Collection
Date of Gazette: 15 November 1918
Place/Date of Birth: Hunslet, Leeds, Yorkshire; 16 February 1892
Place/Date of Death: Dagenham, Essex; 7 July 1964
Grave: Upminster Crematorium, South Essex. 'Sgt. L. Calvert, VC and MM,
  born 16.2.1892 died 7.7.1964'
Memorial: Plaque in the Garden of Remembrance, South Essex Crematorium,
  Upminster

Town/County Connections: Leeds and Conisbrough, Yorkshire; Dagenham, Essex

Significant Remarks: Chevalier de l'Ordre de Leopold II (Belgium)

Account of Deed: On 12 September 1918 at Havrincourt, France, severe enfilade machine-gun fire was creating a difficult situation and Sergeant Calvert went forward alone against a machine-gun team, bayoneting three and shooting four. His valour and determination in capturing single-handed two machine-guns and killing their crews ensured the success of the operation. His personal gallantry inspired all ranks.

Biographical Detail: Born in Leeds, Calvert was educated locally before joining the Territorials on 17 April 1914. He was married with three children. After the war Calvert initially settled in Conisbrough and lived at 19 Beech Terrace. At some point soon after, a special ceremony was held at which he was presented with the Military Medal and the Belgian Croix de Guerre, plus £500 worth of War Bonds, in addition to the sum of £35 raised by a village collection. He joined the King's Own Yorkshire Light Infantry from the Denaby & Cadeby Colliery Company. Later he moved to Dagenham, when he was offered a job as a commissionaire for the National Provincial Bank in London. He died on 7 July 1964.

CHAFER, George William [1916]

Rank/Service: Private; 1st Battalion, East Yorkshire Regiment
VC Location: Prince of Wales's Regiment Museum, York
Date of Gazette: 5 August 1916
Place/Date of Birth: Bradford, Yorkshire; 16 April 1894
Place/Date of Death: Rotherham, Yorkshire; 2 March 1966
Grave: Rotherham Crematorium
Town/County Connections: Epworth, Lincolnshire; Bradford and Rotherham, Yorkshire

Account of Deed: On 3/4 June 1916, east of Meaulte, France, during a very heavy bombardment and attack on our trenches, a man carrying an important written message to his commanding officer was half-buried and rendered unconscious by a shell. Private Chafer, at once grasping the situation, on his own initiative took the message from the man's pocket and, although severely wounded, choking and blinded by gas, ran along the ruined parapet under heavy shell and machine-gun fire. He just succeeded in delivering the message before he collapsed from the effects of his wounds.

Biographical Detail: George W. Chafer was born at Bradford on 16 April 1894, son of Lucy Chafer (1894–1966). Before the war he worked down a coal mine. Returning to Rotherham after the war, he worked in dairy and poultry farming for a while before joining the Civil Service. He retired in 1958 and died aged seventy-one on 1 March 1966. He was cremated at Rotherham Crematorium.

COOPER, Edward [1917]

Rank/Service: Sergeant (later Major); 12th Battalion, King's Royal Rifle Corps
Other Decorations: Medaille Militaire (France)
VC Location: Green Dragon Museum, Stockton
Date of Gazette: 14 September 1917
Place/Date of Birth: Stockton-on-Tees, Yorkshire; 4 May 1896
Place/Date of Death: Stockton-on-Tees, Yorkshire; 19 August 1985
Grave: Teesside Crematorium, Middlesbrough
Memorial: Stockton-on-Tees public library
Town/County Connections: Stockton-on-Tees, Yorkshire

Account of Deed: On 16 August 1917 at Langemarck, Belgium, enemy machine-guns from a concrete blockhouse 250 yards away were holding up the advance of the battalion on the left and also causing heavy casualties to Sergeant Cooper's own battalion. With four men he rushed towards the blockhouse, firing at the garrison from very close range (100 yards), but the machine-guns were not silenced; as a consequence Sergeant Cooper ran straight at them and fired his revolver into an opening in the blockhouse. The machine-guns ceased firing and the garrison surrendered. Seven machine-guns and forty-five prisoners were captured.

Biographical Detail: Sergeant Edward Cooper was not sent on leave until 15 January 1918, nearly five months after the action at Langemarck, and when he left the front he still did not know anything about an award. He was sitting in a YMCA cafe at King's Cross railway station when he happened to see a newspaper carrying a list of the new VCs. The name of Chavasse caught his eye – Captain Noel Chavasse had just won a Bar to his VC, one of only three men ever to do so – and next was the name Cooper, E. It was not until Cooper had read and re-read the name and the regimental number that he realised he was reading his own citation. The small shy sergeant said nothing, but when his train finally reached Darlington, where he had to change, Cooper was astonished to find his father and his elder brother waiting for him. Then, to his enormous embarrassment, there was a civic reception for him at Stockton-on-Tees.

For thirty-five years he lived in modest obscurity until the Victoria Cross Association was formed in 1953 and someone tracked him down. Suddenly he was a hero all over again. On 24 July 1985 Edward Cooper VC was given the Freedom of Stockton, but he died less than four weeks later, on 19 August 1985.

On Thursday 16 September 2010 an interesting lot came up for auction. It comprised a unique group of VC memorabilia including Major Cooper's KRRC cap badge, worn in 1917, a copy of a photograph showing the present-ation of Cooper's VC by King George V and a transcript of the citation with a signed dedication in pen (to the vendor) from Major Cooper. In addition there was a framed photograph showing the vendor and Major Cooper at the presentation and plaque unveiling in Stockton-on-Tees on 16 August 1977, together with transcripts of the speeches and an audio cassette recording of the ceremony. Estimate: £300–£500.

COVERDALE, Charles Henry [1917]

Rank/Service: Sergeant (later Second Lieutenant); 11th Battalion, Manchester
   Regiment
Other Decorations: MM
VC Location: Private (Not on public display)
Date of Gazette: 18 December 1917
Place/Date of Birth: Manchester, Lancashire; 21 April 1888
Place/Date of Death: Huddersfield, Yorkshire; 20 November 1955
Grave: Edgerton Cemetery, Huddersfield. 'In loving memory of Clara
   Florence beloved wife of Harry Coverdale VC 1890–1940. Also the above
   Harry Coverdale, VC, MM 1888–1955'
Town/County Connections: Manchester, Lancashire; Huddersfield, Yorkshire

Account of Deed: On 4 October 1917, south-west of Poelcapelle, Belgium, when close to the objective, Sergeant Coverdale disposed of three snipers. He then rushed two machine-guns, killing or wounding the teams. He subsequently reorganised his platoon in order to capture another position, but after getting within 100 yards of it was held up by our own barrage and had to return. Later he went out again with five men to capture the position, but, seeing a con-siderable number of the enemy advancing, he withdrew his detachment man by man, he himself being the last to retire.

CUNNINGHAM, John [1917]

Rank/Service: Private; 12th (S) Battalion, East Yorkshire Regiment
VC Location: Prince of Wales's Regiment Museum, York
Date of Gazette: 13 January 1917
Place/Date of Birth: Scunthorpe, Lincolnshire; 28 June 1897

Place/Date of Death: Hull, Yorkshire; 21 February 1941
Grave: Western Cemetery, Hull
Town/County Connections: Scunthorpe, Lincolnshire; Hull, Yorkshire

Account of Deed: On 13 November 1916, after the enemy's front line had been captured opposite the Hebuterne Sector, France, Private Cunningham went with a bombing section up a communication trench, where much opposition was met and all the rest of the section were either killed or wounded. Collecting all the bombs from the casualties, Private Cunningham went on alone. When he had used up all the bombs he returned for a fresh supply and again went up the communications trench, this time meeting a party of ten Germans. He killed all ten and cleared the trench up to the new line.

Biographical Detail: John was born in Swains Yard off Manley Street, Scunthorpe, and was the eldest son of Charles and Mary Cunningham. He was nineteen years old and when he won his VC on 13 November 1916 he was serving with the 12th (Service) Battalion (the Hull Sportsmen's Pals Battalion), the East Yorkshire Regiment, 31st Division, at the Battle of the Somme. In June the following year John married Eva Harrison at Hull and they had two children, Annie, who died in infancy, and John, who was born in 1920 at Hull. John Cunningham died on 20 February 1941 at 5 Beaufort Terrace, Campbell Street, Hull, aged forty-three years and his funeral took place in Hull on 24 February 1941. John is buried in grave no. 17509, compartment no. 180 at the Western Cemetery, Hull.

DANIELS, Harry [1915]

Rank/Service: Company Sergeant-Major (later Lieutenant Colonel);
    2nd Battalion, Rifle Brigade (Prince Consort's Own)
Other Decorations: MC
VC Location: Royal Green Jackets Museum, Winchester
Date of Gazette: 28 April 1915
Place/Date of Birth: Wymondham, Norfolkl; 13 December 1884
Place/Date of Death: Leeds, Yorkshire; 13 December 1953
Grave: Lawnswood Cemetery, Leeds
Memorial: The Rifle Brigade Memorial, Winchester Cathedral
Town/County Connections: Wymondham, Norfolk; Leeds, Yorkshire
Significant Remarks: Chief Recruiting Officer, NW Division 1933–42

Account of Deed: On 12 March 1915 at Neuve Chapelle, France, when the advance of the battalion was impeded by wire entanglements and by very severe machine-gun fire, Company Sergeant-Major Daniels and another soldier,

C.R. Noble VC, voluntarily rushed to the front and succeeded in cutting the wires. They were both wounded at once, and Noble died of his wounds the next day.

Biographical Detail: Harry Daniels was the thirteenth child of a baker in Wymondham, Norfolk. Orphaned at an early age, he grew up in an orphanage, where he was nicknamed 'Spitfire'. Twice he ran away. On the first occasion he lived for two days on turnips he found growing in the fields before returning to the home. The second occasion was more successful and he worked for two months on board a fishing smack before he returned.

Shortly after that he received news that his elder brother had been killed while serving with the Guards in South Africa. Harry waited the few months until he was old enough and then in 1903 enlisted in the army, as his brother had done before him. Eventually his service took him out to India, and it was there, at a Christmas Dance at Calcutta in 1913, that he first met Miss Mary Kathleen Perry. Nearly two years went by before they married but it was a whirlwind courtship just the same. For, apart from that dance, he saw her only twice more before they became engaged.

Miss Perry went home to England, Sergeant-Major Daniels to the North-West Frontier. From somewhere in the foothills of the Himalayas he wrote to her asking her to be his wife. She said 'yes' and returned to India, where they were married in January 1914. She died at their Leeds home in Thornfield Road, West Park, in 1949.

On the outbreak of the First World War CSM Daniels went with his regiment to France, and on a cold March day in 1915 he won his Victoria Cross; a year later, with the rank of second lieutenant, he won a Military Cross for bravery under fire. From that date his rise through the ranks was steady: lieutenant (1918), captain (1927), brevet-major (1929), lieutenant-colonel (1934). From 1933 to 1942, when he left the armed forces, he was the army's Chief Recruiting Officer in the north-west division.

On leaving the army Colonel Daniels worked for a short period at the Odeon cinema, Leeds, at which time he became friendly with John Beaumont from the neighbouring Grand Theatre, and accepted an offer to transfer up the street. His knowledge of theatre management was hardly profound, yet it might be supposed that he was early proof of the present-day theory, rapidly gaining ground, that the army provides the best school of management in the world. There was no doubt that his flair for organisation, not to mention his undeniable charisma, benefited the Grand.

Colonel Daniels was also an athlete, who retained a life-long interest in outdoor sports. He was with the British Olympic Games team at Antwerp in

1920, he competed as a horseman and was particularly keen on fishing, fencing and boxing. Even when he was well over sixty he could astonish friends by doing handstands.

When 'Dan VC', as he was known, died after a long illness in December 1953, a Union Jack adorned the coffin at his Lawnswood funeral. His VC and other medals went on show at Leeds Museum before being handed to the Regimental HQ at Winchester, together with a cartoon of him by Bruce Bairnsfather, which he had presented to John Beaumont. He was also made a Freeman of the City of London, and a road is named after him in his home town of Wymondham.

DRESSER, Tom [1917]

Rank/Service: 28425 Private; 7th Battalion, Yorkshire Regiment (Alexandra, Princess of Wales's Own)
VC Location: Green Howards Museum, Richmond
Date of Gazette: 27 June 1917
Place/Date of Birth: Huby, Nr Easingwold, Yorkshire; 6 April 1891
Place/Date of Death: Middlesbrough, Yorkshire; 9 April 1982
Grave: Thorntree Cemetery, Middlesbrough (name not on family stone)
Town/County Connections: Middlesbrough and Pickering, Yorkshire
Significant Remarks: The Beck Isle Museum, Pickering, North Yorkshire, holds several photographs, considerable research material and documentation relating to Tom Dresser and his family, including his birth certificate

Account of Deed: On 12 May 1917 near Roeux, France, Private Dresser, in spite of having been twice wounded on the way and suffering great pain, succeeded in conveying an important message from battalion headquarters to the front-line trenches, which he eventually reached in an exhausted condition. His fearlessness and determination to deliver this message at all costs proved of the greatest value to his battalion at a critical period.

Biographical Detail: Tom Dresser's grandfather Tom was born at Whenby in 1825. A local farmer with 506 acres, he employed six men and three boys. His son Thomas was also born at Whenby in 1863 and was first a groom by occupation; he lived at Little Langton in North Yorkshire, where he possibly met Clara Ward, a farmer's daughter. The family moved around the country for a number of years, and a sister was born in Pontefract in 1887, before settling for a period at Lawnd House Farm, Huby, near Easingwold, where Tom was born on 6 April 1891. Sometime between 1902 and 1917 his father moved from farming at Westgate, Pickering, and bought a newsagent's business in Middlesbrough.

Detail of an illustration depicting Queen Victoria awarding Victoria Crosses at the investiture in Hyde Park on 26 June 1857.

The Victoria Cross.

General Outram leads the first relieving force into Lucknow. (*Mansell Collection*)

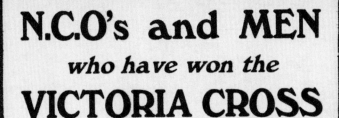

N.C.O's and MEN
who have won the
VICTORIA CROSS

BATTERY-SERGT-MAJOR (NOW SECOND-LIEUT.)
G. T. DORRELL, " L" Battery, Royal Horse Artillery
SERGEANT D. NELSON (NOW SECOND-LIEUT.)
" L" Battery, Royal Horse Artillery
CORPORAL C. E. GARFORTH, 15th (The King's) Hussars
BOMBARDIER E. G. HARLOCK (NOW SERGEANT),
113th Battery, Royal Field Artillery
LANCE-CORPORAL F. W. HOLMES, 2nd Battalion
(The King's Own) Yorkshire Light Infantry
PRIVATE S. F. GODLEY, 4th Battalion, Highland
Light Infantry
DRIVER J. H. C. DRAIN, 37th Battery, Royal Field
Artillery
DRIVER F. LUKE, 37th Battery, Royal Field Artillery

**There is room for
your name on this
Roll of Honour.**

THESE HEROES would never have won
the VICTORIA CROSS by staying away
from the RECRUITING OFFICE.
They enlisted for their Country's sake, and fought
as only brave men do.

Is *your* name to be known from one end of the world
to the other as one of the Empire's *bravest* sons?

ENLIST TO-DAY.

The more men we have, the sooner the war will end.

At any Post Office you can obtain the address of the
nearest Recruiting Office. Enter *your* name to-day on the
Nation's Roll of Honour, and do *your* part.

GOD SAVE THE KING.

A recruitment poster from 1915 utilising Victoria Cross winners.

Captain Bell of the Royal Welsh Fusiliers, with the assistance of Private Syle of the 7th Fusiliers, capturing a Russian gun at the Battle of Alma (Crimea, 1854) from which all VC medals have been made.

Possibly the most iconic and recognisable war poster of any conflict. It is an image that has often been transformed into a caricature in the minds of later generations through changing standards and values, and many times has been misused in other contexts.

A popular boys comic of the 1970s told the stories of famous war exploits. In one edition it include the story of Jack White.

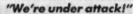

CONTINUED FROM
FRONT PAGE

AAAARGH!

YUUURGH!

GOOD GRIEF! WE'RE
UNDER ATTACK!

QUICK! TURN THE PONTOON
ROUND. IT'LL BE OUR TURN
NEXT!

AAAARGH!

EUGH!

WE WALKED INTO THAT
ONE. WE DIDN'T GET
ROUND IN TIME!

KEEP DOWN! THEY
MAY THINK WE'RE ALL
DEAD.

BUT WE'RE DRIFTING TOWARDS
THEIR BANK, SIR. STRAIGHT
INTO THEIR BLOOMIN' TURKISH
PAWS!

WATCH YOURSELF,
WHITE. THERE'S
NOTHING YOU CAN
DO.

I'M THE ONLY BLOKE NOT DEAD
OR WOUNDED IN THIS PONTOON,
SIR. GOT TO DO SOMETHING.
I'LL BE ALL RIGHT . . . I
HOPE.

THERE! ONE STILL ALIVE!
KILL HIM!

C'MON, YOU BIG AWKWARD
TUB. GET MOVING!

IF I CAN GET IT INTO THOSE
REEDS. THEY'LL NOT BE ABLE TO
SPOT US.

WE MADE IT, SIR. HANG ON,
WHILE I GET IT TIED UP.
THEN WE CAN GET THE DEAD
AN' WOUNDED ASHORE.

WHITE . . . YOU'VE SAVED ALL THE
WOUNDED AND THE EQUIPMENT IN
THIS PONTOON. YOU DESERVE A
MEDAL . . . AND I'LL SEE YOU GET
ONE.

AW, THAT'S ALL RIGHT,
SIR. ONLY DOIN' A JOB
O' WORK.

*For his outstanding courage and resourcefulness at
a time of desperate emergency, Private Jack White
was awarded a medal—the Victoria Cross.*

Look out for another great true war story NEXT WEEK!

Arthur Aaron in civilian attire prior to enlisting.

A.L. Aaron as an air crew cadet.

Flight Sergeant Arthur Aaron RAFVR, 12 August 194[...]

Private Eric Anderson VC, East Yorkshire Regiment, 8 April 1943.

Lance-Corporal Thomas Bryan VC receiving his medal from King George V at a field investiture. (*Dix Doonan Webb*)

William Boynton Butler VC (*left*) being congratulated by a colleague.

Town Hall Square, Bradford, looking towards Tyrell Street, as George W. Chafer VC would have known it.

Sergeant Edward Cooper VC, KRRC.

Lieutenant-Commander
Eugene Esmonde VC, RN,
12 February 1942.

Swordfish aircraft in flight.
(RAF Museum)

The lower reaches of the River Hull in 1937, when it was still a hive of activity. John Harrison VC would have been familiar with such scenes. His father was a ship's boilermaker.

Company Sergeant-Major Stanley Hollis VC.

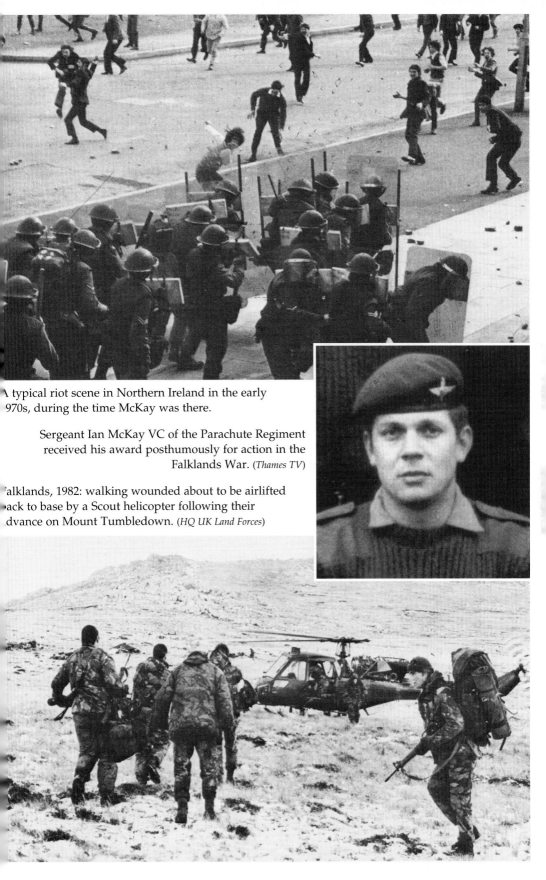

A typical riot scene in Northern Ireland in the early 1970s, during the time McKay was there.

Sergeant Ian McKay VC of the Parachute Regiment received his award posthumously for action in the Falklands War. (*Thames TV*)

Falklands, 1982: walking wounded about to be airlifted back to base by a Scout helicopter following their advance on Mount Tumbledown. (*HQ UK Land Forces*)

Assaulting a redoubt during the Second Maori War in New Zealand. Colour Sergeant Edward McKenna was awarded his VC in just such an action. (*Mansell Collection*)

Leading Seaman James Magennis VC, RN,
31 July 1945.

Leading Seaman Magennis undergoing training.

Leading Seaman James Magennis VC (*left*) and Lieutenant Ian Fraser VC, DSC.

A contemporary illustration showing how Magennis fixed limpet mines to a Japanese cruiser in the Johore Straits.

Ilkley from the famous Cow and Calf Rocks on Ilkley Moor, the birthplace of Second Lieutenant Thomas Maufe VC.

Ilkley from Cow and Calf Rocks.

Lance-Corporal Nicholls VC, 3rd Battalion, Grenadier Guards, 21 May 1940.

VC heroes at Buckingham Palace on 22 June 1945. (*Left to right*) Lt B. Place, Lt-Cdr S. Beattie, L.Cpl H. Nicholls, Lt D. Cameron and (*seated*) Maj F. Tilston of the Canadian Infantry.

Somewhere in France British soldiers rest and snatch a quick meal. (*TPS/3L Photos*)

Lieutenant R.D. Sandford VC at Buckingham Palace to receive his award.

Serving grog aboard a battleship in 1899, a typical scene enacted throughout the navy. Boatswain 1st Class John Shepherd VC, CGM, RN would have been familiar with such activities. (*RN Museum*)

Class 6P5F 4–6–00 No. 45537 *Private E. Sykes VC.*

Detail from Lady Butler's painting 'The Roll Call', showing the Grenadier Guards after the hard-fought Battle of Inkerman, in which Sergeant Symons VC, DCM, took part. (*National Army Museum*)

The tomb of the Unknown Warrior. Seventy-four VC holders made up the honour guard at the interment in Westminster Abbey on Armistice Day, 11 November 1920. Among them was Harry Blanshard Wood.

Tom was educated at St John's and Hugh Bell High School in Middles-brough and left to find employment with Dorman Long Steelworks at the Dock Street foundry.

On 8 February 1916, aged twenty-two, he enlisted into the 6th Yorkshires and then transferred to the 5th Yorkshires. After thirteen weeks at Rugeley training camp, he sailed for France and arrived on the Somme with the 7th Yorkshires in early September 1916. A month later his brother Joe was killed in action with the 9th Battalion, York and Lancaster Regiment; his brother was a well-known cross-Channel swimmer.

Tom survived the wounds he received on 12 May, and when he came out of hospital he was posted to the 74th Machine Gun Corps with a new number 138867; he served with the MGC until he was demobilised on 27 April 1919.

Dresser returned to work at the Dorman Long steel works until he took over the family newsagent's at 65 Marton Road, Middlesbrough. He lived above the shop with his wife Theresa (née Landers), whom he had married in 1924. They had four sons, all born before 1939. During the Second World War he served with G Company, 8th North Riding (Middlesbrough) Battalion, Home Guard.

Tom Dresser died on Good Friday, 9 April 1982, three days after his ninetieth birthday, and was interred in Thorntree Cemetery, Middlesbrough. His Victoria Cross and other medals are on loan from the family to the Green Howards Regimental Museum in Richmond.

EDWARDS, Wilfrid [1917]

Rank/Service: Private (later Captain); 7th Battalion, King's Own Yorkshire
   Light Infantry
VC Location: York Castle Museum, York
Date of Gazette: 14 September 1917
Place/Date of Birth: Norwich, Norfolk; 16 February 1893
Place/Date of Death: Leeds, Yorkshire; 4 January 1972
Grave: Oldfield Lane Cemetery, Lower Wortley, Leeds
Town/County Connections: Leeds, Yorkshire

Account of Deed: On 16 August 1917 at Langemarck, Belgium, when all the company officers were lost, Private Edwards, without hesitation and under heavy machine-gun and rifle fire from a strong concrete fort, dashed forward at great personal risk, threw bombs through the loopholes, surmounted the fort and waved to his company to advance; three officers and thirty other ranks in the fort were taken prisoner by him. Later he did most valuable work as a runner and eventually guided most of the battalion out through very difficult ground. Throughout he set a splendid example and was utterly regardless of danger.

Biographical Detail: Wilfred Edwards was born on 16 February 1893 in Norwich, Norfolk. He enlisted and fought in the First World War. Following his VC exploits, he was commissioned as a second lieutenant in December 1917 and was demobilised in June 1919 with the rank of major. He later moved to Leeds and re-enlisted in the army in the Second World War. On returning from the war, he took up a position with the old Leeds Gas Department. He initiated an annual dinner for Leeds Victoria Cross holders. On his death, Edwards left instructions that his VC be donated to the York Castle Museum along with his Mons Star and six other medals won in both world wars. He died in January 1972 at Leeds.

ESMONDE, Eugene Kingsmill [1942]

Rank/Service: Lieutenant-Commander RN; 825 Squadron, Fleet Air Arm
Other Decorations: DSO
VC Location: Private (Not on public display)
Date of Gazette: 3 March 1942
Place/Date of Birth: Thurgoland, Barnsley, Yorkshire; 1 March 1909
Place/Date of Death: Straits of Dover; 12 February 1942
Grave: Catholic section of Woodlands Cemetery, Gillingham, Kent
Town/County Connections: Borrisokane, Co. Tipperary, Ireland
Significant Remarks: His great-uncle Lieutenant Colonel T. Esmonde was
    awarded a Victoria Cross in 1857

Account of Deed: On 12 February 1942 the German battlecruisers *Scharnhorst* and *Gneisenau* and the cruiser *Prinz Eugen*, strongly escorted by some thirty surface craft, entered the Straits of Dover. Lieutenant Commander Esmonde was told that his squadron must attack before the enemy ships reached the sandbanks north-east of Calais, and soon after noon he led his squadron of six Swordfish to the attack; after ten minutes' flight they were attacked by a strong force of Luftwaffe fighters, numbering about fifteen Messerschmitt 109s and Focke-Wulf 190s. Detached from their escorting fighters (just ten in number) by the enemy fighters, all the aircraft of his squadron were damaged. However, Esmonde flew on, cool and resolute, serenely challenging the hopeless odds, to encounter the deadly fire of the battlecruisers and their escort, which shattered the port wing of his aircraft. Esmonde nevertheless continued the run-in towards his target until his machine burst into flames and crashed into the sea. The squadron went on to launch a gallant attack, but not one of the six aircraft returned.

Biographical Detail: He was born on 1 March 1909 at Thurgoland near Barnsley, South Yorkshire, where his father Dr John Joseph Esmonde (1862–1915) was in temporary general practice. Though by birth English, his parents were from Ireland and he returned to the family's ancestral home of the Esmonde Baronets in Drominagh, North Tipperary, as a boy; he was educated by the Jesuits, first at Wimbledon College in London and then at Clongowes Wood College in Co. Kildare, Ireland.

He had three elder half-brothers from his father's first marriage, Sir John Esmonde, 14th Baronet, who served in the First World War, Second Lieutenant Geoffrey Esmonde (1897–1916) who was killed in action in the First World War serving with the 26th Tyneside Irish Battalion of the Northumberland Fusiliers, and Sir Anthony Esmonde, 15th Baronet.

Esmonde was commissioned into the Royal Air Force as a pilot officer on probation on 28 December 1928. During the early 1930s he served first in the Royal Air Force but then transferred to the Fleet Air Arm, serving in the Mediterranean until the expiry of his commission five years later. On leaving the RAF, Esmonde joined Imperial Airways as a First Officer on 9 August 1934. He flew on the mail-carrying routes between London and Glasgow, and, as Imperial Airways expanded its service, to the Middle East and India. In 1935 he flew on the regular service between Rangoon and Mandalay in Burma, and survived a serious accident when his aircraft crashed into the Irrawaddy. He was promoted to captain on 3 July 1937, and was one of the first to fly the giant flying-boats that introduced the first airmail service between the UK and Australia. On 3 May 1939 Esmonde resigned to take up a commission as a lieutenant commander in the Fleet Air Arm.

Esmonde was on the carrier HMS *Courageous*, when it was torpedoed and sunk in the Western Approaches on 17 September 1939. Following this, he served at RNAS Lee-on-Solent and other naval air stations in the south of England. He was then appointed to the aircraft carrier HMS *Victorious*. On the night of 24 May 1941 he led a squadron of nine Swordfish aircraft, armed with torpedoes, to make a 120-mile flight in foul weather and into head-winds to attack the German battleship *Bismarck*. Esmonde's aircraft attacked through intense anti-aircraft fire from *Bismarck*, and scored one hit amidships on the starboard side. Esmonde received the DSO for this action on 11 February 1942.

Esmonde's next appointment was on HMS *Ark Royal*, and his air squadron rescued members of the ship's company when the ship was sunk off Gibraltar on 13 November 1941. By the end of November Esmonde was back at Lee-on-Solent, remaining there until 12 February 1942, the day when the German battlecruisers *Scharnhorst* and *Gneisenau*, with the cruiser *Prinz Eugen*, and a strong escort of surface craft, made their 'Channel dash' from Brest back to Germany. In the Straits of Dover Esmonde led the 825 Squadron of six Swordfish aircraft to attack the German ships.

The courage of the gallant Swordfish crews was particularly noted by friend and foe alike. Admiral Bertram Ramsay later wrote, 'In my opinion the gallant sortie of these six Swordfish aircraft constitutes one of the finest exhibitions of self-sacrifice and devotion to duty the war had ever witnessed', while Admiral Otto Ciliax in the *Scharnhorst* described, 'The mothball attack of a handful of ancient planes, piloted by men whose bravery surpasses any other action by either side that day.' As he watched the smoking wrecks of the Swordfish falling into the sea, Captain Hoffmann of the *Scharnhorst* exclaimed, 'Poor fellows, they are so very slow, it is nothing but suicide for them to fly against these big ships.' Wilhelm Wolf aboard the *Scharnhorst* wrote, 'What a heroic stage for them to meet their end! Behind them their homeland, which they had just left with their hearts steeled to their purpose, still in view.'

Esmonde was remembered in Winston Churchill's famous broadcast speech on 13 May 1945, 'Five Years of War', as having defended Ireland's honour:

> When I think of these days I think also of other episodes and personalities. I do not forget Lieutenant-Commander Esmonde, VC, DSO, Lance-Corporal Kenneally, VC, Captain Fegen, VC, and other Irish heroes that I could easily recite, and all bitterness by Britain for the Irish race dies in my heart. I can only pray that in years which I shall not see, the shame will be forgotten and the glories will endure, and that the peoples of the British Isles and of the British Commonwealth of Nations will walk together in mutual comprehension and forgiveness.

Esmonde's body floated back to Britain and was fished out of the mouth of the River Medway. He was buried in the Woodlands Cemetery, Gillingham, in Kent.

FIRTH, James [1901]

Rank/Service: Sergeant; 1st Battalion, Duke of Wellington's (West Riding) Regiment
VC Location: Lord Ashcroft VC Collection
Date of Gazette: 11 June 1901
Place/Date of Birth: Sheffield, Yorkshire; 15 January 1874
Place/Date of Death: Sheffield, Yorkshire; 29 May 1921
Grave: Burngreave Cemetery, Sheffield
Town/County Connections: Sheffield, Yorkshire

Account of Deed: On 24 February 1900 at Plewman's Farm, near Arundel, Cape Colony, South Africa, Sergeant Firth picked up and carried to cover a lance corporal who was lying wounded and exposed to heavy fire. Later in the day, when the enemy had advanced to within a short distance of the firing line, Sergeant Firth rescued a second lieutenant who was dangerously wounded, and carried him over the crest of a ridge to safety. He himself was shot through the nose and eye while doing so.

Biographical Detail: James Firth was born on 15 January 1874 to Charles and Elizabeth Firth (née Lister). His birth certificate states that his place of birth was in the registration district of Wortley, sub-district of Ecclesfield, in the county of York, West Riding. His mother registered his birth on 12 February 1874, giving their address as Upper Wincobank, Ecclesfield.

The 1881 Census lists the family address as Dwelling 1, Court No. 1, Eben Street, Brightside Bierlow, York, England.* The family is listed as follows: 'Charles FIRTH Head M Male 45 Leeds, York, England, Furnaceman; Ellen BULLAS Servant M Female 22 Brightside, York, England, Housekeeper (Dom); Clara FIRTH Daughter Female 13 Wincobank, York, England, Scholar; Arthur FIRTH Son Male 10 Wincobank, York, England, Scholar; James FIRTH Son Male 6 Wincobank, York, England, Scholar; Annie BULLAS House-keepers Daughter Female 5 Wincobank, York, England, Scholar; Henry BULLAS Son Male 3 Wincobank, York, England; Florence BULLAS House-keepers Daughter Female 4 M Brightside, York, England.' (The 1871 Census had shown the family living in Ecclesfield. James then had an elder brother William (aged eight) and two older sisters Martha (aged six) and Mary (aged four) who do not appear with the family on the 1881 Census. Clara and Arthur are aged three and four months respectively.)

The 1891 Census shows James's father Charles living in Jarrow with his second wife and family.

He had arrived in Tyneside as a steel smelter and worked initially at the Newbridge foundry. James went to school in Swalwell, Gateshead. His father then moved to Jarrow and worked at Palmers blast furnaces as part of Palmers Shipyard. James lived in Jarrow for a short period and was employed at a local chemical works. There is a plaque to James (and others) at Palmers Hospital as a VC holder and a favoured son of 'Jarrow'. This was unveiled in 2008 and was reported in the local paper, the *Shields Gazette*.

James Firth joined his regiment in July 1889. By the time the Boer War broke out, he had achieved the rank of sergeant. In June 1897 he married Mary

* Sheffield Family History Library Film 1342128; PRO Reference RG11 Piece/Folio 4664/117, p. 33.

Florence Edwards at Emmanuel Church, Attercliffe, Sheffield; she was the only daughter of Thomas Edwards of Swineshead, Lincolnshire, and they had three children, Joseph Wallis Firth (who was born in 1902 and died at the young age of ten in 1912. He was buried in Burngreave Cemetery), Alleyne G. Firth, born on 25 June 1903, and Cecil J. Firth, born on 18 December 1907.

In 1900, after the injuries he sustained in the war, James was discharged from the services as medically unfit. Although he recovered from his wounds, Firth wore an eye-patch for the remainder of his life. He was presented with his Victoria Cross by King Edward VII on Thursday, 25 July 1901. It was reported in *The Times*, on Friday, July 26, 1901.* He applied for service again in 1914 at the outbreak of the First World War but was turned down on medical grounds. After a long period of disability he died of tuberculosis in May 1921.

On 3 June 1921 the *Sheffield Daily Telegraph* carried a brief report of James's funeral, under the headline: 'SHEFFIELD VC BURIED'.

> The funeral of Sergeant James Firth, Sheffield's first VC, took place yesterday at Burngreave Cemetery in the presence of thousands and friends from Neepsend, where he lived for several years. A service was held at St Michael's Church, Neepsend, conducted by the Rev. H.H. Everson (Vicar) and the Rev. C.F. Wardby. From the church, the coffin draped with the Union Jack was carried to a gun carriage by six sergeants and a regimental sergeant major of the Duke of Wellington's (WR) Regiment (Sergeant Firth's old regiment, who came from the depot at Halifax). Following the coffin was a firing party from the Cheshire Regiment from Hillsborough Barracks carrying arms at the reverse. The service at the Cemetery, simple and impressive, was concluded by the sounding of the Last Post and the firing of three volleys over the grave.

His last will and testament gives the following information:

> WILLS & BEQUESTS 1921
> Mr James Firth VC of 193 Douglas Road, Parkwood Springs, Neepsend, Sheffield, and formerly of Swalwell, Durham, formerly Sergeant, Duke of Wellington's (West Riding) Regiment, who was awarded the Victoria Cross in 1900 for conspicuous bravery in the Boer War and who died on May 29 last, left estate valued for probate at £359.

*Issue 36517, p. 3, column E, Court Circular.

The testator left to his son Alleyne Gatehouse Firth, on attaining majority, his Victoria Cross and his South African Medals, the silver watch, No. 34188, presented to him by the people of Swalwell, his Queen Victoria chocolate box, the card bidding him to the investiture at St James Palace to receive the Victoria Cross and his gold snake ring, and further on the decease of his (testators) widow or earlier at her discretion the black marble clock and two bronze horses presented to him by Messrs Vickers Son and Maxim Limited, and the enlarged photograph of himself in his red tunic.

An article in the *Sheffield Star* dated Tuesday, 16 March 2004 reported that after the end of the Boer War Sergeant Firth, who was born in Jarrow, County Durham, in 1874, lived in Neepsend, Sheffield.*

His wife Mary Florence and two of their sons were later buried alongside him. In the 85 years that followed, his grave, in the north eastern section of the cemetery close to the War Memorial, became lost and forgotten and the inscriptions on the ornate stone headstone were eaten away by years of pollution . . . [efforts were made to locate the grave] . . . Mr. Johnson was helped by local historian Albert Jackson and Christine Stevens of the Friends of Burngreave Cemetery.

Alan Johnson, aged fifty-four, of Manor Way, Hoyland, said: 'I had only ever vaguely heard of Sgt. Firth before I found the letter which said he was my father's uncle. It's intriguing really. My eldest aunt says she remembers him visiting the house – apparently he was very tall and used to run his hand along the top of doors to see if there was any dust!'

GLENN, James Alexander *see* SMITH, James

GRANT, Robert [1860]

Rank/Service: Sergeant; 1st Battalion, 5th Regiment, Northumberland Fusiliers
VC Location: Lord Ashcroft VC Collection
Date of Gazette: 19 June 1860
Place/Date of Birth: Harrogate, Yorkshire; 1837
Place/Date of Death: London; 23 November 1874

---

* After leaving the army James became a foreman in a local steel works. In 1925 his wife Mary was living at 193 Douglas Road, Neepsend, Sheffield.

Grave: Highgate Cemetery, London (common grave under a footpath)
Memorial: Regimental Museum of the Royal Northumberland Fusiliers,
    Alnwick Castle, Northumberland
Town/County Connections: Harrogate, Yorkshire; London

Account of Deed: On 24 September 1857 at Alum Bagh, India, Sergeant Grant
went, under very heavy fire, to save the life of a private whose leg had been shot
away. With the help of a lieutenant, Sergeant Grant carried the wounded man
to the safety of the camp.

Biographical Detail: After ten years in the army, which he had joined at the age
of seventeen, Grant became a police constable in the Metropolitan Police
(PC 306), and served in the Y Division Holloway area covering Kentish Town,
until his death from consumption in 1874 aged forty-seven. Penniless and
apparently without family, he was buried, at the expense of the parish, in a
paupers' grave, number 15054, with nine others, where they lay forgotten. In
time, research carried out by assistant gravedigger and local historian Phil
Seaton revealed the unmarked grave of Sergeant Robert Grant VC. This
prompted Kentish Town crime prevention officer Dave King to press Scotland
Yard to honour a man who had served in the Met's old Y Division based in
Highgate, until he died of 'inflammation of the lungs'.

The culmination of the research resulted in Sir Ian Blair, Commissioner of
the Metropolitan Police, unveiling a headstone over Robert Grant's grave on
Tuesday, 24 June 2008. Colonel Simon Marr MBE of the Royal Regiment of
Fusiliers was the first to honour the new headstone, erected and rededicated in
Highgate Cemetery, followed by members of the Grant family. The Fusiliers'
regimental secretary Captain Tony Adamson brought Robert Grant's Victoria
Cross to the ceremony from its home in the Royal Northumberland Fusiliers
Museum in Alnwick Castle, Northumberland.

Grant is now also commemorated in his home town of Harrogate with a
plaque at the war memorial.

HACKETT, William [1916]
Rank/Service: Sapper; 254th Tunnelling Company, Royal Engineers
VC Location: Private (Not on public display)
Date of Gazette: 5 August 1916
Place/Date of Birth: Nottingham; 11 June 1873
Place/Date of Death: Givenchy, France; 27 June 1916
Grave: No Known Grave

Memorials: Ploegsteert Memorial, Belgium; Market Hall, Mexborough, Yorkshire

Town/County Connections: Nottingham; Mexborough, Yorkshire

Account of Deed: During 22/23 June 1916 at Shaftesbury Avenue Mine, near Givenchy, France, Sapper Hackett was entombed with four other men in a gallery, owing to the explosion of an enemy mine. After working for 24 hours, a hole was created and the rescue party outside made contact. Sapper Hackett crawled along and helped three of the other men through the hole; he could easily have followed them, but he refused to leave the fourth man, who had been seriously injured, saying, 'I am a tunneller and must look after the others first'. Even when the hole began to get smaller, he still refused to leave his injured comrade. Finally, the gallery collapsed and, although a rescue party worked desperately for four days, they were unable to reach the two men. Hackett's body was never recovered.

Biographical Detail: William Hackett was born to John and Harriet Hackett on 11 June 1873 in Nottingham. Educated at the local school, he left to go down the mines. He married Alice Tooby in 1900 and they had two children, a son and a daughter. After losing his job, he and Alice moved to Mexborough in South Yorkshire where he took a job as a coalminer. He was forty-one years of age at the outbreak of the First World War and volunteered to join the local regiment, the York & Lancaster Regiment, but was turned down three times before being accepted into the 254th Tunnelling Company, Corps of Royal Engineers, in October 1915. He was forty-three years old, and serving as a sapper when he displayed the courage for which he was awarded the Victoria Cross on 22/23 June 1916 at Shaftesbury Avenue Mine.

On Saturday, 19 June 2010 two members of the Nottingham and Nottinghamshire Victoria Cross Committee attended the unveiling of the new William Hackett VC memorial at Givenchy. Mr Derek Price, Tony Higton and Tony's wife Mavis were greeted by the Mayor of Givenchy, Monsieur Jacques Herbaut, at the village hall. The mayor was presented with a scroll of honour from the Nottingham Castle Victoria Cross Memorial project, which also honoured William Hackett. The William Hackett memorial is located on the same site as the memorial to the 55th West Lancashire Division. It faces the fields in which the tunnel was excavated. The memorial has a T-shaped slot which, when looked through, focuses on the position of the shaft to the tunnel where William Hackett chose to remain with his comrade in arms. On the occasion of the unveiling a line of red flags had been set out to illustrate the actual spot where the remains of William Hackett lie. The Royal Engineers from Nottingham provided the honour guard for the parade and the band.

HARPER, John William [1945]

Rank/Service: Corporal; 4th Battalion, York & Lancaster Regiment
VC Location: York & Lancaster Museum, Rotherham
Date of Gazette: 2 January 1945
Place/Date of Birth: Doncaster, Yorkshire; 6 August 1915
Place/Date of Death: Nr Antwerp, Belgium; 29 September 1944
Grave: Leopoldsburg War Cemetery, Belgium
Town/County Connections: Doncaster, Yorkshire

Account of Deed: On 29 September 1944, during an assault on the Depot de
Mendicite, Antwerp, Corporal Harper led his section across 300 yards of
completely exposed ground, with utter disregard for the hail of mortar bombs
and small arms fire from the enemy. He was killed during the action, but the
subsequent capture of the position was largely due to his self-sacrifice.

Biographical Detail: John William Harper was born in Hatfield, Doncaster,
South Yorkshire, on 6 August 1916 to George Ernest Harper and his wife,
Florence (née Parkin).

HARRISON, John [1917]

Rank/Service: Temporary Second Lieutenant; 11th (S) Battalion, East
   Yorkshire Regiment
Other Decorations: MC
VC Location: Prince of Wales's Own Regiment of Yorkshire, York
Date of Gazette: 14 June 1917
Place/Date of Birth: Sculcoates, Hull, Yorkshire; 2 November 1890
Place/Date of Death: Oppy, France; 3 May 1917
Grave: No Known Grave
Memorials: Arras Memorial, France; outside KC stadium, Hull
Town/County Connections: Sculcoates, Kingston-upon-Hull, Yorkshire

Account of Deed: During an attack on 3 May 1917 at Oppy, France, owing to
darkness, to smoke from the enemy barrage and our own, and to the fact that the
objective was in a dark wood, it was impossible to see when the barrage had
lifted off the enemy front line. Nevertheless, Second Lieutenant Harrison twice
led his company against the enemy trench under terrific rifle and machine-gun
fire, but was repulsed. Then finally he made a dash at the machine-gun, hoping
to knock it out of action and so save the lives of many of his company. Darting
from shell hole to shell hole until he was close enough, he then leapt forward,
hurling the bomb at the enemy gunners. By the light of a star shell and flare he
was seen to fall as he threw the bomb. The machine gun was silenced but

Harrison was not seen to get back up. Despite this, the attack failed to gain further momentum and troops later fell back to their start line. Isolated groups who had got into the wood or village either fell back or were captured. By nightfall the remnants of the battalion were back in dugouts at the railway cutting near Bailleul. The 11th East Yorkshire War Diary records that eight officers, including Harrison, went missing that day, four more officers were wounded, nine men were killed with 150 wounded and a further ninety-eight went missing (mostly killed). Harrison was later reported missing, believed killed.

Biographical Detail: The shipyards of Hull around the turn of the twentieth century might seem an unlikely place to forge a sporting icon and a Victoria Cross recipient, but it did both in the form of John Harrison. Known as 'Jack', he was born at Sculcotes on 2 November 1890. As he grew, his parents recognised that he had academic skills and intelligence that would allow him to break out from following his father as a ship's boilermaker. With their help and encouragement, he left school to be trained as a teacher, first in St John's College, York, then at Lime Street School, back in his native Hull.

While at York, Harrison pursued his interests in cricket and rugby football. His sprinter's speed and strong build helped mould him into a valuable winger or centre in the college line-up. Finding himself a permanent starter on the First XV exposed him to scouts for the York Northern Union Rugby League Club, which desperately needed new and vibrant talent. Turning out for them five times in the 1911/12 season, he scored three tries and further enhanced his standing by doing so. Unfortunately, Jack's relationship with York was destined to be short-lived, and having completed his teacher training he returned to his home town of Hull in the summer of 1912 and married his sweetheart Lillian.

The newly married couple took up residence at 75 Wharncliffe Street in Hull. Jack was now an assistant schoolmaster, but still showed an interest in rugby. Hull, the local rugby league team, invited him to join them for the 1912/13 season. Running out in the famous 'black and white' of Hull for his first game in September 1912, he made an immediate impact on both the game and the fans. At five feet eight inches, he was reasonably tall for the era and was able to command space physically. Allied with his ability to read passes and to 'make the plays', he was a good team player who also, to the joy of fans, regularly scored tries with his speed and panache. Playing alongside Harrison in the Hull side was record signing Billy Batten, bought in for a not inconsiderable £600.

In the 1913/14 season Harrison scored a remarkable fifty-two tries – a record that still stands today. He went on to score a total of 106 tries in 116 matches for Hull up to 1916. He scored one of the two tries scored by Hull in the Challenge Cup victory over Wakefield Trinity at Halifax in 1913 and was selected to tour Australia in 1914, but the tour was cancelled due to the outbreak of hostilities.

His wife Lillian gave birth to their son John in 1915, and it appears that, having seen the pregnancy through, Jack volunteered for duty in the army and enlisted in the Inns of Court Officer Training Corps (OTC) on 4 November 1915. Stationed for this period of training in Hertfordshire, he had temporary digs at 55 Kitsbury Road, Berkhamsted. It is possible that he carried on playing the occasional game for Hull even while under training. When he resigned from the OTC in August 1916 to take up a commission, however, there was no longer any time for playing at Hull.

Harrison was posted initially to the 14th Battalion, East Yorkshire Regiment, a reserve unit based at Whittington Barracks in Lichfield. The East Yorkshire Regiment, like many other regionally recruited regiments, answered the call of Lord Kitchener in 1914 to form locally recruited and raised units that would train, serve and fight together. Initially 100,000 volunteers were required to form the New Army but this figure was achieved so quickly that second and subsequent batches soon followed.

Unfortunately, it was not all plain sailing for the 'Pals' recruiting idea. A letter in the 1914 *Hull Daily Mail* from 'Middle Class of Newland' commented, 'many men were not enlisting because they did not like the idea of having to herd with all types of men now being enlisted. It is keeping young athletes and men of good birth and training from joining the colours.' He continued, 'Larger employers in Hull should use their influence to organize a corps of middle class young men, Clerks, Tailors, Drapers, Grocers, Warehousemen and Artisans.' His was clearly not a lone voice and soon, with the blessing of Lord Kitchener, Lord Nunburnholme, the Lord Lieutenant of the East Riding, was authorised to raise a service battalion with the name 'The Commercial Battalion'. Recruiting was brisk and in one day more than 600 Hull men signed on. By 12 September 1914 the 'Commercials' was full and a second battalion started, this time for 'Tradesmen'. In three days that too was full. Wishing to encourage still more men, the *Hull Daily Mail* urged, 'If you mean to play the Game, join at once.' The third battalion of Hull men was to be called the 'Sportsmen' and its ranks were swelled (though not entirely) by men from football, rugby, cricket and other sporting backgrounds. During December 1914 the battalions were renumbered to bring them into line with a more standardised army system. Thus the 'Commercials' became the 10th Battalion, the East Yorkshire Regiment, the 'Tradesmen' became the 11th and the 'Sportsmen' the 12th. When the final Pals unit was raised, it lacked a specific name and contained a rare mix of all sorts, so the 13th Battalion gained the humorous title of Hull t'others'!

Eventually Jack Harrison joined B Company, 11th East Yorkshire Regiment as a second lieutenant just before Christmas 1916, and was soon in the thick of fighting.

After the action on 3 May 1917 at Oppy, France, the news was soon passed to Lillian that Jack was listed as missing, and one can only imagine what agonies she went through. Investigations began to find out what had happened to Jack after the attack. Red Cross officials were asked to see if he was listed as captured by the German guardsmen, while enlisted men were asked if they had seen him or his body. Months passed with no news of Jack, but in the meantime Lillian was told of the award of the Victoria Cross. The testimony of Private Blake, today held at the National Archives within Harrison's Service record, says, 'He was our Platoon Officer. I saw him hit by a shell at Ypres [*sic*] on May 3rd, in the open. He was killed outright, I saw him brought in but do not know where they buried him. Blake, Private 1534.31/8/1917 Etaples.' A stretcher-bearer who later wrote of the period in his diary, tells proudly of scouring the area and not leaving any bodies uncovered, but stacking the bodies up like logs for later burial.

A communiqué from the War Council to Lillian Harrison dated 13 December finally announced that sufficient time had elapsed to inform her that Second Lieutenant Harrison's death must be accepted. It is highly likely that Jack was buried somewhere near Oppy and today lies beneath the headstone of an 'Unknown Soldier', but he is listed on the Arras Memorial to the Missing.

Lillian was invited to Buckingham Palace in 1918 to receive Jack's VC. Her plight as a war widow with a young son was recognised by the local community, who raised funds in 1923 to pay for his education. St Johns College and Lime Street School both erected memorial plaques for Jack Harrison VC, MC and a development of flats in Hull was named Jack Harrison Court in the 1980s. The latest evidence that Jack has not been forgotten by the rugby world is the Jack Harrison VC MC Memorial at the KC stadium in Hull. Finally, in honour of this extraordinary soldier and player, the Army Rugby League presented the Jack Harrison VC Memorial Trophy to the Combined Services Rugby League in the year 2000, to be contested annually in the Inter-Services fixture between the army and the Royal Navy.

HEDGES, Frederick William [1919]

Rank/Service: Temporary Lieutenant; Bedfordshire Regiment, attached
   6th Battalion, Northamptonshire Regiment
VC Location: Bedfordshire Regiment Museum, Luton

Date of Gazette: 31 January 1919
Place/Date of Birth: Umballa, India; 6 June 1896
Place/Date of Death: Harrogate, Yorkshire; 29 May 1954
Grave: Stonefall Crematorium, Harrogate
Town/County Connections: Hounslow, Middlesex; Harrogate, Yorkshire
Significant Remarks: Served with the Civil Defence in the Second World War

Account of Deed: On 24 October 1918, north-east of Bousies, France, Lieutenant Hedges led his company with great skill towards their final objective, maintaining direction under the most difficult conditions. When the advance was held up by enemy machine-gun posts, the lieutenant, accompanied by one sergeant and followed at some considerable distance by a Lewis gun section, again advanced, capturing six machine-guns and fourteen prisoners. His gallantry and initiative enabled the whole line to advance and contributed largely to the success of subsequent operations.

Biographical Detail: Frederick William Hedges, known as Fred, Freddie or Bill, was born on 6 June 1896 at Umballa in India and baptised there in the Church of St Paul on 17 December 1896. His father was Henry George Hedges, who was 'born at sea, Bengal Bay' around 1857 and his mother was Mrs Harriet Eliza (née Loader) Hedges, born in India around 1865.

His father Henry had served as a bandsman in the 12th Royal Lancers at Bangalore, and later served as the bandmaster in the 18th Hussars. In 1901 the family were living at 24 Landsdowne Road, Hounslow, Middlesex. Henry was then a superintendent (assurance). Freddie, the seventh of nine children, was educated at Grove Road Boys' School and Isleworth County School.

Freddie enlisted into the Queen Victoria's Rifles on 6 August 1914, when his address was given as Davies Street, London. He was posted as Rifleman 2182 to the 1st/9th (City of London) Battalion, the London Regiment (Queen Victoria's Rifles) on 8 August 1914 and left for France with the battalion on 5 November 1914. He took part in the First Battle of Ypres in 1914. He was admitted to hospital in France suffering from frostbite on 28 January 1915 and evacuated to No. 3 Northern General Hospital in Sheffield, where he remained until 15 March 1916.

On 6 July 1915 Hedges was commissioned as a second lieutenant in the Bedfordshire Regiment and on 10 July he went to the Felixstowe School of Instruction before joining the 9th Reserve Battalion as a musketry officer. After a year spent training recruits in musketry, on 2 September 1916 he left for France again, joining the recently arrived 6th Battalion, Bedfordshire Regiment, which was engaged in the Battle of the Ancre between 13 and 15 November 1916 and the Battle of Arras in April 1917. On the night of

10 April 1917 he was wounded in the right hand by shrapnel while the battalion dug in astride the Le Bergere crossroads, a few yards south of Monchy le Preux, in the snow. He was evacuated to Rouen and thence to England aboard the *St George* on 19 April and was admitted to No. 5 General Hospital in Portsmouth; he later went to Osborne House on the Isle of Wight. On 12 October 1917 he returned to light duties with the 3rd Reserve Battalion as a machine-gun instructor and his promotion to lieutenant came through on 1 July 1917.

Hedges returned for a third tour on the Western Front, arriving on 29 September 1918. As his battalion had been disbanded that summer, he was attached to the 6th Northamptons, with whom his service on the front line would end. He served in the final battles of the war, specifically at the Battles of Epehy on 29 September, and the Selle on 23 and 24 October (where he won his Victoria Cross); finally, Captain Hedges was, ironically, wounded again. During the fighting at Mormal Forest on 4 November 1918 Freddie was wounded in the right side of the scalp – 'a three and a half inch crack in the skull', according to Sergeant Gibson – and took a 'through and through' bullet in his right shoulder. He was evacuated back to England, arriving at Southampton on 8 November, and heard that the war had ended from a hospital bed in England.

Captain Hedges was awarded the Victoria Cross by the King at Buckingham Palace on 15 May 1919 and was appointed the Commandant of No. 8 POW Camp on 10 June. On 26 July 1919 Freddie married Mollie Lorna Kenworthy, but soon afterwards, on 27 September 1919, he suffered a compound fracture of his right leg in an on-duty collision between his motorcycle and a car (driven by the managing director of Leyland Motors as it turned out) at Fulwell, England. Subsequent medical examinations revealed the fracture had healed but other remarks show, with hindsight, that Freddie was not entirely well, and was probably suffering 'shell shock' from his experiences in the war.

Captain Hedges VC relinquished his commission on completion of his service on 14 April 1920, but retained the rank of lieutenant. He and his wife Mollie attended the Buckingham Palace Garden Party for Victoria Cross holders in 1920 and the House of Lords dinner for VC holders in 1929.

Taking a senior position with the Prudential Assurance Company, he became very active in British Legion affairs during the 1930s, serving as Vice-Chairman and Chairman of the Teddington branch, and assisting former servicemen to make benefit claims.

On 5 February 1924 Mollie gave birth to their son, John Grosvenor Hedges. It was a difficult birth and the couple avoided any further pregnancies. They were a contented family group and a year or so later they relocated from her parents' home to one of their own in The Avenue, Sunbury. With the exception of the death of Freddie's father at the end of 1936, it seems to have been a period of contentment as their son grew.

In 1939 Freddie was elected Chairman of the Teddington branch of the British Legion, having served previously as Vice-Chairman. But in September the declaration of war was to cast a dark shadow over their lives. Freddie promptly attempted to re-enlist but was rejected, which preyed on his mind. Meanwhile Mollie was deeply upset that he had not consulted her about it, or even mentioned his intention beforehand. It was to cause a lasting rift in their relationship. He became a Civil Defence Co-ordinator, and as Chairman of the British Legion he was given charge of the annual Remembrance Day Parade in 1941.

Four days later, on the evening of 13 November 1941, their son John, then aged seventeen, left home as usual, in full equipment for duty with the local Home Guard unit, the 31st Middlesex, where he was on Upper Thames shore patrol. On this occasion, however, he was setting out to attend a friend's birthday party at Thames Ditton, south of the river. From the party, taking the shortest route, he arrived at Sunbury Lock at around two o'clock in the morning of 14 November. His colleague on duty rowed across from the Middlesex bank to collect him. A few yards from the destination landing stage, John noticed his feet getting wet – the boat was taking in water. They both stood upright and the dinghy, unbalanced, capsized. The ferryman swam to the landing stage, removed his great coat and attempted to rescue his passenger, but in vain. He then reported the incident to the police. The police subsequently dragged the river in that area, a particularly deep and fast-flowing section, a number of times with no success.

A month later, on 13 December, a body was reported floating in the backwater of a downstream island. It proved to be John. A former neighbour formally identified the body. The Coroner's verdict was accidental death due to drowning. The body was cremated at the Mortlake Crematorium on Friday, 19 December, and the death was registered the following day. John had been the focal point of his parents' lives and, inevitably, his loss placed added strain on the marriage.

In the office, Freddie was much appreciated and in 1942 the company offered him the position of branch manager of their Leeds office – promotion with relocation. His subsequent celebratory drink(s) led to him being arrested on the charge of being drunk-in-charge. The magistrates accepted his plea – based on the then widely accepted medical opinion that head injuries were often associated with increased susceptibility to alcohol – and dismissed the case.

In Leeds he continued his Rotarian and British Legion associations and his support for former servicemen. Mollie, however, was less tolerant of the more industrial nature of the area and missed her friends. They weren't completely isolated as his position allowed him some latitude, and he was regularly called upon to return to the London area for meetings, accompanied by his wife. On at least one of their visits, in 1947, they were photographed at Hemel Hempstead, having called in on Mollie's younger cousin (her former bridesmaid) and her family. In or before autumn 1949 they, together with his widowed mother-in-law, relocated to the more pleasant surroundings of Harrogate, where Mollie's mother died in 1950.

Freddie had taken up his father's habit of drinking beer, but recognising and making allowances for any lunchtime intake resulting from entertaining clients. On the tenth anniversary of John's death, however, he was charged once again with being drunk-in-charge. When the case was heard, he was already in a clinic receiving treatment. This magistrate, however, was not sympathetic to his plea, as put by the company's solicitor. He was fined £50 and had his driving licence suspended for two years.

Within two days of being charged, he had accepted the company's offer of further private treatment in a local clinic at their expense and had been admitted. His treatment seems to have been based on the then textbook opinion of a link between head injuries and sensitivity to alcohol. Having signed an Alcoholic's Promise to abstain, his treatment may have comprised little more than a course of anti-depressant medication, and a few sessions each of counselling and occupational therapy while in the clinic. He was discharged from treatment in late January 1952.

At the end of February he wrote a progress letter to the clinic physician. At the beginning of the month he had kept an early appointment in London with the governors. They still felt he should return to the London area; he had argued against this, believing that his anxieties had been resolved and that all his important friends and connections in Yorkshire wanted him back. The general manager had then visited the Leeds office. In Freddie's own words: 'When a Yorkshireman has once accepted you he doesn't fail to give you a helping hand when necessary. Without my knowledge many of them wrote to London expressing their view. Last week my General Manager came up and interviewed a wide cross-section of these people and others, and came to the conclusion that it would be safe to recommend to the Governors I should resume duties here.'

He returned to work the following Monday, 3 March 1952. Two years later, about the end of March 1954, he retired on the grounds of ill health. His (now late) colleague and successor was of the opinion that the governors maintained their wish for him to return to a London area appointment, albeit reducing the pressure they put on him. Mollie, on the other hand, had never fully accepted life away from the London area, although having her widowed mother with them until her death in 1950 had ameliorated the situation.

Mollie's view of Freddie was that he had been depressed ever since their son's death and he was treated for nervous anxiety for most of that time. In May 1954 he was confined to bed, being visited daily by his GP. On 27 May he seemed much better and was allowed to get up; during that day and the next and the morning of the 29th he had seemed quite well, in good spirits and cheerful. Mollie left the house about 10.30 that morning, leaving him in the house. When she returned about forty-five minutes later she found him hanging from the landing newel post.

At the inquest, the Coroner found that Freddie had taken his own life while the balance of his mind was disturbed; he was quoted as saying it was 'tragic that the holder of the highest honour for gallantry, the Victoria Cross, should end his life in this way'. At his cremation at the Stonefall Crematorium, Harrogate on 2 June 1954, the chief mourners were his wife and elder sister (her childhood nursemaid), a few close friends and his doctor. Large numbers of his former colleagues and members of the local (Leeds and Harrogate) Rotary Clubs and the insurance industry also turned out. His ashes were collected on behalf of his widow and sister, who are believed to have scattered them discreetly over the flower beds of the local public gardens in which he had enjoyed walking.

Attitudes of the period towards suicide, however, meant that there was no discussion of him. Even mention of his name was avoided because of the 'shame' of his action. However, Mollie, and later Madge (her main beneficiary – her young cousin and former bridesmaid), did keep a few items that identified him: portraits of him as a newly commissioned second lieutenant and as a new captain at his desk, together with a small plaque presented to him by the Old Boys of Isleworth County School.

HILL-WALKER, Alan Richard [1882]

Rank/Service: Lieutenant (later Major); 2nd Battalion, Northamptonshire
    Regiment
VC Location: Private (Not on public display)
Date of Gazette: 14 March 1882
Place/Date of Birth: Northallerton, Yorkshire; 12 July 1859
Place/Date of Death: Thirsk, Yorkshire; 21 April 1944

Grave: St Michael & All Angels Church, Maunby. 'In loving memory of Major Hill-Walker, VC, the Northamptonshire Regt. Born 1869 died 1944 and of his son Thomas Henry Lieut. Commander, RN, killed in action 1940'

Town/County Connections: Richmond and Thirsk, Yorkshire

Significant Remarks: He changed his surname from Hill to Hill-Walker

Account of Deed: On 28 January 1881 at Laing's Nek, South Africa, Lieutenant Hill remained behind when the retreat was ordered and tried to carry out of danger another lieutenant who was lying on the ground severely wounded. Unable to lift the man into the saddle, he carried him in his arms until he was shot dead. Lieutenant Hill then brought another wounded man out of action on his horse and afterwards returned and rescued another. All this was carried out under very heavy fire.

Biographical Detail: Richard was born at Northallerton, the county town of North Yorkshire. He joined the army and in October 1881 he was promoted from second lieutenant to lieutenant. Six years later in October 1887 Captain Hill VC, serving with the 1st Battalion, was made Adjutant of the 3rd/4th Battalions. He was promoted to major in September 1896 and served with the 1st Battalion in India, where he gained the India Medal with clasps for his actions at the Punjab Frontier and Tirah. He retired in October 1901, at which date he changed his name to Hill-Walker. He died in Thirsk, North Yorkshire, at the age of eighty-four.

HIRSCH, David Philip [1917]

Rank/Service: Acting Captain; 4th Battalion, Yorkshire Regiment (Alexandra, Princess of Wales's Own)

VC Location: Green Howards Regimental Museum, Richmond

Date of Gazette: 14 June 1917

Place/Date of Birth: Leeds, Yorkshire; 28 December 1896

Place/Date of Death: Wancourt, France; 23 April 1917

Memorial: Arras Memorial to the Missing, France

Town/County Connections: Leeds, Yorkshire

Significant Remarks: Mentioned in Despatches, 9 April 1917

Account of Deed: During an attack on 23 April 1917 near Wancourt in France, Captain Hirsch arrived at his unit's first objective; although wounded, he made his way back over fire-swept slopes to satisfy himself that the defensive flank was being properly established. The enemy machine-gun fire was so intense that it was necessary for him to be continuously moving up and down the line encouraging and steadying his men. He stood on the parapet, in the face of machine-gun fire and counter-attack, until he was killed.

Biographical Detail: David Hirsch was born in Leeds on 28 December 1896, the eldest son of Harry and Edith Hirsch of Westwood Grove, Leeds. In May 1908 he entered Willeston School, Nantwich, where in time he became head boy. Known as 'Pip' to his parents, he was a fine all-round athlete: he took more wickets for the school than any previous bowler, and held the school record for the mile. He was also a gifted pupil, and won an open exhibition in history to Worcester College, Oxford.

Hirsch left school in December 1914 and went straight into training with the Leeds University Officer Training Corps (OTC), obtaining a commission on 7 April 1915 in the 11th West Yorkshire Regiment. On 22 September he was transferred to the Yorkshire Regiment (the Green Howards) as a second lieutenant. He attended a machine-gun course just before he went to France to join the 4th Battalion in April 1916.

His battalion fought through the Battle of the Somme, and Hirsch was wounded at Eaucourt L'Abbaye, commanding the battalion's machine-guns; he was promoted to temporary lieutenant on 23 September 1916, aged only nineteen years. He was appointed acting captain on assuming command of Y Company on 16 November. On 10 February 1917 he moved with his battalion to Foucaucourt, and then relieved units of the French Army to become the extreme right battalion of the British Line on the Western Front. He was Mentioned in Despatches on 9 April 1917.

His name is listed on Bay 5 of the Memorial to the Missing at Arras. His parents paid for a swimming pool in his memory to be built at Willesden School, now an ecumenical Theological College. There is a Hirsch Close in Nantwich, Cheshire, and a plaque in his memory outside Leeds City Art Gallery.

In 1918 Hirsch's Victoria Cross became the property of his brother Major Frank Hirsch, who died in 1995, when it passed to Phil Kilpin, a nephew who lived in Elgin, South Africa. He loaned the VC and other medals to the Green Howards Regimental Museum in September of that same year. The Hirsch Papers were presented to the Liddle Collection in the Brotherton Library, Leeds University, by Mrs Dorothy Kilpin in July 1997.

HOLLIS, Stanley Elton [1944]

Rank/Service: 4390973 Company Sergeant-Major; 6th Battalion, Green
   Howards (Alexandra, Princess of Wales's Own Yorkshire Regiment)
VC Location: Green Howards Museum, Richmond
Date of Gazette: 17 August 1944

Place/Date of Birth: Middlesbrough, Yorkshire; 21 September 1912
Place/Date of Death: Middlesbrough, Yorkshire; 8 February 1972
Grave: Acklam Cemetery, Middlesbrough
Town/County Connections: Middlesbrough, Yorkshire
Significant Remarks: The only VC awarded at the D-Day landings

Account of Deed: On 6 June 1944 in Normandy, France, Company Sergeant Major Hollis went with his company commander to investigate two German pillboxes that had been bypassed as the company moved inland from the beaches. He rushed forward to the first pillbox, taking all but five of the occupants prisoner, and then dealt with the second, taking twenty-six prisoners. Throughout the day he appeared wherever the fighting was heaviest, displaying the utmost gallantry. It was through his heroism and resourcefulness that the company's objectives were gained and casualties were not heavier. He saved the lives of many of his men.

Biographical Detail: Hollis was born in Loftus on 21 September 1912, the eldest son of fishmonger Alfred Edward and Edith Hollis, who had three sons, one of whom died in infancy. He attended the local school until he was twelve years old. In 1926 his parents moved to Robin Hoods Bay on the North Yorkshire coast, where Stan worked for his father in the fish shop. At the age of seventeen he was apprenticed to the Rowland & Marwood Shipping Company of Whitby, to learn to be a navigation officer. He later transferred to the Elder, Dempster Line, making regular voyages to West Africa, where in 1930 he fell ill with blackwater fever, which ended his merchant naval career.

Hollis returned to North Ormesby, Middlesbrough, where his parents now owned a fish shop in Beaumont Road, and found employment as a lorry driver. He married Alice Clixby and they had a son and daughter. In 1939 Hollis was employed with the Crossley Brick Company, but he enlisted as a Territorial in the 4th Battalion, Green Howards. When his unit travelled to France in April 1940 to join the British Expeditionary Force (BEF), primarily to construct runways for aerodromes, Hollis was employed as the commanding officer's dispatch rider.

When the battalion escaped from Dunkirk Hollis was promoted from lance corporal to sergeant. He moved with his battalion to Iraq, Palestine and Cyprus, then fought from El Alamein to Tunis in the North African Campaign as part of the Eighth Army. He was promoted to company sergeant major just before the invasion of Sicily in 1943. He was wounded at the Primasole Bridge and recommended for, but not awarded, the DCM. He was wounded at Normandy on 6 June 1944 and evacuated to England in September 1944. He was decorated by King George VI at Buckingham Palace on 10 October 1944.

After the war jobs were scarce in North Ormesby and Hollis spent several years as a sandblaster in a Middlesbrough steelworks. He then worked for, and became a partner in, Horobin's motor repair business in Darlington before joining a Canadian-registered ship as its third engineer in 1950. He spent the next four years sailing in the Far East, returning to train as a publican with Vaux Breweries. In 1955 he became the successful manager of the Albion public house in Market Square, North Ormesby, which was renamed The Green Howards. When it was demolished in 1970, he moved to become the tenant of the Holywell View public house at Liverton Mines near Loftus.

Stanley Hollis died in North Ormesby Hospital on 8 February 1972, aged fifty-nine. He was buried at Acklam Cemetery in Middlesbrough on 12 February. In 1982 his medals were auctioned at Sotheby's, where they fetched the (then) record sum of £32,000. In November 1997 his Victoria Cross and medals were presented to the Green Howards Regimental Museum as a gift by Sir Ernest Harrison OBE.

On a return trip to Gold Beach years later Sergeant Major Hollis gave a talk to Army cadets about his D-Day experiences:

> We made sure our weapons were working and the company commander, Major Lofthouse, gave me a square box. He said, 'Give one of these to each of the men.' They were boxes of French letters [condoms].
>
> 'Are we going to fight them or f*** them?' I asked. They were for waterproofing the Bren guns and they did work when we landed waist-deep in water.
>
> The man in front of me, Sergeant Hill, had been a very good soldier all through the war. A real fighting man. He jumped out first into a shell hole under the water. The landing craft went over him and he couldn't come up with all the stuff he was carrying. The propellers cut him to bits.
>
> We dashed over the beach. A lot of the boys had been seasick and were only too glad to get out of those boats. We ran up to the top and along the ridge, where there was just rolled wire. Believe it or not, there were two or three birds sat on this wire. This Irishman, Mullaly, who was next to me, said: 'No bloody wonder they're there, Sergeant Major. There's no room in the air for them.' He was killed a few minutes later, going up the road.
>
> We knew the gunfire was coming from up above us somewhere, but we didn't know exactly where. We crawled up this hill and when we got to the top Major Lofthouse and I saw it was coming from a

pillbox. It was well camouflaged but I saw guns moving in the slits. I got my Sten gun and rushed at it, just spraying it hosepipe fashion. They fired back at me and missed.

They must have been more panic-stricken than me and I got on top of it and threw a grenade through the slit killing the two men inside. There was a communicating trench from that pillbox to another and I took eighteen or twenty prisoners there.

We didn't bother with escorts. We just pointed the way down to the beach and they were happy to go by themselves.

A few hours later Hollis was in action again:

These chaps were starting to shoot at us from behind a wall and I saw a man running along the top. I borrowed a rifle off one of the chaps and took a shot at him and, to my amazement, I hit him. At the same time I got hit in the face. There wasn't a lot of damage but there was a lot of blood. Then the firing ceased.

By that time I was in charge of 16 Platoon. Lieutenant Kirkpatrick of 2 Commando had been killed.

In the village of Crepon Hollis once more led from the front:

On closer inspection I saw a field gun, or what appeared to me to be a field gun. So I went back and told the company commander. He told me we would see what we could do about it but, before I went back, I told seven or eight of 16 Platoon to dash across and engage whatever was in that hedge. Just open up with Bren guns and shoot that hedge up. They ran out and all seven or eight were killed – stone dead straight away.

I went back to report to the company commander and he told me to get an anti-tank gun and a couple of Brens and crawl towards it through this patch of rhubarb. Three of us crawled through and I poked the anti-tank gun through and had a shot. As was usual with me, I missed – then the field gun fired and blew the top off the building which sheltered us. There were bricks, stones and masonry flying all over the place so I thought we'd better get out of it and leave it to somebody better equipped.

I crawled back out and walked back up the road to join the company about 100 yards away. Then we heard a terrific racket coming from ahead of us and somebody came and told me that the two Bren gunners I had brought in were still in the rhubarb. They were pinned down. I said to Major Lofthouse: 'I took them in. I will try to get them out.'

I waited until there was a lull in the firing and ran straight for the Bren guns. I was able to shout to these two lads to get out and come back and join me.

Later that day Sergeant Major Hollis continued his heroics:

We were down on our hands and knees and I could see the firing was coming from a tree and one side of the lane was getting casualties. I could see these two Germans getting up, firing a burst down that side of the lane, then getting down. I watched them for a few seconds – it seemed quite a long time. They would bob up, fire and get down, so I felt in my Bren pouch for a grenade – and found I had a pair of socks and a shaving brush. This after I had made sure everybody else had their equipment and ammunition!

I turned to the chap behind me and said, 'For Christ's sake give me a grenade,' and I waited until I got the rhythm of what they were doing bobbing up and down and shooting. The last time they bobbed up, I threw this grenade; I could never throw a grenade like the army taught you. I used to throw them like cricket balls.

The Germans saw it coming and got down. I followed the grenade up straight away – but I hadn't pulled the bloody pin out. Of course, the Germans didn't know that and they kept down, waiting for it to go off. By the time they realised I was on top of them and I shot them.

On the way back Sergeant Major Moffat and I picked up one of our captains, Captain 'Bolo' Young. He was a very good officer and we put him on a tank. He had been badly wounded.

We had completed our job. We had done what we set out to do.

Author's note: this account is adapted from an article in the *Sun* newspaper. A full version of the account appears in P. Liddle, *D-Day by Those Who Were There* (Pen & Sword Books, 2004).

HOLMES, Joel [1858]

Rank/Service: Private; 84th Regiment (later York & Lancaster Regiment)
VC Location: York & Lancaster Regiment Museum, Rotherham
Date of Gazette: 18 June 1858
Place/Date of Birth: Gomershall, Yorkshire; 1821
Place/Date of Death: Halifax, Yorkshire; 27 July 1872

Grave: All Souls' Cemetery, Halifax
Town/County Connections: Halifax, Yorkshire

Account of Deed: On 25 September 1857 at Lucknow, India, Private Holmes was the first man to respond to a call for volunteers to assist in working under very heavy enemy fire one of the guns from which all the artillerymen had become casualties.

HUGHES, Matthew [1857]

Rank/Service: Private (later Corporal); 7th Regiment (later Royal Fusiliers)
VC Location: Royal Fusiliers Museum, Tower of London
Date of Gazette: 24 February 1857
Place/Date of Birth: Bradford, Yorkshire; 1822
Place/Date of Death: Bradford, Yorkshire; 9 January 1882
Grave: Undercliffe Cemetery, Bradford (erected 1997). 'Erected to the memory of Pte Matthew Hughes, VC the 7th Regiment the Royal Fusiliers in which he won the Victoria Cross in the Crimea on 7 June 1855. Interred 9 January 1882 Aged 60 years'
Town/County Connections: Bradford, Yorkshire

Account of Deed: On 17 June 1855 in the Crimea, at the storming of the Quarries at Sebastopol, Private Hughes went twice across open ground under heavy fire to fetch ammunition. He also went to the front and brought in a soldier who was severely wounded. On 18 June he volunteered to bring in a badly wounded lieutenant, and in so doing was severely wounded himself.

Biographical Detail: Hughes was among the first recipients of the Victoria Cross to be presented with their medals by Queen Victoria in Hyde Park on 26 June 1857, a 'proud and gratifying day'. A perusal of the Royal Fusiliers' list of VC recipients provides a mixed picture of Matthew Hughes. According to the scant but telling records, Hughes was born in 1822 and at the age of eighteen joined the 7th Royal Fusiliers. Four years later he was discharged by purchase in January, but then re-enlisted in June of the same year. During this period of service the diminutive Hughes, who stood just five feet tall, spent a month 'in custody of the Civil Powers' during 1845, then achieved the rank of corporal in 1855. He was further promoted to sergeant in September 1855. This was the pinnacle of his military career. There then followed a court martial, demotion to private, reinstatement, a further court martial – and his record lists twenty-one entries in the regimental defaulters' book. Hughes finished his twenty-five-year service aged forty-three, still a private.

HULL, Charles [1916]

Rank/Service: Private Shoeing Smith (later Corporal); 21st Lancers (Empress of India's)

VC Location: Queen's Royal Lancers Museum, Belvoir Castle

Date of Gazette: 3 March 1916

Place/Date of Birth: Harrogate, Yorkshire; 24 July 1890

Place/Date of Death: Leeds, Yorkshire; 13 February 1953

Grave: Woodhouse Lane Cemetery, Leeds

Town/County Connections: Harrogate and Leeds, Yorkshire

Account of Deed: On 5 September 1915 at Hafiz Kor on the North-West Frontier Private Hull rescued an officer from certain death at the hands of tribesmen. The latter's horse had been shot, but Hull took the officer up behind on his own horse, under heavy fire at close range, and galloped to safety.

Biographical Detail: Charles Hull attended Western Council School.

On 12 November *1919 the Harrogate Herald* published a detailed report about him:

> The Harrogate VC, Corporal Charles Hull, of the 21st Lancers, son of Mr and Mrs John Hull, of Albert Terrace, Harrogate, reached home on Monday night, after being away some nine years. His arrival was totally unexpected by his family, as, though it was known late in the day that the ship in which he had crossed had docked at Portsmouth on Saturday, the messages he had sent from the ship were delayed in transit, and he was still believed to be in the South. As a matter of fact, Corporal Hull had journeyed north on Sunday night, and the train on its way to the Ripon Dispersal Camp ran through Harrogate early on Monday morning. The VC kept a sharp look-out at Harrogate to recognise friends and acquaintances, but at half-past six o'clock there were very few people about, and none that he knew. He was busy with kit matters at Ripon during the day, and in the evening he came to Harrogate and pleasantly surprised his parents by his appearance. Corporal Hull looked the picture of health after the Indian campaign, and has grown and filled out after the nine years abroad, so much that his acquaintances have to look twice to recognise in the stalwart soldier the man who went away. He has nearly twelve years' service in the Army, and is on a month's furlough, at the end of which he is taking leave of the Army. Corporal Hull was a postman in Harrogate before he joined the Colours. His father is an old employee of the Harrogate Corporation.

Corporal Hull won the VC in the 1915 operations on the north-west frontier of India by gallantly going to the rescue of Captain G.E.D. Learoyd, who had been unhorsed and was surrounded by his enemies, and who would have been killed but for the behaviour of Corporal Hull. The Harrogate soldier got his officer up behind him on his horse, and carried him to safety from amid the native enemy. Captain Learoyd died in Risalpur about a year ago. He was suddenly taken ill with influenza, and this turned to pneumonia, to which he succumbed in hospital.

Corporal Hull, in addition to the VC, was awarded the Croix de Guerre by the French. The father of Captain Learoyd presented the Harrogate VC with a handsome gold watch and chain, suitably inscribed.

The parents of Corporal Hull received the following letters from Captain Learoyd's father:

Launds Abbey, Leicester

Dear Sir,

I have only just become acquainted with your address, and hasten to congratulate you and Mrs Hull on your son's well-earned VC for his very gallant and brave action in saving my son in the action at Shabkadir. You may well imagine how grateful Mrs Learoyd and I and all our family feel towards your son and we look forward to the day when we may thank him personally. I also intend coming to see you sometime, but shall have to postpone the pleasure, as I am not very well at present. With our kindest regards to you and Mrs Hull.

Believe me, yours very sincerely,

A.E. Learoyd

Dear Mr Hull,

I am very sorry I could not find time to come over to Harrogate to hand you the watch and chain for your gallant son, so I decided to send it you by post. Again I should like to say how grateful my family feel towards your son, and how sincerely we congratulate you, his parents, in owning such a splendid fellow for a son. May he soon come to you safe and sound.

Yours very sincerely,

A.E. Learoyd

PS. It would be in accordance with the fitness of things if the towns-people were given an opportunity of publicly welcoming Corporal Hull back to his native town.

On 7 February 1917 the *Harrogate Herald* reproduced a very long and inter-esting letter by Private D.T. Wilks from India. Part of it read:

> ... Our camp is not far away from my old comrade, Charles Hull, but up to now I have not got into touch with him, though I did hear, from one of our YMCA friends, that he had been acting as 'best man' at the wedding of the officer [Captain G.E.D. Learoyd] whose life he saved when he got the VC ...

And on 6 October 1920 there was a further report about him in the *Harrogate Herald*:

> Mr Charles Hull, VC, of Harrogate, who won the bronze cross as a shoeing-smith with the 21st Lancers on the Indian Frontier in 1916, and who is now a constable in the Leeds Police Force, was married at All Hallows' Church, on Saturday afternoon, to Mrs Eliza Ann Brown, of Rosebank Grove, Leeds. The ceremony was performed by the Vicar (the Rev. A.B. Fisher) in the presence of a large congre-gation.

And on 4 July 1956 the *Harrogate Herald* reported:

> Lieutenant Colonel G.E.B. Stephenson unveiled a plaque in St Peter's School, Harrogate, on Friday, in memory of the school's two holders of the Victoria Cross, the late Second Lieutenant Donald Simpson Bell, of the Green Howards, and the late Private Charles Hull, of the 21st Lancers, who won their awards in 1916. Present was the Mayor of Harrogate, Councillor Edwin Pickard.

Corporal Hull was one of the honour guards at the interment of the Unknown Soldier at Westminster Abbey on Armistice Day, 11 November 1920.

INGHAM, Samuel *see* MEEKOSHA, Samuel

INSALL, Gilbert Stuart Martin [1915]

Rank/Service: Second Lieutenant (later Group Captain); 11 Squadron, Royal Flying Corps (later Royal Air Force)
Other Decorations: MC
VC Location: Royal Air Force Museum, Hendon
Date of Gazette: 23 December 1915
Place/Date of Birth: Paris, France; 14 May 1894

Place/Date of Death: Scrooby, Bawtry, Yorkshire; 17 February 1972
Grave: Nocton Churchyard, Lincolnshire. 'In memory of Group Captain
   Gilbert Stuart Martin Insall, VC, MC. Passed away on 17th February
   1972'
Memorial: Rose Hill Crematorium, Doncaster
Town/County Connections: Scrooby, Bawtry, Yorkshire
Significant Remarks: Also served in the Second World War; commanded RAF
   Uxbridge in 1940

Account of Deed: On 7 November 1915 near Achiet, France, Second Lieutenant
Insall was on patrol in a Vickers fighter with his observer, First Class Air
Mechanic T.H. Donald, when they engaged an enemy machine, the pilot of
which was eventually forced to make a rough landing in a ploughed field.
Seeing the Germans scramble out and prepare to fire, the lieutenant dived to
500ft and his gunner opened fire, whereupon the enemy fled. After dropping
an incendiary bomb on the German aircraft, he flew through heavy fire, at
200 feet, over enemy trenches. The Vickers' petrol tank was hit, but Insall
managed to land near a wood 500 feet inside Allied lines and he and his gunner,
after repairing the machine during the night, flew back to base at dawn.

Biographical Detail: Born in Paris on 14 May 1894, Gilbert Stuart Martin Insall
was training to be a dentist when the First World War began. He joined the
Royal Fusiliers in September 1914 but transferred to the Royal Flying Corps in
1915, and that summer he was sent to the Western Front, where he earned the
Victoria Cross on 7 November 1915 near Achiet-le-Grand, France. Unfortunately, Insall could not personally receive his VC, however, as he and Donald
had been captured on 14 December 1915 after engaging Hauptmann Martin
Zander and his gunner. As a prisoner in Germany, he made a number of daring
escape attempts, which included the use of elaborate disguises. He escaped on
his third try, on 28 August 1917, after tunnelling out from Ströhen camp, near
Hanover. After walking for nine days, covering 150 miles, he reached neutral
Holland on 6 September. He won the Military Cross in 1918.

   He returned to duty in November 1917 as the Flight Commander of
A Flight, 51 Squadron, and continued to serve his nation through to 30 July
1945. After the war Insall remained in the RAF, and during a flight one clear
day in 1925 he spotted a strange formation of pits in the ground below him.
He took a photograph, and from this one photograph came the rediscovery of
the Bronze Age site now known as Woodhenge, 2 miles from Stonehenge
(Crawford, *Air-Photography for Archaeologists*, 1929). In 1929 he similarly discovered Arminghall Henge.

Lieutenant Robert Hughes-Chamberlain, who served as a pilot in 11 Squadron, RFC, wrote an interesting account of Insall's achievements in respect of his VC award:

> Major Dawes was the squadron commander. Dawes simply didn't like Insall, I can't think of any particular reason but they didn't get on, until he did this job and then he was racing about the place to get Insall this VC: to the French, to get reports from them; reports from all over the place. It made a very good story.
>
> I was in the office, the squadron office, and Dawes was cursing Insall up hill and down dale because he hadn't arrived back in the squadron. 'What the hell's the fellow doing now?' – that sort of stuff. Then the telephone rang and he picked it up and he started to blaspheme until Insall got it into his head to tell him, 'We've shot down a German aircraft over the French lines'.
>
> Then he proceeded to describe how they'd followed him down to the ground, the two men had got out and run and then Insall started to shoot them up. The men disappeared into the hedge at the back of a field or something so Insall's observer dropped a small bomb, about as big as your fist, and it fell on the German machine and set it alight. Smoke and so on came up. Then Insall discovered that he was practically on the floor, it was getting dark and he hadn't any petrol left to speak of and he couldn't get upstairs once more, so he'd shouted to Donald [First Class Air Mechanic T. H. Donald, Insall's observer] and said, 'Look, we'll hedge-hop over the trenches and trust to luck.' Their luck didn't hold because a bullet came from a trench on the German side and went through the petrol tank. Well, when that happens, it's goodbye. He could just land in a field on the other side, whereupon the Germans started chucking shells across. Insall and Donald went and bunked for the hedges and watched the bombardment but it didn't hit the machine at all and darkness supervened.
>
> Insall, who was educated in Paris, his father was something or other there, he spoke French like a native and went down and saw the colonel commanding that part of the French line and explained what he wanted. He said, 'I'm the aeroplane pilot, I want to let my squadron know that the tank's busted,' and the French colonel gave him every assistance and that's how Dawes heard Insall's voice coming through [on the telephone], telling him all about it.
>
> So Dawes was highly excited and he yelled for Rees, the chief flight commander of 11 Squadron, who came along and he said,

'Take a tender, a new tank and all the appliances and petrol and everything else that you want and some mechanics to run the show. He's on the French line, 15 miles away.' Rees, who was very good indeed at anything of that kind, a first-class man, he went and took all the apparatus necessary and under masked lights they took out the old tank, put in the new one, filled it up and got it generally ready to start and then Insall got in and flew it away at dawn. That's how the citation ended.

Well, they made a good thing out of it but it wasn't a VC job in my opinion, it was very ordinary, shooting down a machine and escaping over the trenches. I should have reversed it. What he did in escaping from Germany was a VC job in my opinion; he told me the whole story one day at Dover when I was in command there and I always thought that was an extraordinary job, the other one was an MC job. He got them both but the wrong way round.

Insall served again in the Second World War and died in 1972. His headstone is in Nocton Churchyard, Lincolnshire.

JACKSON, Thomas Norman [1918]

Rank/Service: Lance-Corporal; 1st Battalion, Coldstream Guards
VC Location: Coldstream Guards RHQ Museum, Wellington Barracks
Date of Gazette: 27 November 1918
Place/Date of Birth: Swinton, Yorkshire; 11 February 1897
Place/Date of Death: Graincourt, France; 27 September 1918
Grave: Sanders Keep Military Cemetery, France
Town/County Connections: Swinton, Lancashire; Swinton, Yorkshire

Account of Deed: On 27 September 1918 at the Canal du Nord near Graincourt, France, Lance Corporal Jackson was the first to volunteer to follow his company commander C.H. Frisby VC across the canal in his rush against an enemy machine-gun post. With two comrades Jackson followed his officer; rushing the post, they captured two machine-guns. Later that morning Jackson was the first to jump into a German trench, which his platoon had orders to clear, but he was almost immediately killed.

LAMBERT, George [1858]

Rank/Service: Sergeant-Major (later Lieutenant Adjutant); 84th Regiment
  (later York & Lancaster Regiment)
VC Location: York & Lancaster Regiment Museum, Rotherham
Date of Gazette: 18 June 1858

Place/Date of Birth: Market Hill, Co. Armagh, Ireland; December 1819
Place/Date of Death: Sheffield, Yorkshire; 10 February 1860
Grave: Wardsend Cemetery, Sheffield. 'In memory of George Lambert, VC,
   Lieutenant and Adjutant 84th Regiment who died at Sheffield 10th
   February 1860 aged 41 years. This tablet was erected by his brother
   officers'
Memorial: Mullaghbrook Church, Co. Armagh, Ireland
Town/County Connections: Mullaghbrook, Armagh; Sheffield, Yorkshire

Account of Deed: On 29 July 1857 at Oonao, India, Sergeant Major Lambert
acted with distinguished bravery. Also on 16 August 1857 at Bythoor, when the
rebels were driven at the point of the bayonet out of a strong position, and on
25 September 1857 at the passage through Lucknow, India, to the Residency.

Biographical Detail: George Lambert was born in Market Hill, Co. Armagh,
Ireland, in December 1819. He served in the ranks from 6 June 1840 to
11 December 1857; on the following day he became an ensign without purchase
and was further promoted to adjutant on 2 July 1858, again receiving promotion on 17 December that same year to lieutenant without purchase. George
Lambert died at Sheffield on 10 February 1860, having gone to live there on
leaving the army the previous year.

   The *Sheffield and Rotherham Star* carried an account of his funeral:

> The funeral of Lieutenant and Adjutant Lambert, of the 84th Regi-
> ment, took place on Thursday, at the St Philip's burial ground. The
> ceremony was conducted with military honours, the band of the regi-
> ment marching at the head of the procession, and playing the 'Dead
> March' in Saul. Most of the deceased's brother officers were present,
> and his charger was led after the body, bearing his master's boots
> reversed. The usual volleys were fired over his grave at the con-
> clusion of the service, and the procession then returned to the
> Barracks. Lieutenant Lambert was greatly respected by all who knew
> him, and his sudden decease is greatly lamented. His death was
> caused by the breaking of a blood vessel on Friday week, whilst on
> the parade ground of the Barracks. He had been somewhat unwell
> for several weeks, but not so seriously as to cause any apprehension,
> or to prevent him from fulfilling a part of his duties. He had risen
> from the ranks, having been in the service about 18 years, and had
> earned his honours in India.

George Lambert died on the parade ground at Hillsborough Barracks; his
death certificate records the cause of death as due to an aortic aneurism that

ruptured and flooded his right lung with blood. His funeral took place eight days after his death on 18 February 1860. The *Sheffield and Rotherham Independent* noted, 'The ceremony was conducted with military honours, the band of the regiment marching at the head of the procession and playing the Dead March ... his charger was led after the body bearing his masters boots reversed. The usual volleys were fired over the grave at the conclusion of the service and the procession then returned to the barracks.'

Lambert's grave is in the cemetery at Wardsend, and in time it became overgrown and neglected.

On 28 June 2010 t*he Sheffield Star* published the following article under the title 'Shame of "forgotten" city war Hero's Grave':

> The grave of a war hero who was awarded the Victoria Cross has been abandoned in a state of disrepair and surrounded by drug addicts' heroin needles in a Sheffield cemetery. The plot where the body of Lieutenant George Lambert lies is one of hundreds forgotten and overgrown at Wardsend Cemetery in Owlerton.
>
> Dave Ogle, from High Green, Sheffield, went to pay his respects at the grave after researching Victoria Cross recipients on the internet. He said: 'I couldn't believe it when I got there – it was overgrown, there were headstones knocked over, and there were heroin needles surrounding it.'
>
> Lieutenant Lambert was born in 1819 in County Armagh, Northern Ireland, but was based at Hillsborough Barracks. He fought all over the world and was awarded the Victoria Cross for acts of bravery during the Indian Mutiny in 1857. He survived the fierce fighting to make it back to Sheffield where he died on the parade ground at his barracks in 1860. The Victoria Cross is the highest military decoration that can be awarded for bravery. Only 1,356 have been handed out since the award was introduced in 1856.
>
> Mr Ogle said: 'I think it's disgusting that we forget our fallen heroes like this. This man was awarded the Victoria Cross, which not many people receive, and his grave is left like this. It's in a terrible state and whoever is in charge of the cemetery should be ashamed.'
>
> The cemetery, which is behind the Bassett's factory in Owlerton, was last used for burials in the 1970s, and its chapel, which was deemed unsafe, was demolished. It was until this year managed by a charitable trust, but was taken over by Sheffield Council just ten weeks ago.

Councillor Shaffaq Mohammed, Cabinet member for Communities, said: 'It's very sad that this historic cemetery has fallen into a state of disrepair. Now that we have taken over maintenance of the site, we're determined to both clean it up and stop people using it as a dumping ground. It's not going to be an easy job as some of the memorials will need a lot of attention, but we're going to work hard to make the area safe for the public to visit, and preserve the cemetery in a respectable condition.'

A volunteers group called The Friends of Wardsend Cemetery exists to try to oversee the restoration of the Victorian cemetery. Its secretary, George Proctor, said:

'We are only a small group and do what we can, but we need the help of those in charge to help restore the cemetery. We have a lot of problems with security with people riding their off-road bikes around and people firing air rifles – often at rabbits that can be found in the area. It's a beautiful cemetery, with lots of local history, but it needs a lot of care and attention to make it accessible to those who want to use it.'

Interestingly, the *Sheffield and Rotherham Independent* dated 2 June 1860 reported, 'Our townsman, Mr Edwin Smith, of the Sheffield Marble Works, has just executed a neat marble tablet to the memory of the above respected officer, and which has just been forwarded to his parents in the county of Armagh. It consists of a stainary marble tablet, supported upon trusses on the pediment of which is neatly carved two swords, suspended from which is the Victoria Cross, encircled with a ribbon, on which is engraved, 'For Valour.' The whole is placed on a black marble background. The tablet has the following inscription: 'In memory of Lieutenant George Lambert, VC. Adjutant HM 84th Regiment, who died at Sheffield, February 10th, 1860, aged 39 years.' This tablet was presented to his parents by his brother officers, as a token of their esteem, and in appreciation of his gallantry during the Indian campaign of 1857 and 1858.

LOOSEMORE, Arnold [1917]

Rank/Service: Private (later Sergeant); 8th Battalion, Duke of Wellington's
    (West Riding) Regiment
Other Decorations: DCM
VC Location: Private (Not on public display)
Date of Gazette: 14 September 1917

Place/Date of Birth: Sheffield, Yorkshire; 7 June 1896
Place/Date of Death: Sheffield, Yorkshire; 11 April 1924
Grave: Eccleshall Cemetery, Sheffield
Memorial: Cross in churchyard at Eccleshall, Sheffield
Town/County Connections: Sheffield, Yorkshire

Account of Deed: On 11 August 1917, south of Langemarck, Belgium, Private Loosemore's platoon was held up by heavy machine-gun fire during an attack on a strongly held enemy position. Loosemore crawled through the partially cut wire, dragging his Lewis gun with him, and single-handedly dealt with a strong party of the enemy, killing about twenty of them. Immediately afterwards his Lewis gun was destroyed and three of the enemy rushed at him, but he shot them with his revolver. Later he shot several enemy snipers, and, on returning to the original position, he brought back a wounded comrade under heavy fire.

Biographical Detail: Arnold was born on 7 June 1896 and was the sixth son of George Harry and Selina Loosemore (née Hoyland). His father George was born in Brinsworth, Rotherham, but must have moved to the Ecclesall area of Sheffield soon after for the 1901 Census has the family living in Dyson Lane. George's occupation is given as domestic gardener. His wife Selina was the daughter of Joshua (1826–1895) and Mary (*b.* 1830) Hoyland. Her father was a stone quarryman while her mother was employed as a charwoman. She had two younger brothers and two younger sisters according to the 1881 Census. There is no entry for Selina or George in the 1881 Census but there is an entry for Selina's family which shows them living on Greystones Road* in the Ecclesall Bierlow district of Sheffield.

George and Selina were married in Sheffield on 17 December 1882 and they had eight children. Arnold attended Clifford Church of England School on Psalter Lane in Sheffield and then worked on a farm in the Fulwood district of Sheffield. He had left there and was working for a local coal merchants as a carter when he enlisted in January 1915. His age on his enlistment form is given as nineteen years and seven months and his address as 1 Lescar Lane, off Sharrow Vale Road, Sheffield.

Arnold was posted to the Yorkshire & Lancaster Regiment and after initial training was sent to Suvla Bay and the Dardanelles to take part in the Gallipoli campaign. He was then drafted to the 8th Battalion, the Duke of Wellington's (West Riding) Regiment, and trained as a machine-gunner, operating the

*RG11 Piece 4639, f. 51, p. 9

then-new Lewis gun. It is rumoured that Arnold shot down a German aircraft while it was chasing a British plane over his unit's camp. It was while serving with the 8th Battalion that Arnold was awarded the Victoria Cross.

Arnold was presented with his Victoria Cross by King George V, and the occasion was noted in *The Times*.* As Sergeant Loosemore he was also awarded the Distinguished Conduct Medal (DCM) for his actions at Zillebeke on 19 June 1918. He must have been promoted since the award of the VC.

On 18 October 1918 Loosemore was badly wounded in both legs by machine-gun fire in an attack on a ridge near Villers-en-Cauchies. Such was the extent of the injuries that his left leg was eventually amputated. After demobilisation, Arnold returned to Sheffield and married Amy Morton on 24 August 1920 at St Andrews Church, Sharrow, Sheffield. His occupation was given as 'poultry farmer'. They had a son the following year, named George after his father.

Douglas Lamb, in his book *Lest We Forget*, details what happened to the family after the war. The Sheffield Rotary Club provided Arnold and his family with a bungalow and a pony and trap. Sadly the long-term effects of Arnold's wounds led to his early death on 10 April 1924, at the age of just twenty-seven. Max Arthur, in his recently published book on VC holders, gives Arnold's home address as Stannington, and ascribes his death to tuberculosis. Arnold was buried five days later on 15 April 1924 in the new churchyard of All Saints, Ecclesall. It appears that the grave was purchased by a relative who had died a few days earlier.

Arnold's bereaved wife Amy and their three-year-old son were left without financial resources when the British government refused to pay her a War Widows pension on the grounds that as she had been aware of his injuries when she married him and he was no longer a serving soldier at the time of the marriage in 1920, so she was not entitled to any monies. The government/ army did not even ensure that Arnold had a grave to himself for the one in the churchyard in Ecclesall is a shared one. Lloyd George's call for 'a country fit for heroes' has rarely sounded so hollow.

To add insult to injury, the Council sent his penniless widow a bill for the whole of the city's lavish funeral arrangements! This story was corroborated by a relative in later years:

> I can verify the fact that a bill for the lavish funeral was received by Amy Loosemore, his wife. Her sister was my grandmother Mary Worth (née Morton). Aunty Amy stayed with us, holidaying in

* Thursday, 3 January 1918, p. 9, column A, Court Circular.

Folkestone with her sister and brother-in-law, as did Arnold's son and wife and three children, my second cousins or is it first cousins once removed? I was too young to appreciate the significance of the First World War and a VC, but my Auntie Joan, my father's sister, told me the same story some years ago having heard it from Amy and her own mother Mary.

Arnold's Victoria Cross was sold at Sotheby's on 1 May 1969 for £1,080. The buyer is not known.

McKAY, Ian John [1982]

Rank/Service: Sergeant; 3rd Battalion, Parachute Regiment
VC Location: Lord Ashcroft VC Collection
Date of Gazette: 11 October 1982
Place/Date of Birth: Wortley, near Sheffield, Yorkshire; 7 May 1953
Place/Date of Death: Mount Longdon, East Falkland; 12 June 1982
Grave: Aldershot Military Cemetery
Memorial: Aldershot Military Cemetery, Hampshire
Town/County Connections: Rotherham, Yorkshire; Aldershot, Hampshire

Account of Deed: During the night of 11/12 June 1982 the 3rd Battalion, Parachute Regiment, mounted a silent night attack on an enemy battalion position on Mount Longdon, an important objective in the battle for Port Stanley in the Falkland Islands. Sergeant McKay was the platoon sergeant of 4 Platoon, B Company, which, after the initial objective had been secured, was ordered to clear the northern side of the long east–west ridge feature, held by the enemy in depth, with strong mutually supporting positions.

By now, the enemy troops were fully alert and resisting fiercely. As 4 Platoon's advance continued, the Paras came under increasingly heavy fire from a number of well-sited enemy machine-gun positions on the ridge, and took casualties. Realising that no further advance was possible, the platoon commander Lieutenant Andrew Bickerdike ordered his men to move from their exposed position to seek shelter among the rocks of the ridge itself. Here they met up with part of 5 Platoon. The enemy fire was still both heavy and accurate, and the position of the platoons was becoming increasingly hazardous. Taking Sergeant McKay, a corporal and a few others, and covered by supporting machine-gun fire, the platoon commander moved forward to reconnoitre the enemy positions but was hit by a bullet in the leg, and command devolved upon Sergeant McKay.

It was clear that instant action was needed if the advance was not to falter and casualties to increase. Sergeant McKay decided to convert this reconnaissance into an attack in order to eliminate the enemy positions. He was in no doubt of the strength and deployment of the enemy as he undertook this attack. He issued his orders, and, taking three men with him, broke cover and charged the enemy position. The assault was met by a hail of fire. The corporal was seriously wounded, one private was killed and another wounded. Despite these losses, Sergeant McKay, with complete disregard for his own safety, continued to charge the enemy position alone. On reaching it, he dispatched the enemy with grenades, thereby relieving the position of the beleaguered 4 and 5 Platoons, who were now able to redeploy in relative safety. Sergeant McKay, however, was killed at the moment of victory, his body falling on the bunker.

Without doubt, Sergeant McKay's action retrieved a most dangerous situation and was instrumental in ensuring the success of the attack. His was a coolly calculated act, the dangers of which must have been only too apparent to him before-hand. Undeterred, he performed with outstanding selflessness, perseverance and courage. With a complete disregard for his own safety, he displayed courage and leadership of the highest order, and was an inspiration to all those around him.

Biographical Detail: Born on 7 May 1953 at Wortley, near Sheffield, he was educated at Blackburn Primary School, Roughwood Infant and Junior School and Rotherham Grammar School. His father, a steelworker, was not keen on the army as a career for his son and would have preferred him to train as a physical-education teacher. Indeed, he was a talented footballer, and when he left Rotherham Grammar School he was training with Sheffield United and had turned down an offer to become a professional with Doncaster Rovers. Instead, Ian had his own way and became a boy soldier, having told his father that, if he would not give his consent to his enlisting when he was seventeen, he would wait until he was eighteen and enlist then when he did not need his parents' permission.

It was suggested that he stay on in education to get his A-levels, and then try to get into the Royal Military Academy, Sandhurst. However, he was impatient to get on with soldiering and wanted to work his way up through the ranks. Three months after his seventeenth birthday he joined up. Six months later he was a qualified paratrooper and was posted to the 1st Battalion, Parachute Regiment.

In March 1971, while he was still only seventeen, he was sent to Northern Ireland. Soon after he arrived, three young Scottish soldiers, all under eighteen, were killed in a single incident. The victims' youth caused public disquiet. McKay was posted back to England to await his birthday. This was ironic, because three seventeen-year-olds fought and died alongside Ian

McKay on Mount Longdon. One was killed on his eighteenth birthday, while another, Private Jason Burt, was shot dead in the action that earned McKay his VC.

Once McKay's eighteenth birthday passed, he returned to Northern Ireland and was there in time for 'Bloody Sunday'. On 30 January 1972 the Northern Ireland Civil Rights Association organised a peaceful, but illegal, demonstration in Londonderry against the UK government's policy of internment without trial. Around 10,000 people turned out. McKay was with a support company of 1 Para, sent to back up the police, who were trying to prevent the march reaching the city centre. While the main body of the march headed off towards Free Derry Corner, some of the demonstrators confronted the soldiers. Stones and other projectiles were thrown. The troops responded by firing rubber bullets and a water cannon. Although in reserve, 1 Para was the most experienced unit on hand since it was nearing the end of its eighteen-month tour of the province. The brigade commander sent the Paras in to arrest the ringleaders. Who fired the first shot still remains open to question.

Over the next ten years McKay worked his way up to the rank of sergeant. He got married and had two children. His family described him as 'a quiet, introverted character'. However, there was a determined streak in him, perhaps of Yorkshire cussedness. He did not like to lose.

By the time the Falklands War broke out, he was an instructor at Aldershot. Had he not been killed, it is said that he would probably have been persuaded to attend Sandhurst as a senior NCO instructor of cadets. This elite posting was often a stepping-stone to the higher ranks. As it was, he was sent to 3 Para as a platoon sergeant.

Sergeant McKay's action in the Falklands began with three weeks at Goose Green and Port Stanley, after which there was a brief lay-up to regroup. During this period McKay wrote home to his parents: 'I have never known a more black, windswept and wet place in my life. We spend our life with wet feet, trying to dry out and keep warm. The wind blows constantly, but it is cooling rather than drying. You cannot walk 50 paces anywhere, even on the mountain-sides, without walking in a bog. I thought the Brecon Beacons was bad, but this takes the biscuit.'

Just before 3 Para moved into position on Mount Longdon, he penned a few more lines to his parents: 'Mind you things are much quieter now than for some time, and finding things to occupy our time is now a problem. Some clown has put our artillery batteries just behind our positions, and as the Argentinian guns try to range in on them, they sometimes drop one in around our position . . . the papers we get mention only the Marines and the Guards, so if we aren't officially here we might as well come home.'

In fact, McKay was well aware that after one final effort the whole thing would end. On 9 June he wrote, 'Things should be over one way or another in a week ... we will be home hopefully about two week afterwards.' Sadly, and perhaps prophetically, he was right. However, that one last push was to take his life.

Marcia McKay received her husband's VC at Buckingham Palace on 9 November 1982. Their daughter Melanie, aged five, was photographed wearing it pinned to her black velvet dress. His father Ken McKay was also present at the ceremony. Sergeant McKay was buried along with fifteen comrades in Aldershot on 26 November 1982. The last two men to see him alive helped to carry his coffin; they were Corporal Ian Bailey, himself wounded in the same action, and Colour Sergeant Brian Faulkner. Ian McKay was just twenty-nine years old when he died. His was one of the sixty-four bodies brought back from the Falklands on the *Sir Bedivere*, to be greeted at Marchwood military port by a lone piper.

Ian McKay's old school, Rotherham Grammar, unveiled a plaque in his honour and in June 1988 Princess Margaret opened the McKay Memorial Cottages in Barnsley. A portrait of him hangs in Rotherham Town Hall. There is another portrait in 3 Para's sergeants' mess and a painting of him winning the VC in the officers' mess. The 3 Para band plays the Ian McKay VC commemorative march and a statuette of him, with a grenade in one hand and a rifle in the other, is presented annually to the winner of an inter-platoon competition designed to test marching, shooting and other individual battle skills.

Marcia McKay later presented her husband's medals to the Parachute Regiment, which put them on display in the Imperial War Museum. In 2000 she sold them and they are now in one of the biggest private collections of VCs.

McKENNA, Edward [1864]

Rank/Service: Colour Sergeant (later Ensign); 65th Regiment (later York & Lancaster Regiment)

VC Location: Auckland War Memorial Museum, Wellington, New Zealand

Date of Gazette: 16 January 1864

Place/Date of Birth: Leeds, Yorkshire; 15 February 1827

Place/Date of Death: Palmerston North, New Zealand; 8 June 1908

Grave: Terrace End Cemetery, Palmerston North, NZ. 'Edward McKenna, V.C. late ensign, 65th Reg, also N.Z.R., died 8 June 1908 aged 79; also Elizabeth Gordon, wife of the above. RIP'

Town/County Connections: Leeds, Yorkshire

Account of Deed: On 7 September 1863 near Cameron Town, New Zealand, after both his officers had been shot, Colour Sergeant McKenna, with a small force, heavily outnumbered by the enemy, charged through the enemy position with the loss of one man killed and one missing. The colour sergeant's coolness and intrepidity amply justified the confidence placed in him by the soldiers brought so suddenly under his command.

Biographical Detail: In October 1865 McKenna's regiment was recalled to England, but he had grown attached to the colony so he sold his commission and remained. He joined the New Zealand Railways as a clerk and soon rose to be stationmaster at Kaiapoi, Ashburton, Invercargill, Gore, Greatford, Halcombe and, in the early 1880s, Palmerston North. He eventually retired to Palmerston North, where he later died. Edward McKenna and Elizabeth Gordon had thirteen children between them and today there are a large number of his relatives throughout New Zealand.

McNESS, Frederick [1916]

Rank/Service: Lance Sergeant (later Sergeant); 1st Battalion, Scots Guards
VC Location: Scots Guards RHQ, Wellington Barracks
Date of Gazette: 26 October 1916
Place/Date of Birth: Bramley, Nr Leeds; 22 January 1892
Place/Date of Death: Bournemouth, Hampshire; 4 May 1956
Grave: Bournemouth Cemetery
Town/County Connections: Leeds, Yorkshire; Bournemouth, Hampshire

Account of Deed: On 15 September 1916 near Ginchy, France, during a period of severe fighting, Lance Sergeant McNess led his men forward with great dash in the face of heavy shell and machine-gun fire. When the first line of enemy trenches was reached it was found that the left flank was exposed and that the enemy were bombing down the trench. Sergeant McNess thereupon organised and led a counter-attack; despite being very severely wounded in the neck and jaw, he did not give up. Finally he established a 'block' and continued encouraging his men and throwing bombs until exhausted by loss of blood.

Biographical Detail: Sadly, in 1956 McNess took his own life while 'the balance of his mind was disturbed'.

MAGENNIS, James Joseph [1945]

Rank/Service: Acting Leading Seaman; Royal Navy
VC Location: Lord Ashcroft VC Collection
Date of Gazette: 13 November 1945

Place/Date of Birth: Belfast, Ireland; 27 October 1919
Place/Date of Death: Halifax, Yorkshire; 12 February 1986
Grave: Nab Wood Crematorium, Shipley, Yorkshire
Memorial: Grounds of City Hall, Belfast
Town/County Connections: Belfast, Ireland; Bradford, Yorkshire

Account of Deed: On 31 July 1945 in the Johore Straits Leading Seaman Magennis, a diver in the midget submarine *XE3*, attached limpet mines to the Japanese cruiser *Takao* under particularly difficult circumstances. He had to squeeze through a narrow space in the partly open diving hatch, and then scrape barnacles off the bottom of the cruiser before attaching the limpets. During this time his breathing apparatus was leaking and he returned to the submarine after completion of his task very exhausted. When they began to withdraw, *XE3*'s commander, Ian Fraser VC, found that one of the limpet carriers that should have been jettisoned would not release itself, and Magennis immediately volunteered to free it. This he did after five minutes of nerve-racking work with a heavy spanner.

Biographical Detail: James Joseph Magennis was born in the Catholic area of West Belfast on 27 October 1919. His home was in one of the many side streets that spread from the Falls Road and Springfield Road, both of which became all too familiar to the British public during the Troubles of the 1970–1980s.

Belfast in Magennis's childhood was going through great political, religious and sectarian agitation. Although the First World War was over, Ireland was still in a state of turmoil. The Anglo-Irish Treaty of 1922 divided the country into the six counties of Northern Ireland and the twenty-six counties of the Irish Free State (later, the Republic). This did not, however, stop the unrest and Belfast was a hotbed of sectarian tensions. Many people from both sides lost their lives.

James, or 'Mick' as he became better known, attended St Finian's School on the Falls Road. He did not join in the team sports of Gaelic football or hurling but excelled, significantly, at swimming.

On 3 June 1935, at the age of fifteen, Mick enlisted in the Royal Navy as a boy seaman and for the first time left Ireland for England. He travelled to the Suffolk training establishment of HMS *Ganges* near the port of Harwich. After nine months of arduous training, on 6 March 1936 First Class Boy Seaman Magennis joined the battleship HMS *Royal Sovereign* at Portsmouth.

After just three weeks at sea he was transferred to the cruiser HMS *Dauntless*. When he reached Ceylon, he was drafted again to join the 7,550-ton cruiser HMS *Enterprise*. The following year he gained promotion to Able Seaman and transferred to the old First World War aircraft carrier HMS *Hermes*.

After serving on board four ships that had been built during and after the First World War, Mick was at last to get a new ship.

On the outbreak of the Second World War Mick was drafted to the newly built 1670-ton destroyer HMS *Kandahar*. After months of patrolling in the North Sea, *Kandahar* had her first encounter with the enemy in May 1940. She had sailed from Greenock in the company of her sister ship, HMS *Kelly*, commanded by Louis Mountbatten. As dusk approached, there was a tremendous explosion. A torpedo smashed into *Kelly* by the forward boiler-room and burst with a terrifying blast. A great lick of flame roared up into the night, the masthead silhouetted black and stark against its flare. Men lay dead, dying, wounded and stunned. *Kelly* canted over to starboard in a cloud of hissing steam and smoke with a great hole torn in her side from her keel almost to her upper deck. Then out of the blackness appeared a German E-boat racing along at forty knots. It ploughed into *Kelly*'s sloping deck, disappeared in the darkness astern and sank.

At dawn the following day HMS *Kandahar* put her stern alongside the remains of HMS *Kelly* and took off the wounded. Mick recalled his feelings in an interview in 1969:

> Fear is a word people never mention to me, as though they don't think I could ever be afraid. But fear came to me when the smoke of battle had died down; when all that lingered was a dawn mist that hung like funeral crepe ... and death. The action was over. Enemy E-boats had torpedoed *Kelly*. Her sister ship *Kandahar* was edging alongside to take off the injured. It was the sight of the dead and dying that struck real fear into me for the first time in my life. It made me sick. It paralysed me. I remembered the remedy my old gunner's mate gave for everything – 'Fight it.'

On 22 May 1941 HMS *Kandahar* was again involved in rescuing survivors, this time from the destroyer HMS *Greyhound*, sunk during the Battle of Crete. Under heavy air attack, *Kandahar* was forced to abandon its rescue attempt with many of the survivors still in the water.

After seeing much action in the Mediterranean theatre, *Kandahar*'s luck ran out. On 19 December 1941 she struck a mine off Tripoli. The crew abandoned ship and were rescued by HMS *Jaguar*.

The following year, after a spell at torpedo school, Magennis joined the Submarine Branch, and then volunteered for 'special and hazardous duties', which he soon learnt meant midget submarines – the new X-craft four-man submarines. Mick chose special services with the X-craft and on 15 March

1943 he was sent to the high security training facility at Loch Striven in Scotland.

One of his first assignments took place in September 1943, when six little X-craft left their Scottish base towed by a mother submarine and headed out into the unfriendly North Sea. Their destination was Altenfjord in northern Norway and their target was the 44,000-ton German battleship *Tirpitz*. For his efforts in this notable enterprise, Magennis received a Mention in Despatches. However, it was for his extraordinary courage in the midget submarine *XE3* attacking the Japanese cruiser *Takao* on 31 July 1945 that he was awarded his VC. Following this exploit, Mick Magennis was drafted to HM Submarine *Voracious*, stationed at Sydney, Australia. It was here one September morning that he was told by Lieutenant Fraser that he had won the Victoria Cross.

Fraser and Magennis received their medals from King George VI at Buckingham Palace on 11 December 1945. Mick Magennis was the only junior rating in the submarine service to be awarded the Victoria Cross.

While Mick's family and neighbours were overjoyed at the news of the award, the politicians in Belfast were thrown into a quandary. The Unionists, who ran the city, were embarrassed that a Catholic Navy man had been awarded the highest decoration for bravery, but had to acknowledge the fact with a civic ceremony; however, they stopped short of offering Mick the Freedom of the City. On the other side, the Nationalists were trying to make political capital out of it, but at the same time were scornful that Mick was a member of His Majesty's Navy.

Among his family and neighbours in Ebor Street and the surrounding area Mick's award was received with unconditional pride. A fund was set up and the substantial sum of more than £3,000 was collected for him.

Mick's final years in the service, however, were not happy. He was reduced in rank, served time in Portsmouth's Detention Quarters and removed from the submarine service. One happy event, however, was his marriage to a Yorkshire girl, Edna, from Barnsley, and they were soon blessed with a son, James, to be followed by David and Paul. Mick returned to Belfast with his family in 1949. Settling into civilian life after fifteen years of service was far from easy. It was made even harder to cope when Mick's son David was killed by a trolley bus. The family were devastated.

By 1952 the fund he had received was exhausted, for Mick had over-generously spent and shared the money among his family and friends, and he had lost his job. Shortly afterwards he was forced to sell his Victoria Cross to a dealer for £75. Unfortunately the press got hold of the story and vilified Mick for selling his award, and so the public came to know of his humiliation. The dealer promised the Ulster Museum that the medal would be presented to them, although Mick later claimed that it was only on loan. For the benefit of everyone but Mick, the return of his Victoria Cross was performed in front of a journalist and photographer. His enemies from both sides of the political and religious divide revelled in his misfortune. Mick later recalled that unhappy time: 'The dealer had promised to keep quiet about it, but after a few weeks he announced publicly he would present it to the Belfast Museum. My name was on it and everyone knew it was my VC. What a stink it caused; what a blow up. The world protested. I received hundreds of letters condemning me. Some were sympathetic; others, rude and scurrilous . . .'

This was the beginning of a period of re-evaluation for Magennis. The people of Belfast no longer appeared to hold him in high regard; some people even tried to downgrade his act of bravery. He realised that the limelight he had basked in was gone for ever. His critics had come out into the open and he now knew where he stood. It was clear he was not wanted in Protestant Unionist East Belfast and neither was he wanted in Catholic Nationalist West Belfast. His only option was to go to England.

On 7 February 1955 Mick and his family moved to Rossington near Doncaster, where he found work as an electrician at the local coal mine. Here he found the comradeship of the Yorkshire miners very much akin to his early experiences in submarines.

In the late 1950s the Magennis family moved to Bradford, and Mick lived here for the remainder of his life. After years of suffering from chest problems, he finally died of acute bronchitis on 12 February 1986, only hours before his heroism was honoured on a first-day cover issued by the Royal Navy Philatelic Office.

This brave sailor was cremated and his ashes scattered in the Garden of Remembrance at Shipley. His adopted home paid tribute to Mick with a memorial service at Bradford Cathedral, which prompted Ireland's leading daily newspaper, the *Irish Times*, to headline a report with 'Belfast Hero Ignored, Remembered in Bradford'. It took until 1999 before a suitable memorial to Belfast's only VC recipient was belatedly created.

Regarding the exploits against the Japanese cruiser, Lieutenant Ian Fraser VC, the commander of *XE3*, left a description of the entire affair:

> In 1944 I was made first lieutenant of a submarine called *H44*, which was one of these old 1914–18 War types of submarine. We were based in Londonderry doing Asdic-running: a very unexciting period of my life. Then a signal came from the Admiralty one day asking for volunteers for special and hazardous service. I had a sub

lieutenant with me, the third hand, and we both volunteered; I wanted to get away from this ping-running and do something more exciting. And as a result of that we both found ourselves sent to HMS *Varbel*, the shore base at Rothesay for the 12th Submarine Flotilla, which was the submarine flotilla that dealt with all the special projects like midget submarines, human torpedoes and all the different types of underwater craft.

I was quite surprised when I saw my first midget submarine. They weren't like human torpedoes where you put on a diving suit and sat astride; they were proper submarines. They were about fifty-seven feet long, about thirteen feet from top to bottom and the actual hull width was about six feet. You could stay at sea for up to three weeks if you had your own food; you had a Gardner diesel engine; you had a range of about a thousand miles on the surface, two periscopes: a proper submarine.

The war in Europe was coming to an end and they decided that there was nothing further there that X-craft could do. So we six X-craft were all hoisted on board a depot ship called HMS *Bonaventure*, which was a converted Clan liner, she had a very heavy lifting derrick fore and aft, and we were taken in her to Australia. There we went to the Barrier Reef and started doing some working-up exercises on getting underneath ships and cutting submarine telephone cables and various things like that. Eventually we went to a place called Labuan, in Borneo, and I was delegated an operation to go into Singapore harbour to attack and stick limpet mines under a Japanese battle cruiser called the *Takao*.

We set sail in July 1945 being towed by a submarine called the *Stygian* and we were towed from Borneo to the entrance of the Singapore Straits – a tow of about 600 miles – and there we did the crew change: the passage crew got off and my operational crew and I got on. We then slipped the tow and we made the passage up the Straits of Singapore until we came to the island of Singapore itself.

Now this cruiser that we'd been detailed to attack was lying at the old Admiralty dockyard which was on the north side of Singapore Island and it meant going some twelve miles up a narrow channel, which is called the Johore Strait. So we went through the boom at the entrance to the harbour, the gate of which was open, at about nine o'clock in the morning on 31 July 1945 and navigated our way up this channel – I suppose it was about half a mile or a mile wide – until we saw the *Takao*.

It was heavily camouflaged, lying very close inshore on the north end of Singapore Island with its stern towards the island and its bows pointing up towards Burma. Once I'd sighted it I let all my crew have a look through the periscope, the other three chappies of the crew. One of them was a New Zealander, 'Kiwi' Smith, I had an engine-room artificer called Charlie Reed and my diver was Leading Seaman Magennis. I thought it was quite an exciting thing to see and I thought that they'd like to see it and I let them all have a look at the *Takao* through the periscope before we started the attack.

Eventually we got close enough and we started to attack it, we ran in and went underneath it. You go under very slowly, as slow as you can possibly go. There's a porthole in the top of the submarine which you can look through and it's bright daylight and then you suddenly see it getting darker and darker and darker and you suddenly see the plates of the hull with the weeds hanging down and the rivet holes, the rivets, all that sort of thing. Then you stop the submarine, give it a little bit astern, and stop dead. And we settled on the bottom, opened the door and put the diver out.

When Magennis got out, he found that the bottom of the ship was heavily encrusted with barnacles – it had been there a long time. He took the limpet mines out but he had to scrape the bottom of the ship with his diving knife to get a bit of clear plate for him to attach the magnets and he had quite a considerable job to do it. It took him about forty minutes to put six limpet mines on. He then came back into the submarine, we flooded down, and we couldn't get out, because the tide had gone out. We were in a very narrow hole under this thing, there was hardly any room, and the tide had gone out a foot or so and the ship had sunk down and we just couldn't move.

I was a bit frantic then – I really did feel frightened then. And it took me about twenty minutes of going ahead, full astern, blowing tanks, filling tanks, just trying to nudge a hole in the seabed so we could climb out, and eventually we did, we came out and went up a bank and on to the seabed proper. Here we found that one of the side charges hadn't come off and it was stuck – once the limpet mines had been placed you just release the side charges because you don't want to be towing those back with you, it made you lop-sided. So Magennis had to go out again in his diving suit and lever this thing off, which he did, about fifty yards away from this cruiser in about thirty feet of water, very clear water. If they had looked there, looking down, the enemy must have been able to see a black shape out there; and to make matters worse his diving suit was leaking so he was sending a stream of bubbles up to the surface all the time. Eventually he released the charge and got in again and we made our way back out of the Johore Strait. The gate was still open and we got out through the gate and out to sea and eventually we were picked up by the larger submarine and towed back to Singapore.

When I got back to Labuan a couple of days later I went up with Captain Fell, the captain of the *Bonaventure*, and had a look at aerial photographs that had been taken over the spot. The old *Takao* was still there, albeit sitting on the bottom, presumably, but you couldn't really tell, she hadn't blown into smithereens. Captain Fell said, 'Well, we've got to do something about this. You'll have to go back again and have another go at it.' Well, that really did upset me: having done one what I thought was a considerably successful attack, to have to go back again. But nevertheless we said 'OK' and we fixed to go back seven or eight days later. I always remember sitting on the deck of *Bonaventure* watching a film – we'd got vittled up with new stores and everything ready to go – and the film was stopped and the captain came out and told us that they'd dropped an atomic bomb and the operation had been put off for a while. And then of course they dropped the second one and the Japanese capitulated so we didn't have to go back to Singapore. I was very grateful for that.

Eventually I was awarded the Victoria Cross, with Magennis, and we were both ordered to be flown back to the UK to get our Victoria Crosses at Buckingham Palace. It was suggested that I should go to Singapore on the way and find out what had happened to the *Takao*, which I did and I spent fourteen days there. I was taken on board by Japanese officers – one of them had been educated at Oxford, spoke with a very refined Oxford accent – and they showed me over the ship. All the charges had gone off and the whole of the ship had sunk and sat on the seabed about six feet deeper than it was before we started the attack. I went right down to the bottom and they were opening all sorts of hatches. As a matter of fact, I was a bit frightened. I thought, 'God, knowing the Japanese mentality, they're going to chuck me down one of these holes and lock me in'. But that didn't actually happen.

MAUFE, Thomas Harold Broadbent [1917]

Rank/Service: Second Lieutenant (later Captain); 124th Siege Battery, Royal
   Garrison Artillery
VC Location: Private (Not on public display)
Date of Gazette: 2 August 1917
Place/Date of Birth: Ilkley, Yorkshire; 6 May 1898
Place/Date of Death: Ilkley, Yorkshire; 28 March 1942
Grave: Ilkley Cemetery, Yorkshire. 'In loving and devoted memory of
   Thomas Harold Broadbent Mauffe, VC, captain Royal Artillery, who gave
   his life for his country March 28th 1942 aged 43 years. Also his beloved
   wife Gwen who died January 20th 1978'
Town/County Connections: Ilkley, Yorkshire

Account of Deed: On 4 June 1917 at Feuchy, France, Second Lieutenant Maufe,
on his own initiative and under intense artillery fire, repaired, unaided, the
telephone wire between the forward and rear positions, thereby enabling his
battery to open fire on the enemy. He also prevented what could have been a
disastrous occurrence by extinguishing a fire in an advanced ammunition dump
caused by a heavy explosion, regardless of the risk he ran from the effects of gas
shells in the dump.

Biographical Detail: Thomas Maufe was the son of Frederick Broadbent and
Helen Mann Maufe of Warlbeck, Ilkley, West Yorkshire. The family name was
originally Muff but was changed to Maufe in 1909. The family owned the
former Bradford department store Brown, Muff. In response to their rising
fortunes they left Bradford and changed their name to Maufe, thereby
inspiring the local rhyme:

> *In Bradford 'tis good enoof*
> *To be known as Mrs Muff*
> *But in Ilkley by the river Wharfe*
> *'Tis better to be known as Mrs Maufe!*

He was nineteen years old and a second lieutenant serving with the 124th Siege
Battery, Royal Garrison Artillery during the First World War when he per-
formed the deed for which he was awarded the VC. By the end of the war he
had achieved the rank of major, one of the youngest men to hold that rank.
After the war he completed his interrupted education at Clare College,
Cambridge, and the Royal School of Mines.
    Maufe served in the Home Guard as a volunteer during the Second World
War in the 28th West Riding (Otley) Battalion. He was killed on 28 March

1942, at the age of forty-three, when a trench mortar misfired during training with the Home Guard near Ilkley. He is buried in Ilkley Cemetery.

Maufe's name is listed on a war memorial on the gates of his former preparatory school, Nevill Holt, near the village of Medbourne, Leicestershire, along with other casualties of the world wars. He married Miss Mary Gwendolen Carr.

MEEKOSHA, Samuel [1916]

Rank/Service: Corporal (later Captain); 1/6th Battalion, West Yorkshire
  Regiment (Prince of Wales's Own)
VC Location: Private (Not on public display)
Date of Gazette: 22 January 1916
Place/Date of Birth: Leeds, Yorkshire; 16 September 1893
Place/Date of Death: Blackwood, Monmouthshire; 8 December 1950
Grave: Glyntaff Cemetery, Pontypridd, Mid Glamorgan, South Wales
Town/County Connections: Leeds and Bradford, Yorkshire; Penarth,
  Glamorgan; Oakdale, Monmouthshire
Significant Remarks: In 1939 he changed his name to Ingham by deed poll

Account of Deed: On 19 November 1915 near the Yser, France, Corporal Meekosha was with a platoon of about twenty NCOs and men holding an isolated trench. During a heavy bombardment six of the platoon were killed and seven wounded, while the rest were more or less buried. When there were no senior NCOs left in action, Corporal Meekosha took command, sent for help and, in spite of more heavy shells falling within twenty yards of him, continued to dig out the wounded and buried men in full view of the enemy at close range. His courage saved at least four lives.

Biographical Detail: Samuel Meekosha was the first child of Warsaw-born Alexander Meekosha and his English wife Mary Catherine Cunningham, and was born in Leeds on 16 September 1893. When Samuel was a baby the family moved to Bradford, where he spent his formative years. The First World War interrupted Samuel's education at Bradford Technical College.

He was nineteen years old, and a second lieutenant in the 124th Siege Battery, Royal Garrison Artillery when he undertook the deed for which he was awarded the VC. He was invested with his Victoria Cross by King George V at Buckingham Palace on 4 March 1916. That same year he returned to Bradford to marry his fiancée Bertha.

Meekosha was commissioned into the West Yorkshire Regiment in 1917 and joined the British Army's Territorial Force, serving with the Bradford-based

1st/6th Battalion, Prince of Wales's Own (West Yorkshire Regiment) of the 49th (West Riding) Infantry Division. He was promoted to lieutenant in 1918 and captain in 1919. Before the war ended in 1918 he survived being shot in combat in the right wrist and left temple. He transferred to the Corps of Military Accountants in 1919, retiring in 1926.

After the First World War Meekosha became a representative for the tobacco company John Player. In 1940 he rejoined the West Yorkshire Regiment as a captain and transferred to the Royal Army Ordnance Corps, based in Leicestershire, later the same year. He was subsequently promoted to major. He was a very private and modest man, who found himself instantly recognised because of his VC, and the fact that Britain was again at war with Germany led to a huge resurgence in praise from strangers. Determined to avoid the limelight, he changed his name by deed poll to Ingham. (Speculation continues as to whether Meekosha's new name derived from his mother's maiden name Cunningham, or his second wife's name, Mary Constance Ingham.)

Major Ingham died on 8 December 1950, aged fifty-seven, at his home in Oakdale, Monmouthshire (now Gwent) and was cremated at the Glyntaff Crematorium, Pontypridd. His ashes were taken by his family. There is no memorial.

In the year 2000 the *Yorkshire Post* reported that Meekosha, along with twelve others, had been honoured with a permanent exhibition at Bradford City Hall. He was Bradford's first VC winner.

The sale of the Victoria Cross awarded to Corporal Samuel Meekosha took place at the auctioneers Sotheby's on 3 May 2001; it was sold to a private buyer for the hammer price of £92,000.

MORRELL, Thomas *see* YOUNG, Thomas

MOUNTAIN, Albert [1918]

Rank/Service: Sergeant; 15/17th Battalion, West Yorkshire Regiment (Prince of Wales's Own)

Other Decorations: Croix de Guerre and Medaille Militaire (France)

VC Location: Prince of Wales's Regiment Museum, York

Date of Gazette: 7 June 1918

Place/Date of Birth: Leeds, Yorkshire; 19 April 1895

Place/Date of Death: Garforth, Leeds, Yorkshire; 7 January 1967

Grave: Lawnswood Crematorium, Leeds

Town/County Connections: Leeds, Yorkshire

Account of Deed: On 26 March 1918 at Hamelincourt, France, the British were being driven back by the Germans' 'Big Push'. The situation was critical, when Sergeant Mountain, with a party of ten men, attacked an advance enemy patrol about 200 strong with a Lewis gun, killing half of them. The sergeant then rallied his men in the face of overwhelming numbers of the main body of the enemy to cover the retirement of the rest of the company – this party of one NCO and four men held at bay 600 of the enemy for half an hour. Sergeant Mountain later took command of the flank post of the battalion, holding on for twenty-seven hours until finally surrounded.

MOYNIHAN, Andrew [1857]

Rank / Service: Sergeant (later Captain); 90th Regiment (later
   The Cameronians – Scottish Rifles)
VC Location: Cameronians (Scottish Rifles) Museum, Hamilton
Date of Gazette: 24 February 1857
Place / Date of Birth: Wakefield, Yorkshire; 8 September 1831
Place / Date of Death: Floriana, Malta; 19 May 1867
Grave: La Braxia International Cemetery, Malta
Town / County Connections: Wakefield, Yorkshire

Account of Deed: On 8 September 1855 in the Crimea Sergeant Moynihan was with the storming party at the assault on the Redan at Sebastopol, where he personally encountered and killed five Russians. He also rescued from near the Redan a wounded officer under very heavy fire.

Biographical Detail: The village of Dukinfield has proud memories of Andrew Moynihan, who came to Crescent Road as a child, his family having moved from Wakefield in West Yorkshire. He went to the Wesleyan Methodist School in Ashton-under-Lyne and afterwards worked at Flash Hall Mills on Old Street before moving to James Ogden's Mill at Hall Green.

At the age of seventeen he joined the army, enlisting in the 90th Regiment, Perthshire Volunteers, stationed in Ashton. The following six years were spent in Ashton and in 1853 he married Ellen Parkin at Ashton parish church. With the outbreak of the Crimean War in 1854, Moynihan was sent to the front and in September 1855 his gallantry merited the Victoria Cross. He received a hero's welcome on his return to Dukinfield in 1856. A special reception took place at the Astley Arms and presentations to him included an inscribed watch from the local people. The following year he received his Victoria Cross from Queen Victoria.

Moynihan was promoted to sergeant major and in 1856 was commissioned into the 8th Foot. He was promoted to lieutenant the following year and to captain in 1863. Moynihan later served during the Indian Mutiny and was then stationed in Ireland and Gibraltar. His final posting was to Malta in the 1860s, where he was also the musketry instructor for the island.

Tragically in May 1867 Moynihan contracted 'Malta Fever' through drinking unsterilised goat's milk. He died aged only thirty-six, leaving a widow and several children. He is buried in La Braxia Cemetery and his Victoria Cross is displayed at the Cameronians Regimental Museum in Hamilton, Lanarkshire, Scotland.

Moynihan's only son (b. 2 October 1865) subsequently became a prominent surgeon, being raised to the peerage as Berkeley Moynihan, 1st Baron Moynihan of Leeds in the County of York, on 9 March 1929. After his death on 7 September 1936 the title passed to his son Patrick Berkeley [Moynihan], 2nd Baron Moynihan OBE, born 29 July 1906. A noted surgeon, he was President of the Royal College of Surgeons of England from 1926 to 1932.

NAPIER, William [1858]

Rank/Service: Sergeant (later Sergeant Major); 1st Battalion, 13th Regiment
   (later Somerset Light Infantry, Prince Albert's)
VC Location: Somerset Light Infantry Museum, Taunton, Devon
Date of Gazette: 24 December 1858
Place/Date of Birth: Keighley, Yorkshire; 1828
Place/Date of Death: Rochester, Victoria, Australia; 2 June 1908
Grave: Bendigo General Cemetery, Victoria, Australia
Town/County Connections: Bingley, Yorkshire

Account of Deed: On 6 April 1858 near Azimgurh, India, Sergeant Napier was on baggage guard when he coolly bandaged and defended, and finally rescued, a private of his regiment who was severely wounded, while surrounded by sepoys and under heavy fire.

Biographical Detail: William Napier was born at Keighley in Yorkshire on 20 August 1828, the son of Samuel Napier and his wife Mary (née Horsfall). William grew up in a military family and was educated at a private school. His uncle William Napier fought at the Battle of Waterloo in 1815 with the Grenadier Guards (2nd Battalion); he gave his Waterloo Medal to William. By the time William had left school he had the urge to join the army. On 10 December 1846 he enlisted at Leeds, Yorkshire, with the 13th Light Infantry.

In 1855 William Napier left England with the 1st Battalion, 13th (1st Somersetshire) (Prince Albert's Light Infantry) Regiment of Foot under General

Lord Mark Kerr GCB, and arrived at Balaklava in the Crimea by sea on 29 June 1855. In 1897 William described his experiences at Sebastopol:

> The mortality was fearful, but the losses in battle were not more than one half of those caused by fever, and the hardships of camp life in that rigorous climate. Not long before the outbreak of the war, I saw a regiment of the Grenadier Guards paraded at Gibraltar, 900 strong. Afterwards I saw them paraded in the Crimea, when only 82 of all ranks answered the roll call. Of the 800 odd who were absent, not more than 300 had fallen in battle.

In October 1862 Sergeant Major William Napier VC was in transit to Calcutta, and on 8 December 1862 he was discharged. He left Calcutta on 21 December 1862 at 8:38pm on the *Madras* and arrived in Melbourne, Australia, in January 1863.*

William found work as a clerk and later met and married Elizabeth Slater, the daughter of William and Margaret Slater of Ripon, Yorkshire, on 16 September 1863 in Melbourne. They had two children, Alfred and Mary, but both died in infancy. Elizabeth herself died on 25 April 1867, aged thirty-seven. William subsequently married Ruth Ann Hirst, widow of Joseph Graham Hirst of Thornes by Wakefield, Yorkshire, and daughter of Thomas Crompton Booth of Sowerby, Yorkshire, on 5 November 1869 at Bendigo, Victoria.

After initially working as a clerk, William found employment for a short time as a miner and then became a cordial manufacturer based in Mackey Street, Rochester. William was a member and treasurer of the Rochester branch of the Masons.

Sergeant Major William Napier moved to Melbourne after his property burnt down. After a few years in Melbourne he became sick and returned to Rochester in 1907. He stayed with John and Ethel Abbey in Mackey Street, next to his former home. He died there on 2 June 1908, leaving his wife Ruth and their adopted stepdaughter Eliza. Ruth and Eliza moved to Western Australia, and Eliza married William Henry Winch, ancestor of Lord John Napier-Winch of Western Australia. Ruth died at her grandson Ernest Alfred Winch's home in 1924. William Napier's personal belongings are now held by Lord John Napier-Winch.

NICHOLLS, Henry [1940]

Rank/Service: Lance Corporal; 3rd Battalion, Grenadier Guards
VC Location: Grenadier Guards Museum, Wellington Barracks

---

* The *Weekly Times*, Victoria, 3 July 1897.

Date of Gazette: 30 July 1940
Place/Date of Birth: The Meadows, Nottingham; 21 April 1918
Place/Date of Death: Leeds, Yorkshire; 11 September 1975
Grave: Southern Cemetery, Nottingham
Town/County Connections: Nottingham; Leeds, Yorkshire

Account of Deed: On 21 May 1940 near the River Escaut in Belgium, Lance Corporal Nicholls, although suffering from shrapnel wounds in his arm, continued to lead his section in a counter-attack against overwhelming opposition. He advanced over a ridge and, when the position became critical, he rushed forward, putting three enemy machine-guns out of action. He then attacked massed enemy infantry beyond a second ridge until his ammunition ran out and he was taken prisoner.

Biographical Detail: Henry Nicholls, known as 'Harry', was the son of John Clarke Nicholls (1877–1945) and Florence Mary (1884–1965) and elder brother of William 'Billy' (1927–1988). After the event he was posted 'Missing believed killed', and his 'widow' received his VC on 6 June 1940 from King George VI. However, in September 1940 he was reported alive and well in an enemy hospital. He was then transferred to a PoW camp in Poland, where he spent the rest of the war; during this time Nicholls was presented with his VC ribbon by the German commandant. He was released from captivity in 1945. He was then asked to return his VC to Buckingham Palace, whereupon the king personally presented Nicholls with his medal on 22 June 1945. This is a unique instance of a VC being presented twice for the same action, and the only occasion where a VC was presented by the enemy.

ORMSBY, John William [1917]

Rank/Service: Sergeant; 2nd Battalion, King's Own Yorkshire Light Infantry
Other Decorations: MM
VC Location: KOYLI Museum, Doncaster
Date of Gazette: 8 June 1917
Place/Date of Birth: Dewsbury, West Yorkshire; 11 January 1881
Place/Date of Death: Dewsbury, West Yorkshire; 29 July 1952
Grave: Dewsbury Cemetery, West Yorkshire
Town/County Connections: Dewsbury, West Yorkshire

Account of Deed: On 14 April 1917 at Favet, France, during operations that culminated in the capture of an important position, Sergeant Ormsby, acting as his unit's colour sergeant major, showed complete indifference to the heavy machine-gun and rifle fire and set a fine example. After clearing a village he pushed on and drove out many snipers from localities further forward. When the only surviving officer was wounded, he took command of the company and led the men forward under heavy fire for 400 yards to a new position, holding it until relieved.

Biographical Detail: After he left the army, he was presented with a horse and cart and £500 to enable him to set up as a greengrocer.

PEARSON, John [1859]

Rank/Service: Private (later Sergeant); 8th Hussars (King's Royal Irish)
VC Location: Lord Ashcroft VC Collection
Date of Gazette: 26 January 1859
Place/Date of Birth: Seacroft, Leeds, Yorkshire; 19 January 1825
Place/Date of Death: Ontario, Canada; 18 April 1892
Grave: Eastnor Township Cemetery, Lion's Head, Ontario, Canada
Memorial: Plaque in Memorial Park, Lion's Head, Ontario, Canada
Town/County Connections: Leeds, Yorkshire

Account of Deed: On 17 June 1858 at Gwalior, India, Private John Pearson, together with Captain Charles Heneage VC, Sergeant Joseph Ward and Farrier Hollis, took part in a gallant charge made by a squadron of the 8th Hussars, supported by a division of the Bombay Horse Artillery and the 95th Regiment, which routed the enemy. Charging through a rebel camp into two batteries, they captured and brought into their own camp two of the enemy's guns, despite coming under a heavy and converging fire from the fort and town. Pearson was wounded in the action, suffering a sword-cut to the right shoulder.

Biographical Detail: Information about John Pearson's early life is sketchy. He may have been the son of Stephen Pearson (gardener) and Elizabeth Darley, and born in Seacroft on the outskirts of Leeds. He married Selina Smart in the General Baptist Church in Trowbridge, Wiltshire, on 6 April 1851. At that time he was listed as twenty-five years old and a private in the 8th Hussars, living in the barracks in Trowbridge. Selina was twenty, the daughter of Edward Smart. It is known that John Pearson enlisted as a private in the 8th King's Royal Irish Hussars in January 1844. He embarked with his regiment aboard the horse transport vessel *Wilson Kennedy* on 2 May 1854, bound for the Crimea. He served with the 8th Hussars throughout the Crimean War, his regiment forming part of the Light Brigade, which took the second line, along with the 4th (Queen's Own) Light Dragoons and the 11th (Prince Albert's Own) Hussars, during the famous charge on 25 October 1854. The first line was taken by the 13th Light Dragoons and the 17th Lancers. For service during the Crimean War John Pearson was awarded the Crimea Medal with clasps for 'Balaclava' and 'Sebastopol'.

In 1857 he sailed from Cork to India aboard the SS *Great Britain*, six months after the outbreak of the Indian Mutiny. Following the action described above, it was the soldiers themselves who elected Pearson, along with a captain, a sergeant and a farrier, to receive the VC. Pearson's medal was presented to him by Lieutenant General Sir Henry Somerset, the commander-in-chief of the Bombay Army.*

Five years after the charge at Gwalior, in November 1863, Pearson transferred to the 19th Hussars as a private, being promoted back to corporal the following month; he was made a sergeant on 6 August 1865. Pearson was awarded the Meritorious Service Medal on 3 October 1867 with an annuity of £15, and, in the following month was invalided home to England from Meerut.

Following his discharge from the army Pearson lived with his wife and family in Halifax, West Riding. In the 1881 Census they were living at 11 Melville Place, Halifax. John was listed as a Chelsea Pensioner (retired Army) aged 56, and his wife Selina was fifty. Their children were listed as Albert, Frank, Selina, Ida and Mary. Some time later the family emigrated to Canada to begin a new life as farmers. By 1888 John owned a farm near Little Pike Bay, 9 miles west of Lion's Head on the Bruce Peninsula, Ontario.

John Pearson died on 18 April 1892 and is buried in Eastnor Township Cemetery, Lion's Head. A plaque erected to his memory in the Memorial Park, Lion's Head, is inscribed: 'John Pearson VC, 1825–92. Born in England, Pearson served in the Crimea War and won his decoration for outstanding gallantry during the Indian Mutiny. He later emigrated to Canada and settled near Lion's Head.'

His Victoria Cross and other campaign medals were sold at auction in November 2004 by London auctioneers Morton & Eden for the hammer price of £78,000. The VC group was purchased on behalf of the Michael Ashcroft Trust, the holding institution for Lord Ashcroft's VC Collection.

---

* *London Gazette*, 28 January 1859: Gwalior, Indian Mutiny, 17 June 1858, Private John Pearson, 8th King's Royal Irish Hussars. 'Selected for the Victoria Cross by their comrades in the gallant charge made by a squadron of the Regiment at Gwalior, on the 17th June 1858, when, supported by a division of the Bombay Horse Artillery, and Her Majesty's 95th Regiment, they routed the enemy, who were advancing against Brigadier Smith's position, charged through the rebel camp into two batteries, capturing and bringing into their camp two of the enemy's guns, under a heavy and converging fire from the Fort and Town (Field Force Orders by Major-General Sir Hugh Henry Rose GCB, Commanding Central India Field Force, dated Camp Gwalior, 28th June 1858: Elected by the Regiment).

POULTER, Arthur [1918]

Rank/Service: Private; 1/4th Battalion, Duke of Wellington's (West Riding) Regiment
VC Location: Duke of Wellington's Regiment Museum, Halifax
Date of Gazette: 28 June 1918
Place/Date of Birth: East Witton, North Yorkshire; 16 December 1893
Place/Date of Death: Leeds, Yorkshire; 29 August 1956
Grave: New Wortley Cemetery, Leeds
Memorial: Brick plinth at the south end of the Rue Delpierre, Erquinghem–Lys, Armentieres
Town/County Connections: Leeds, Yorkshire

Account of Deed: On 10 April 1918 at Erquinghem, Lys, France, Private Poulter, who was acting as a stretcher-bearer, on ten occasions carried badly wounded men on his back through particularly heavy artillery and machine-gun fire. Two of the wounded were hit a second time while on his back. Again, after a withdrawal over the river had been ordered, Private Poulter returned in full view of the enemy and carried back another wounded man who had been left behind. He bandaged forty men under fire and was seriously wounded when attempting another rescue in the face of the enemy.

Biographical Detail: Born in East Witton, Middleham, in 1894, Arthur Poulter was the youngest of twelve children but he grew into a big strong man. He farmed until he was nineteen, when he went to Leeds and joined the brewers Timothy Taylor & Co. The ease with which he handled the heavy bags of malt was later to stand him in good stead when carrying in the wounded on the Western Front. He then worked for a firewood dealer, marrying his step-daughter Ada Briggs in August 1916. They were to have two daughters and eight sons, one of whom died in 1947 as a result of deprivation suffered as a prisoner of war in Germany. Meanwhile, Poulter had tried to enlist in the Royal Navy. He was turned down for dental reasons but was accepted by the Duke of Wellington's and joined the 1/4th Battalion in March 1916.

In a later engagement with the enemy, Private Poulter was hit and badly wounded near Kemmel on 27 April 1918 when a bullet struck him behind the ear and came out below his eye, temporarily blinding him. He managed to walk to the dressing station but his war was over. His eight brothers all survived the war but two of them were also wounded. He eventually regained his sight and after several operations made a full recovery before his discharge from the army in 1919. He had several jobs before joining Price (Tailors) Ltd, where he was to stay for the rest of his working life. In 1953 he was hit and badly injured by a police vehicle. He retired early in 1956 and died, two years after his wife, on 29 August 1956, aged sixty-two.

After the war, Poulter's young son took the VC medal out his father's drawer and swapped it with another boy for a bag of marbles. When the transaction was discovered, the medal was returned (as presumably were the marbles).

On 14 November 1998 the great-grand-daughter of Poulter VC jointly unveiled a memorial at the place where he had carried so many men to safety eighty years before. Plaques in English and French telling the story of his exploits were mounted on a brick plinth by the Erquinghem–Lys Historical Society and the project was organised by Monsieur Jack Thorpe, himself the son of a Normandy veteran. After an impressive ceremony, beer was provided by Timothy Taylor & Co.

PROCTER, Arthur Herbert [1918]

Rank/Service: Private (later Reverend); 1/5th Battalion, King's (Liverpool) Regiment
VC Location: King's Regiment Museum, Liverpool
Date of Gazette: 5 August 1916
Place/Date of Birth: Bootle, Lancashire; 11 August 1890
Place/Date of Death: Sheffield, Yorkshire; 27 January 1973
Grave: City Road Crematorium, Sheffield (ashes buried in All Saints' Chapel, Sheffield Cathedral)
Memorial: Sheffield Cathedral
Town/County Connections: Bootle, Lancashire; Sheffield, Yorkshire
Significant Remarks: Served as a chaplain with the RAF during the Second World War, having been ordained in 1927. He was the first British soldier to be decorated with the Victoria Cross on the battlefield

Account of Deed: On 4 June 1916 near Ficheux, France, Private Procter noticed that two wounded men lying in full view of the enemy about 75 yards in front of the trenches were moving. At once, on his own initiative, he ran and crawled to the two men; although heavily fired at, he got them under cover of a small bank, dressed their wounds and promised that they would be rescued after dark. He then left them with warm clothing and returned to his trench, again under heavy fire. The men were rescued at dusk.

Biographical Detail: Arthur was born in Bootle, Lancashire, and educated at Port Sunlight and Exeter. His first employment was at the Corn Exchange in Liverpool as a wholesale provisions grocer. In November 1914 Arthur joined the war effort, enlisting with the 1/5th Battalion, the King's (Liverpool) Regiment; Territorial Forces. He was presented with his medal by King George V at Amiens on 9 August 1916. He was the first British soldier to be decorated with the Victoria Cross on the battlefield.

Following the war, Proctor returned to Liverpool, where he received a hero's welcome, being paraded through the streets and given a gold watch. In 1918 Arthur married Hilda Codd at Birkenhead and a year later they had a son, also called Arthur. He returned to his old occupation of wholesale grocer but around 1925 Arthur decided to pursue a new vocation and began training for entry into the Church. He was ordained in 1927.

During the 1930s he was vicar of St Stephens Church, Bennett Street, Hyde. In the Second World War he served as a chaplain in the Royal Air Force, and after leaving the services in 1946 became Rector of St Mary's Church in Droylsden near Manchester. In 1951 he moved to St Peters Church in Claybrook, Leicester. Between 1963 and 1965 he was vicar at the parish church in Bradworthy, Devon, but he finally retired to Sheffield. He spent the last years of his life in a bungalow for retired clergymen, where he died in January 1973, aged eighty-two.

RAYNES, John Crawshaw [1915]

Rank/Service: Acting Sergeant (later Battery Sergeant Major); A Battery, 71st Brigade, Royal Field Artillery
VC Location: Royal Artillery Museum, Woolwich
Date of Gazette: 18 November 1915
Place/Date of Birth: Ecclesall, Sheffield, Yorkshire; 28 April 1887
Place/Date of Death: Leeds, Yorkshire; 13 November 1929
Grave: Harehills Cemetery, Leeds
Town/County Connections: Sheffield and Leeds, Yorkshire

Account of Deed: In October 1915 his battery was based at Fosse 7 de Bethune, France, a pithead on the road from Bethune to Lens. Used as an artillery site, it was heavily involved in what became known as the Battle of Loos. On 11 October 1915 the site was heavily bombarded by armour-piercing and gas shells. When his gun was ordered to cease firing, Sergeant Raynes went out under intense enemy shelling to assist his friend Sergeant Ayres, who was lying wounded forty yards away. He bandaged him, but returned to his gun when it was again ordered into action. A few minutes later 'Cease fire' was again ordered, owing to the intensity of the enemy's fire, and Sergeant Raynes, calling on two gunners to help him – both of whom were killed shortly afterwards – went out and carried Sergeant Ayres into a dug-out. A gas shell then burst at the mouth of the dug-out, and Sergeant Raynes once more ran across the open to fetch his own smoke helmet, which he put on Sergeant Ayres; then, despite being badly gassed himself, he staggered back to serve his gun. (Sadly; despite all of John's efforts, Sergeant Ayres did not survive the gassing and died the same day.)

On 12 October 1915 at 'Quality Street', a house was knocked down by a heavy shell, and four men were buried in the rubble of the house and four more in the cellar. The first man rescued was Sergeant Raynes, who was wounded in the head and leg, but he insisted on remaining, under heavy shell fire, to assist in the rescue of all the other men. Then, after having his wounds dressed, he reported himself immediately for duty with his battery, which was again being heavily shelled.

Biographical Detail: John was the son of Stephen Raynes of Sheffield and Harriet Elizabeth Crawshaw. He was one of four children. The Reverend W. Odom in his book *Fifty Years of Church Life 1866–1916* refers to Christ Church, Heeley, Sheffield, and records that John was 'an old scholar of our Day and Sunday Schools, a member of our Boys' Brigade', and goes on to report that 'Sergeant-Major J.C. Raynes, who, on his recovery, visited his old school, received a warm welcome from the vicar, teachers, and scholars, and in a simple, unassuming manner, after handing round his VC to the scholars, offered a few words of advice to the lads ...'

John's parents had moved to the Heeley district soon after their marriage in the Leeds, Wortley district in the March quarter of 1886. The address given in the register is the Sheaf View Hotel in Heeley. John's father was the landlord and was granted the licence by the Sheffield magistrates in 1891. In the application he also disclosed that he worked as an auctioneer's clerk.

Raynes enlisted into the Royal Horse and Royal Field Artillery on 10 October 1904 and served with the regiment for a total of eight years. He married Mabel Dawson at the Leeds Register Office (Leeds: RB/159/149) on 24 April 1907. They had two sons, John Kenneth, who was born on 30 January 1912, and Thomas, who was born around 1925.

After leaving the army in 1912 Raynes joined the Leeds City Police, but at the outbreak of war in August 1914 he was recalled for military service as a reservist. He was discharged from the army on 11 December 1918 as 'physically unfit'. He returned to civilian life and rejoined the Leeds City Police based at the old Milgarth police station, rising to the rank of sergeant. However, he was still suffering from the effects of the gas poisoning suffered during his VC action and struggled to perform his duties as a policeman, eventually being forced to take a desk job. He finally retired from the police in 1926.

John Raynes was invested with his Victoria Cross by King George V at Buckingham Palace on 4 December 1915. *The Times* of 23 November 1915 also makes a brief mention of John being presented with a gold watch by members of the Leeds City Police, the presentation being made by the Lord Mayor at the town hall.

According to his obituary (*The Times*, 14 November 1929), he was bedridden for the final three years of his life and had to rely on his wife for constant support and nursing. His spinal injuries had deteriorated to the extent that his legs were paralysed. Max Arthur, in his recently published book on VC holders, also mentions that John had periods of depression in the final years of his life.

John missed the Victoria Cross reunion dinner on Saturday, 9 November 1929 in the Royal Gallery, House of Lords, but he received a telegram from his fellow Yorkshire VC holders on Monday, 11 November conveying their greetings and expressing their regret that he could not complete the party. He also had a visit from the new Lord Mayor of Leeds, Mr N.G. Morrison, on the same day. Just two days later, on 12 November 1929, John died at his home in Grange Crescent, Chapeltown, Leeds, at the comparatively young age of forty-two, leaving a wife and family.

John's funeral took place on 16 November 1929 and was recorded in a local newspaper as follows:

> The funeral took place in the presence of nineteen Victoria Cross recipients, eight of which were Yorkshire VC holders. The Yorkshire VCs were: Captain George Sanders, Lieutenant Wilfred Edwards, Sergeant Fred McNess, Sergeant Charles Smith Hull, Sergeant Albert Mountain, Lance Corporal Frederick W. Dobson, Private Arthur Poulter [and] Private William Boynton Butler who were acting as pallbearers. The 71st Field Brigade, Royal Artillery provided the gun carriage that carried the coffin of Mr Raynes, followed by the chairman of the Leeds Old Contemptible Association, Captain W.E. Gage, carrying a purple cushion with JCR's medals upon it; a wreath of Flanders poppies and evergreen in the shape of a Victoria Cross was carried by Lieutenant Edwards.
>
> The wreath was intended as a souvenir for JCR from the VC Dinner at the House of Lords. The wreath bore the message 'In affectionate memory from brother VCs of Leeds, who sorely missed their comrade at the Prince of Wales's dinner, whence this emblem was brought for him.' Mr Raynes was intended to go to the dinner but he had to give his apologies, he asked if his son John Kenneth, age 18, would be able to take his place.
>
> Raynes received a telegram on Armistice Day from the other Yorkshire VCs who attended the dinner, stating that they regretted

that he could not attend and complete the party, sending their greetings. They promised him a memento of the dinner (the VC-shaped wreath). The service was held at St Clement's Church, with the Lord and Lady Mayor and the Chief Constable in attendance, along with a squad of police.

He was buried at Harehills Cemetery, Leeds. A firing squad was arranged and provided by the West Yorkshire Regiment and the 'Last Post' was sounded. The cemetery gates had to be closed due to the amount of people that were there to pay their respects, an estimated 25 to 30,000. Such was the popularity of this brave man.

The story of John Crawshaw Raynes and his actions gaining him the VC appeared in the *Yorkshire Evening Post* in 1972 after the discovery of an unknown VC portrait. It was soon found to be the portrait of Sgt Major Raynes. His daughter-in-law, who held the VC at the time, asked for the picture to be forwarded to the regimental museum.

The Times of 18 November 1929 also contained an article on John's funeral, under the heading 'FUNERAL OF LEEDS VC'.

It was while researching into the First World War that West Yorkshire policeman PC Anthony Child learned about the heroic actions of Battery Sergeant Major John Raynes VC. Child discovered that his grave in Harehills Cemetery, Leeds, had fallen into disrepair, and attempts were made to tidy it up in the summer of 2008. Eventually, following a complete refurbishment of the headstone, a ceremony of rededication was held on 13 November 2008, with the West Yorkshire Police chaplain, the Revd Inspector Andrew Earl, officiating.

RIDGEWAY, Richard Kirby [1880]

Rank/Service: Captain (later Colonel); Bengal Staff Corps and 44th Ghurkha Rifles (later 1/5th Ghurkha Rifles), Indian Army
Other Decorations: CB
VC Location: Private (Not on public display)
Date of Gazette: 11 May 1880
Place/Date of Birth: Oldcastle, Co. Meath, Ireland; 18 August 1848
Place/Date of Death: Harrogate, Yorkshire; 11 October 1924
Grave: Lawnswood Crematorium, Leeds
Town/County Connections: Oldcastle, Co. Meath; Harrogate, Yorkshire

Account of Deed: On 22 November 1879, during the final assault on Konoma, on India's Eastern Frontier, under heavy fire from the enemy, Captain

Ridgeway rushed up to a barricade and attempted to tear down the planking surrounding it in order to enable him to gain entrance. While doing this, he was wounded severely in the right shoulder.

SANDERS, George [1916]

Rank/Service: Corporal (later Captain); 117th Battalion, West Yorkshire
   Regiment (Prince of Wales's Own)
Other Decorations: MC
VC Location: Private (Not on public display)
Date of Gazette: 9 September 1916
Place/Date of Birth: New Wortley, Leeds, Yorkshire; 8 July 1894
Place/Date of Death: Leeds, Yorkshire; 4 April 1950
Grave: Cottingley Crematorium, Leeds
Town/County Connections: Leeds, Yorkshire

Account of Deed: On 1 July 1916 near Thiepval, France, after an advance into the enemy's trenches, Corporal Sanders found himself isolated with a party of thirty men. Organising the defences, he detailed a bombing party and impressed upon the men that his and their duty was to hold their position at all costs. Next morning he drove off an attack by the enemy, rescuing some prisoners who had fallen into their hands. Later two more enemy bombing attacks were driven off, and Sanders was finally relieved after thirty-six hours. All this time his party had been without food and water, having given their water to the wounded during the first night.

Biographical Detail: Born on 8 July 1894 at New Wortley near Leeds, George Sanders was the son of Thomas and Amy Sanders. He was educated at Little Holbeck School and indentured as an apprentice fitter at the nearby Airedale Foundry. George enlisted for service on 9 November 1914 and was drafted to the 1/7th Battalion, Prince of Wales's Own Yorkshire Regiment – the Leeds Rifles. After spells of training at York and Gainsborough, the battalion sailed for France and landed at Boulogne in April 1915.

Corporal George Sanders was invested with his Victoria Cross by the King at Buckingham Palace on 18 November 1916. On 27 June 1917 George was awarded a commission with the 2nd Battalion, West Yorkshire Regiment. In April 1918 his unit was involved in bitter fighting at Mount Kemmel during the German Spring Offensive. Acting Captain Sanders was awarded the Military Cross during this action but was taken prisoner on 25 April. He was posted as wounded and missing, having been last seen with leg and right arm injuries, but carrying on with his revolver in his left hand. In July 1918 his father received a letter from George confirming that he was being held prisoner at a camp in Limburg. He was repatriated on Boxing Day 1918 and demobbed in March 1919.

He attended both the Buckingham Palace garden party held in June 1920 and the VC reunion dinner in November 1929.

George Sanders VC, MC died in Leeds on 4 April 1950, aged fifty-six. His funeral was held at the Cottingley Crematorium in the city. It is believed that his son Kenneth Sanders retains his father's medals.

SANDFORD, Richard Douglas [1918]

Rank/Service: Lieutenant; Royal Navy
Other Decorations: Legion d'Honneur (Belgium)
VC Location: Britannia Royal Naval College, Dartmouth
Date of Gazette: 23 July 1918
Place/Date of Birth: Exmouth, Devon; 11 May 1891
Place/Date of Death: Grangetown, Middlesbrough; 23 November 1918
Grave: Eston Cemetery, Middlesbrough, Yorkshire
Memorial: Exeter Cathedral
Town/County Connections: Exmouth, Devon; Middlesbrough, Yorkshire

Account of Deed: On 22/23 April 1918 at Zeebrugge, Belgium, Lieutenant Sandford, commanding HM Submarine *C3*, skilfully placed the vessel between the piles of the viaduct that connected the Mole with the shore, before laying the fuse and abandoning the submarine. He disdained to use the gyro steering that would have enabled him and his crew to abandon the submarine at a safe distance, preferring to position her precisely to make sure that his mission would be successful.

Biographical Detail: Richard Sandford was the seventh son of the Ven. Ernest Grey Sandford, Archdeacon of Exeter,* while his grandfather, the Right Revd Daniel Sandford, had been Bishop of Edinburgh. At the time of his death, his mother was living in Exmouth.

---

*Ernest Grey Sandford was born in Dunchurch, Warwickshire, in the September Quarter of 1839. He married Ethel Maria Poole in Somerset in the March Quarter of 1875. By that time he was Vicar of Landkey, a small parish some 4 miles to the south-east of Barnstaple. They had six children. In 1888 Ernest was appointed Archdeacon of Exeter, a role he held until 1909. The family moved to Exeter to live in the Cathedral Yard, in the shadow of the Cathedral. Ernest Sandford died on 8 March 1910 and is commemorated by a plaque in Exeter Cathedral. After her husband's death, Ethel went to live in Exmouth. Two of their sons are also commemorated on a brass plate in the south aisle of Exeter Cathedral: Captain Francis Hugh Sandford DSO, RN (ob. 1926) 'Croix de Guerre avec Palmes' and Lieutenant Richard Douglas Sandford VC, RN (ob. 1918) 'Legion of Honour'.

Richard attended Clifton College before joining the Royal Navy in 1904. At that time the navy was in the process of rapid change with the new, deadly Dreadnought class warships and the introduction of submarines into the fleet. In 1914, at the age of twenty-three, Sandford volunteered for the submarine service. By the age of twenty-six he was a lieutenant in command of the elderly HMS *C3*. He was known to his crew as 'Uncle Baldy' for his cheerful and mock elder statesman manner.

Lieutenant Sandford survived the war, only to die of typhoid on 23 November in the Eston Council Building, Cleveland Hospital, Grangetown, just twelve days after the signing of the Armistice. He was buried in Eston Cemetery near Middlesbrough. In 1927 a memorial tablet was unveiled to HMS *C3* at the spot where the submarine breached the Mole at Zeebrugge.

The *Devonian Year Book* (1919) records:

> Among those who received the VC in connection with the attack on Zeebrugge on St George's Day 1918 was Lieutenant Richard Douglas Sandford RN, the youngest of seven sons of the late Archdeacon of Exeter, and of Mrs Sandford who now resides in Exmouth.
>
> Educated at Dartmouth and at the Royal Naval College, Osborne, he had only been promoted to his present rank a short time before the outbreak of war, but he had specialised in the submarine branch of the service from the first, and gallantly undertook the perilous task of blowing up the bridge connecting the Mole at Zeebrugge to the mainland.
>
> After pushing the submarine under the piles of the viaduct and setting the fuse, he and his companions* found that the propeller of their launch was broken, and they had to resort to oars and to row desperately hard against the strong current to get a hundred yards away before the charge exploded. They had a wonderful escape from being killed by the falling debris.
>
> They were ultimately rescued by a service picket-boat in charge of his elder brother, Lieutenant Commander Francis H. Sandford DSO, RN, who, in describing the incident in a letter to his mother, said: 'I went with my picket-boat to pick up the bits.' However,

---

* A crew of six men, all single and all volunteers, took part in this dangerous mission. Lieutenant Sandford was awarded the VC and Lieutenant Howell-Price the DSO, while Petty Officer Walter Harner (coxswain), Leading Seaman William Cleave, Engine Room Artificer Allan Roseburgh and Stoker Henry Brindle were decorated with Conspicuous Gallantry Medals (CGMs).

although his brother was wounded in the thigh and right hand, he was able to save him and the others who were wounded and in the water. This little picket–boat covered 170 miles during the voyage to and from the Belgian coast and her gallant commander has been promoted for his services, the official report stating that 'his staff work in the preparation of the demolition arrangements and fitting out of submarines was invaluable'.

SHEPHERD, Albert Edward [1918]

Rank/Service: Rifleman (later Corporal); 12th (S) Battalion, King's Royal Rifle Corps
VC Location: Royal Green Jackets Museum, Winchester
Date of Gazette: 13 February 1918
Place/Date of Birth: Royston, Nr Barnsley, Yorkshire; 11 January 1897
Place/Date of Death: Royston, Nr Barnsley, Yorkshire; 24 October 1966
Grave: Royston Cemetery. 'Treasured memories of a dear husband and father Albert Edward Shepherd, VC, Died October 23rd 1966 aged 69 years. Also his dear wife Gladys Maud, died October 23rd 1982 aged 73 years. Also Mildred daughter of the above named died November 10th 1944 aged 5 years'
Town/County Connections: Royston, Yorkshire

Account of Deed: On 20 November 1917 at Villers Plouich, France, when his company was held up by a machine-gun at point-blank range, Private Shepherd volunteered to rush the gun; although ordered not to, he dashed forward and threw a Mills bomb, killing two gunners and capturing the gun. The company, continuing its advance, then came under heavy enfilade machine-gun fire; when the last officer and NCO had become casualties, Private Shepherd took command of the company, ordered the men to lie down and went back some 70 yards to get the help of a tank. He then returned to his company and led them forward to their last objective.

Biographical Detail: A miner by trade, after the war Shepherd returned to his former occupation. Following his death, a lottery grant was awarded to erect a suitable memorial to him. In due course a suitable celebration took place to mark the unveiling of the memorial, described here by Peter Lyddon MBE and Stuart Anderson:

At Royston, which lies between Barnsley and Wakefield in York-shire, on Wednesday 13th February 2008 there was a gathering of people to dedicate a plaque in memory of Albert Shepherd VC.

Amongst those assembled were several members of the RGJ Association (Yorkshire Branch), including a fair proportion of KRRC
veterans, along with the President of the Branch, Brigadier Peter
Lyddon MBE.

Shepherd VC was invested with the award in March 1918 and when he
returned from Buckingham Palace he was carried shoulder high through the
streets of his native town. For many years his principal memorial has been a
wooden lych-gate set upon a grassy mound within the churchyard. Unfortunately with the passage of time the timbers of the gate themselves have
decayed and action was needed to replace or thoroughly renovate them.

After much discussion between the Royston Branch of the Royal
British Legion and the Church authorities; and with consultation
with Richard Frost, representing the KRRC, it was at last agreed
that a metal plaque be affixed to the Memorial in the churchyard.
The day chosen for the dedication fell a little over ninety years since
Rifleman Shepherd's display of leadership and outstanding bravery
in 1917 when he was twenty years of age.

The 13 February was a lovely still, early spring day. We were
instructed by the Royston Legion Secretary, Mr Cooper, to gather
behind the Pack Horse Inn shortly before mid-day. From there we
would march (later changed to amble), a short distance into the
graveyard. Amongst the crowd awaiting the signal to start were
people of Royston, British Legion members, the RGJ contingent,
the Mayor and Mayoress of Barnsley and Shepherd family members.
At the head of the column strode several standard bearers followed
closely by the church representatives and the principal guests. We
entered the churchyard and wound our way to the Shepherd family
gravestone. The Vicar of Royston, the Very Reverend John Hudson,
officiated at the short ceremony to the accompaniment of the steady
clicking of cameras from the representatives of the *Yorkshire Post* and
several local newspapers. After the ceremony Ken Shepherd, one
of Rifleman Shepherd's two sons, was helped towards his father's
gravestone by his wife and daughter. He and other members of the
family, including Rifleman Shepherd's great-great grandson Devon
Green, sprinkled poppy petals on the grave itself. Also interred in
the grave are his wife Gladys and their daughter Mildred, who was
killed in a tragic accident aged five in 1944. The driver of the bus
involved in the accident was said never to have been able to drive
again.

From the graveside it was a short distance across the main road to the churchyard wherein is situated the Royston War Memorial. We gathered in loose formation on three sides of the stone. On the open side and upon its grassy knoll stood the weather-beaten but distinctive lych-gate. The vicar performed a short ceremony, the new plaque was unveiled and the standards were lowered. Unnoticed by most a musician had taken up position to one side. He was assisted by a large official who held up a sheet of music at arm's length. Due to operational duties and the distance involved it had not been possible to have the services of a Regimental Bugler. The sad notes of the *Last Post* floated over those gathered and after a brief silence *Reveille* was sounded. It was a moment of solemnity as we remembered the courage of Rifleman Shepherd and the great unreturning army that he represented. The Mayor made a short address and Peter Lyddon stepped forward and read out the VC citation. Young Devon Green stepped forward and laid a single rose on the stone beneath his great-great-grandfather's plaque.

After the ceremony photographs were taken and we were all invited to proceed to the Civic Centre where we would find a warm welcome and a splendid buffet waiting. When the joint KRRC/RGJ contingent reached the Civic Centre we were informed that the bar was open and the drinks would come courtesy of a lottery grant of some sort. We pressed forward reluctantly!

Inside the entrance hall is a large photograph of Rifleman Shepherd wearing a dress suit and bow tie. We were also shown a photograph of the steam train that bore his name. When the speeches were over and most of the guests had departed, those of us who remained went to bid farewell to the Shepherd family who, as in the past, had graced the occasion with their friendliness and quiet dignity. Ken had been confined to his home for many months but he had made a special effort to attend the ceremony aided by his wife Jean and daughter Beverley. His brother Eric, who had been a submariner for 22 years, was unable to attend as he was looking after his ailing wife. Ken told a newspaper reporter that you would never have guessed that his father was a hero because he was quiet, unassuming and modest. 'He was my best friend. I still miss him every day.'

The text on the plaque reads:

In memory of a gallant soldier Albert E. Shepherd VC of the King's Royal Rifle Corps, born January 1897 died October 1966. He was awarded the Victoria Cross, the Croix de Guerre with Oak Leaf and the Medaille Militaire in 1918 for valiant efforts beyond the call of duty. 'He was small in stature – but a giant among men.' This plaque was donated by 'Awards for all' lottery funding under the auspices of the Royston Royal British Legion, 2008.

SHEPHERD (or SHEPPARD), John [1857]

Rank/Service: Boatswain's Mate (later Boatswain First Class); Royal Navy (Naval Brigade)
Other Decorations: CGM; Legion d'Honneur (France); AI Valore Militari (Sardinia)
VC Location: National Maritime Museum, Greenwich
Date of Gazette: 24 February 1857
Place/Date of Birth: Hull, Yorkshire; 22 September 1817
Place/Date of Death: Padstow, Cornwall; 17 December 1884
Grave: Padstow Churchyard, Cornwall
Town/County Connections: Hull, Yorkshire

Account of Deed: On 15 July 1855 at Sebastopol in the Crimea Boatswain's Mate Sheppard went into the harbour at night, in a punt that he had especially constructed for the purpose, with an explosive device with which he intended to blow up one of the Russian warships. He managed to get past the enemy's steamboats at the entrance of Careening Bay, but was prevented from getting further by a long string of boats carrying enemy troops. He made a second attempt on 16 August. Although both these actions were unsuccessful, they were all boldly conceived and carried out in the face of great danger.

Biographical Detail: John Sheppard was the fourth person to be awarded the Victoria Cross, and the first from Hull in the East Riding of Yorkshire. He later achieved the rank of Boatswain First Class.

SHORT, William Henry [1916]

Rank/Service: 12067 Private; 8th Battalion, Yorkshire Regiment (Alexandra, Princess of Wales's Own)
VC Location: Green Howards Regimental Museum, Richmond
Date of Gazette: 9 September 1916
Place/Date of Birth: Eston, near Middlesbrough; 4 February 1887
Place/Date of Death: Contalmaison, France; 6 August 1916
Grave: Contalmaison Chateau Cemetery, France, Plot II, Row B Grave 16
Memorials: Grangetown War Memorial; Eston Cemetery, Middlesbrough
Town/County Connections: Eston, Middlesbrough, Yorkshire

Account of Deed: On 6 August 1916 at Munster Alley in France, during the Battle of Contalmaison, Private Short was foremost in an attack, bombing the enemy with great gallantry, when he was wounded in the foot. He was urged to go back but refused, and continued to throw bombs. Later a shell shattered his leg and he was unable to stand, so he lay in the trench adjusting detonators and straightening the pins of bombs for the other men to throw. He died the next day, before he could be carried out of the trench.

Biographical Detail: William Short was born on 4 February 1885 to James Short and Annie Stephenson, who did not marry until 1888. They had five sons and four daughters. The family first lived at 11 William Street, Eston, but subsequently moved to 35 Vaughan Street, Grangetown, in 1900. Known to his family as 'Will', he was a popular local footballer playing for Grangetown Albion and Saltburn and Lazenby United FC.

At the age of sixteen Short went to work as a crane-man at Bolckow, Vaughan & Co. steelworks in Eston until the outbreak of the First World War. He enlisted on 2 September 1914 into the Green Howards, and travelled to France on 26 August 1915 with C Company, 8th Battalion, Yorkshire Regiment.

William Short's medals were sold to the regiment by his youngest and only surviving brother in April 1979, and are presently in the Green Howards Regimental Museum. His name is recorded on the Grangetown War Memorial and the stone obelisk in Eston Cemetery is inscribed with the following: 'This memorial is erected to the memory of WILLIAM SHORT VC 8th Yorkshire Regiment to commemorate the great gallantry and devotion to duty displayed by him at the Battle of Contalmaison August 6th 1916 (Somme Offensive). Subscribed for by Lieutenant Colonel Western, Officers, Non commissioned Officers, and men of his regiment & fellow workers.'

SMITH, James Alexander Glenn [1915]

Rank/Service: Private; 3rd Battalion, Border Regiment, attached
   2nd Battalion
VC Location: Border Regiment Museum, Carlisle
Date of Gazette: 18 February 1915
Place/Date of Birth: Workington, Cumberland; 5 January 1881
Place/Date of Death: Middlesbrough, Yorkshire; 21 May 1968
Grave: Acklam Crematorium, Middlesbrough
Town/County Connections: Workington, Cumbria; Middlesbrough, Yorkshire
Remarks: Real name James Alexander GLENN

Account of Deed: On 21 December 1914, at Rouges Bancs in France, Private Smith and Private Abraham Acton VC voluntarily went out from their trench and rescued a wounded man who had been lying exposed near the enemy's trenches for seventy-five hours. On the same day they again left their trench under heavy fire to bring in another wounded man. They were under fire for a total of sixty minutes while conveying the wounded men to safety.

Biographical Detail: Smith was born James Alexander Glenn on 5 January 1881 and is thought to have taken his mother's maiden name (Smith) so he could enlist at the age of thirteen into the 3rd Militia Battalion. He served as a regular soldier and was discharged into the Army Reserve but was called up in August 1914 and sent overseas. In March 1915, three months after his courageous acts, he was wounded and returned to Workington.

The *West Cumberland Times* recorded how Private Smith arrived home by the last train from Carlisle:

> That he did not manage entirely to avoid the welcome waiting for him was due to his being 'spotted' on the train at Wigton. The news was wired on to Maryport and from Maryport to Workington and when he appeared his modesty was shocked by the reception.
>
> He found himself taken prisoner and hoisted shoulder high before he left the booking hall and he narrowly escaped being carried in triumph through the streets. The artillerymen and band had not heard of his 'second coming' in time and the borough fathers had definitely abandoned hope of surprising him so these were not there. But the others were numerous and amid congratulatory greetings of all sorts he was carried like the hero that he has proved himself, to his father's house in Southey Street.

The newspaper reported that 'an attempt to get him to say a few words at one of the halls as a stimulus to recruiting was fruitless. He could a tale unfold, but he doesn't because he isn't built that way. He has apparently recovered from the wound he received at Chapelle, and he looks fit and capable.'

The Duke Street Mission Hall and the surrounding streets were crowded when Workington's Mayor, Alderman P. Walls made a presentation to the hero. The newspaper records that 'on the platform beside him were Pte Smith and his aged father, and supporting them Lt Col Nash, the officer commanding the Border Depot, Colonel Sparrow, aldermen and members of the Corporation, and the Town Clerk'. The proceedings opened with the national anthem and the mayor told the audience: 'I knew James Smith (Jimmy) when only a youth, a modest, lively, fine fellow. He was born on the Marsh, one of our workers, and I think everybody in Workington feels honoured by Private James Smith's honour on the battlefield.' To loud and prolonged applause, the mayor presented Private Smith with a medal and a purse containing 25 sovereigns and the audience sang 'For He's A Jolly Good Fellow'. Then according to the newspaper: 'Private Smith, modest and hesitant, replied: "Well ladies and gentlemen, I am very pleased that Workington has seen fit to honour me. I thank them all – the council and the people of Workington who have thought so much of me. To one and all I am 'yours truly', a chip off the old block (loud applause)"'.

Then,

> Lieutenant Colonel Nash said he hoped that Private Smith's example would be an inducement to many more to come forward and enlist; but Colonel Sparrow said he was sorry to see that young men were not responding as they might do. They were going about with little bunches of red, white and blue ribbons in their button-holes; which, he said, was very pretty but it was not what they wanted.

The newspaper described the scene as the ceremony ended: 'Outside a dense crowd waited until Private Smith appeared. He was instantly surrounded and amid the hat waving and cheering he had to shake innumerable hands and only with difficulty could the police make a way for him out of the street and towards his home.'

The following day Private Smith left Workington for London to receive his medal from King George V. The *West Cumberland Times* reported that: 'His Majesty shook hands with him and spoke a few words of cordial congratulations.'

The 1 May 1915 edition of the *West Cumberland Times* newspaper reported that 'the marriage of Private James Smith (or Glenn) VC, took place quietly on Tuesday at North Ormesby Parish Church near Middlesbrough, his bride being Miss Eliza Reynolds of Stovin Street, Middlesbrough, where the bridegroom resided before the war'. It further records that when the bridegroom arrived in the town he modestly avoided anything in the nature of a public welcome by keeping the time of his arrival a secret.

Later, at a recruiting rally, Private Smith was presented with 'purses of gold' on behalf of the Ironmasters' Association, the blast-furnace men (he had worked in the trade before the war) and members of the corporation.

Smith served overseas until January 1917, then returned to England and was finally discharged on 8 January 1919. After the war he went back to Middlesbrough. He served with the Home Guard during the Second World War and died in May 1968 at the age of eighty-eight. His medals were bequeathed to the Border Regiment and are on display in the regimental museum at Carlisle Castle.

SYKES, Ernest [1917]

Rank/Service: Private; 27th (8) Battalion, Northumberland Fusiliers
VC Location: Royal Northumberland Fusiliers Museum, Alnwick
Date of Gazette: 8 June 1917
Place/Date of Birth: Mossley, Saddleworth, Yorkshire; 4 April 1885
Place/Date of Death: Lockwood, Huddersfield, Yorkshire; 3 August 1949
Grave: Lockwood Cemetery, Huddersfield
Memorials: Regimental Museum of Northumberland Fusiliers, Alnwick
    Castle; an LMS locomotive, Class 6P5F 4–6–0 no. 45537, named *Private
    E. Sykes VC* in his honour
Town/County Connections: Saddleworth and Huddersfield, Yorkshire

Account of Deed: On 19 April 1917, near Arras in France, his battalion was attacking when it was held up by intense fire from front and flank, and suffered heavy casualties. Private Sykes, despite this heavy fire, went forward and brought back four wounded men. He then made a fifth journey forward and remained there under conditions that appeared to be certain death, until he had bandaged all those too badly injured to be moved.

Biographical Detail: Ernest Sykes was born in Mossley on 4 April 1885 and educated at St George's School in Stalybridge. He later worked as a platelayer for the London & North Western Railway Company at Micklehurst. Sykes was living with his wife and two sons on Bank Street in Mossley when the First World War began, and he immediately joined as a volunteer in the 7th Battalion, Duke of Wellington's Regiment. He was posted to Gallipoli, where he suffered severe injuries to the foot, but several operations succeeded in saving the limb. He then returned to England, where he was passed as fit to serve in the Tyneside Irish Brigade of the 27th Battalion, Northumberland Fusiliers, with whom he served in France and Flanders. It was here that he was awarded the Victoria Cross for 'most conspicuous bravery and devotion to duty near Arras, France, on 19 April 1917'.

Sykes received his Victoria Cross from King George V at Buckingham Palace in July 1917. His return to Mossley was met by public adulation, as people turned out in their thousands to greet him and to witness the presentation of a commemorative gold watch by the mayor in Market Square. He later went on to be awarded the 1914–1919 Star, the British War Medal and the Victory Medal.

Sykes was demobilised prematurely in May 1918 due to illness. He returned to work for the local railway company, where a locomotive was named after him. In 1937 he was awarded the Coronation Medal. During the Second World War Sykes returned to serve with the 25th Battalion, West Riding Home Guard.

Ernest Sykes died at his home in Lockwood near Huddersfield on 3 August 1949 and was buried with honours at Woodfield Cemetery in Lockwood. His Victoria Cross is on display at Alnwick Castle, and a Blue Plaque to honour his memory is located at the George Lawton Hall in Mossley.

SYMONS, George [1857]

Rank/Service: Sergeant (later Captain); Royal Regiment of Horse Artillery
Other Decorations: DCM
VC Location: HQ RLC Officers' Mess, Camberley
Date of Gazette: 20 November 1857, amendment 1 December 1857
Place/Date of Birth: South Hill, Cornwall; 18 March 1826
Place/Date of Death: Bridlington, Yorkshire; 18 November 1871
Grave: Bridlington Priory Churchyard (no headstone)
Town/County Connections: South Hill, Cornwall; Bridlington, Yorkshire

Account of Deed: On 6 June 1855 at Inkerman in the Crimea Sergeant Symons volunteered to unmask the embrasures of a five-gun battery in the advanced Right Attack. He did this under terrific fire from the enemy, which increased with the opening of each embrasure until he came to the last one, when he boldly mounted the parapet and threw down the sandbags. As he was doing this, an enemy shell burst nearby and wounded him severely.

Biographical Detail: Symons was later commissioned into the Military Train, but transferred back to the Royal Artillery in 1862 and reached the rank of captain.

TRAYNOR, William Bernard [1901]

Rank/Service: Sergeant; 2nd Battalion, West Yorkshire Regiment (Prince of Wales's Own)
VC Location: Private (Not on public display)
Date of Gazette: 17 September 1901
Place/Date of Birth: Hull, Yorkshire; 31 December 1870
Place/Date of Death: Dover, Kent; 20 October 1954
Grave: Charlton Cemetery, Dover, Kent. 'In fond remembrance of Frank Traynor who died 12th August 1911 aged 12 years. Also Jane E. Traynor

who died 6th June 1934 aged 59 years. Also William B. Traynor, VC,
husband of Jane who died 20th October 1954 aged 83 years'
Town/County Connections: Hull, Yorkshire; Dover, Kent

Account of Deed: On 6 February 1901 at Bothwell Camp, South Africa, during a
night attack Sergeant Traynor ran out of a trench under extremely heavy fire to
assist a wounded man. While running he was wounded; unable to carry the
man himself, he called for help. Lance-Corporal Lintott came to him and
between the two they carried the wounded soldier into shelter. Afterwards, in
spite of his wounds, Sergeant Traynor remained in command of his section
encouraging his men until the attack failed.

Biographical Detail: William Bernard Traynor was born on 31 December 1870
at 29 Moxon Street, Hull, the son of Francis Traynor of County Monaghan,
Ireland, and Rebecca Traynor, formerly of Hull. He was educated at Pryme
Street (Roman Catholic) School, Hull, and entered the 2nd Battalion, West
Yorkshire Regiment on 14 November 1888. He served for some years in India
and from 1899 to 1901 in South Africa, where he won the Victoria Cross when
serving under Lieutenant G.L. Crossman DSO and Lieutenant Colonel W. Fry
CB. Sergeant Traynor took part in the following operations in South Africa:
Willow Grange (23 November 1899); Colenso; Spion Kop; Vaal Krantz;
operations in Natal from 14 to 27 February, ending at Pieter's Hill; Northern
Natal and Orange River Colony, including action at Laing's Nek, and East and
West Transvaal; severely wounded on 6 February 1901, he arrived in hospital
on 15 February. For his services in this campaign Sergeant Traynor also
received the Queen's Medal and clasps for Tugela Heights, the relief of
Ladysmith, Laing's Nek, Transvaal and the Orange River Colony Clasp for
1901. Owing to his poor state of health he was unable to travel to London to
receive his decoration from the monarch, so his Victoria Cross was presented
to him on 2 July 1902 at York by Colonel Edward Stevenson Browne VC, who
had won his own Victoria Cross in the Zulu War of 1879.

Unfortunately, Traynor's wound was so serious that a telegram was sent to
his wife announcing that he had been killed in action. This was not so, but he
had to be invalided home in 1901, and was discharged as medically unfit from
the service on 29 September 1901. He and his wife settled in Dover and he
became an orderly room clerk with the Royal Artillery. Later he was given the
post of barrack warden at Dover Castle on 8 September 1902, in which capacity
he was mentioned for valuable services in connection with the First World War
on 2 September 1918. Traynor retired from this post in 1935.

On 12 June 1897 at Hunton, near Maidstone in Kent, Sergeant Traynor
married Jane Elizabeth Martin, daughter of Elizabeth and James Martin. They

had six children. Their twin boys, William and Victor (b. 5 April 1905) joined the army, both reaching the rank of major in the Royal Engineers.

It was while in Dover that he became a member of the British Legion and was for ten years Vice-Chairman of the Dover branch. He was also a Freemason, initiated into Military Jubilee Lodge No. 2195 in February 1919, and a founder of Snargate Street Lodge No. 6770 in November 1946.

In 1951 a dinner was held at the town hall to honour the fiftieth anniversary of the award of his Victoria Cross. The programme reveals that the guests enjoyed soup, followed by fish, with a main course of steak pie, creamed potatoes and peas or cabbage, with trifle and coffee to follow. Music was supplied by the band of the 1st Battalion, The Buffs, and there were a number of toasts. That to Sergeant Traynor was proposed by Colonel Tidmarsh, while Sergeant Traynor himself, after responding, proposed a toast to his own old regiment, the West Yorkshires.

In 1953 Sergeant Traynor was one of the few non-Freemen invited to a coronation lunch at the town hall held by the Hereditary and Honorary Freemen.

He died on 20 October 1954, at Buckland Hospital. The funeral was held at St Andrews, Buckland, and was attended by a large congregation, including the mayor, many representatives of the services and veterans, and Freemasonic Lodges. Sergeant Traynor is buried at Charlton, XI8, in the grave of his wife; as the coffin was lowered, the Last Post and Reveille were played, and black-draped standards were dipped.

WALLER, Horace [1917]

Rank/Service: Private; 10th (S) Battalion, King's Own Yorkshire Light
   Infantry
VC Location: Private (Not on public display)
Date of Gazette: 8 June 1917
Place/Date of Birth: Batley Carr, Dewsbury, Yorkshire; 23 September 1897
Place/Date of Death: Heninel, France; 10 April 1917
Grave: Cojeul British Cemetery, St Martin-sur-Cojeul, France; family grave
   in Dewsbury Cemetery, West Yorkshire
Memorial: Horace Waller VC road in Dewsbury Business Park was named
   after him
Town/County Connections: Dewsbury, West Yorkshire

Account of Deed: On 10 April 1917, south of Heninel in France, Private Waller was with a bombing section forming a block in the enemy line, when a very violent counter-attack was made by the enemy on this post, which one officer described as 'the most violent hand-to-hand fighting I have ever witnessed'. Although five of the garrison were killed, Private Waller continued for more than an hour to throw bombs and finally repulsed the attack. In the evening the enemy again counter-attacked and the entire garrison became casualties except Private Waller, who, although wounded later, continued to throw bombs for another half an hour until he was killed.

Biographical Detail: Horace Waller was the son of John Edward and Esther Waller of Laurel Bank, Heald's Road, Dewsbury, Yorkshire. Initially, Private 30144 Horace Waller was reported missing believed killed. His commanding officer paid tribute to him, followed by a tribute from his old school, Batley Grammar School, which was extremely proud of its ex-pupil. His parents received a letter from Captain L. March, commanding C Company, explaining that he had recommended Horace for the highest of all honours, and it had also been endorsed by the colonel.

Horace Waller is buried at Cojeul British Cemetery, C.55, Pas-de-Calais, France. There is a family grave in Dewsbury Cemetery which has inscribed upon it:

> Strickland Waller of Batley Carr, born 1st February 1840 died 7th February 1898. Also Sarah, wife of the above who died September 26th, 1916 aged 71 years. Also John Edward Waller, born February 18th, 1858, died August 20th 1936. Also Esther, wife of John Edward Waller, born April 10th 1871, died July 28th, 1899. Also in loving memory of Sarah Elizabeth, wife of the above J E Waller, died March 29th, 1953 aged 89 years. Also Horace Waller, VC, son of the above born September 23rd, 1896, killed in action at Henin-sur-Gojeul, France April 10th, 1917.

WARD, Charles Burley [1900]

Rank/Service: Private (later Company Sergeant Major); 2nd Battalion, King's Own Yorkshire Light Infantry

VC Location: Private (Not on public display)

Date of Gazette: 28 September 1900

Place/Date of Birth: Hunslet, Leeds, Yorkshire; 10 July 1877

Place/Date of Death: Bridgend, Glamorgan, Wales; 30 December 1921

Grave: St Mary's Churchyard, Whitchurch, Cardiff

Town/County Connections: Leeds, Yorkshire; Bridgend, Glamorgan; Cardiff

Significant Remarks: Last winner of the VC to be decorated by Queen Victoria

Account of Deed: On 26 June 1900 at Lindley, South Africa, about 500 Boers surrounded a piquet of the regiment on three sides and the majority of them were either killed or wounded. Private Ward volunteered to take a message asking for reinforcements to the signalling post about 150 yards away. He eventually gained permission to go, although it seemed certain that he would be shot, but he managed to get across through a storm of bullets. Having delivered his message, Ward returned to his commanding officer across the fire-swept ground; he was severely wounded, but his gallant action saved the post from capture.

Biographical Detail: Born in Leeds, Yorkshire, he died at Bridgend in Glamorgan and was buried in St Mary's Churchyard, Cardiff. Ward was the last winner of the VC to be decorated by Queen Victoria and later achieved the rank of company sergeant major.

A (silent) movie interview with Private Ward following the award of the VC was filmed by the Lancashire cinematographers Sagar Mitchell and James Kenyon; sealed in steel barrels after their company went out of business in the 1920s, the 800 films of their archive were discovered during demolition work in 1994 and have now been restored by the British Film Institute.

As a result of considerable effort by John O'Sullivan, the British Legion, Whitchurch Glamorgan and others, a series of events were arranged to mark the unveiling in 2005 of a War Grave Commission style headstone to the memory of Sergeant Major Charles Burley Ward. Following a processional hymn, the national anthem, a citation, a lesson, an address and prayers, the headstone was unveiled by Major General P.E. de la C. de la Billiere CBE, DSO, KC, General Officer Commanding Wales. Also present were Mrs Susan Williams, Lord Lieutenant of South Glamorgan, Captain Lloyd-Edwards, O.St.J., RD, DL, RKR (Rtd), former Lord Mayor of Cardiff, Councillor Y.P. Herbert, Deputy Lord Mayor, Reverend Canon F.G. Turner, Vicar, and Mr Eddie Chapman VC. Another VC of South Wales, Lord Justice Tasker Watkins, was unable to be present due to another engagement. About twenty members of Ward's family, including his daughter Mrs Edith Chapman from Australia were present. Mr Ward was a widower when he married a second time. At the time of his death he was living at Soberton Avenue off Whitchurch Road, Cardiff. After the ceremony in St Mary's Churchyard, there was a march-past led by the Light Infantry Burma Band, followed by standard bearers and escorts when the salute was taken by General de la Billiere. In the evening there was a reception and entertainment at the Royal British Legion Earl Haig Club, Whitchurch, when a portrait of Sergeant Major Ward VC by Llanrumney artist Ray Chick was unveiled.

WHITE, Archie Cecil Thomas [1916]

Rank/Service: Temporary Captain (later Colonel); 6th Battalion, Yorkshire Regiment (Alexandra, Princess of Wales's Own)
Other Decorations: MC (gazetted 3 June 1918)
VC Location: Green Howards Regimental Museum, Richmond
Date of Gazette: 26 October 1916
Place/Date of Birth: Boroughbridge, Yorkshire; 5 October 1890
Place/Date of Death: Camberley, Surrey; 20 May 1971
Grave: Brookwood Crematorium, Woking
Town/County Connections: Boroughbridge, Yorkshire
Significant Remarks: Army Educational Corps 1920–1947; Principal, City Literary Institute 1948–1956; Member of Senate, University of London 1953–1956; Deputy Colonel-Commandant, Royal Army Educational Corps 1960–1969; Officier d'Academie FKC

Account of Deed: During the period 27 September to 1 October 1916 at Stuff Redoubt, near Thiepval, France, Captain White was in command of the troops holding the southern and western faces of a redoubt. For four days and nights his skilful dispositions enabled him to hold the position under heavy fire of all kinds and against several counter-attacks. Although short of supplies and ammunition, his determination never wavered and, when the enemy attacked in greatly superior numbers and had almost ejected the British troops from the redoubt, he personally led a counter-attack that finally cleared the enemy out of the southern and western faces.

Biographical Detail: Thomas White was born on 5 October 1891, the elder of two sons of Thomas and Jean White (née Finlayson) of Norwood House, Langthorpe, near Boroughbridge. His father ran an outfitters shop in Boroughbridge. Thomas was educated at the same time as Donald Bell VC at Harrogate Grammar School, where he won a scholarship to study English Literature at King's College, London. He graduated in 1912 and became a teacher at Westminster School.

On the outbreak of the First World War he was commissioned into the Green Howards on 14 October, and on 10 December 1914 was made a temporary lieutenant in the 6th Yorkshires. He was made a temporary captain on 1 July 1915 prior to his battalion sailing for Gallipoli. His younger brother, Second Lieutenant John Finlayson White was killed in a night assault on Lala Baba at Suvla Bay on 6/7 August, while Thomas was sick with dysentery.

In addition to winning a VC, White was Mentioned in Despatches and wounded twice, and later won the Military Cross.

White became a staff officer in France, first as a GS03 on 30 June 1917, then a brigade major on 28 March 1918. He was brigade major for the Archangel (Russia) Relief Force between 29 May and 5 October 1919. On 13 November 1920 he relinquished his commission in the Green Howards because he was only offered a peacetime lieutenancy as opposed to a majority in the newly created Army Education Corps, which he joined on 25 November 1920, aged twenty-nine years, with the rank of major.

Major Archie C.T. White VC, MC, became an instructor at RMA Sandhurst between 1921 and 1925. He was Commandant of Queen Victoria's School, Dunblane, between 1925 and 1929, then returned to Sandhurst to become the Senior AEC Instructor from 1929 to 1933. He then took various tours of duty with the AEC in India and Burma before joining the Cypher Office as a lieutenant-colonel at the start of the Second World War. During the war he became Command Education Officer (Northern, Southern and AA Commands) between 1940 and 1943, and Chief Education Officer 21st Army Group between 1943 and 1945. He was again Mentioned in Despatches on 9 August 1945, when he served in South-East Asia, before retiring as honorary colonel on 17 November 1947. He was Deputy Commandant of the RAEC between 1960 and 1969 and wrote *The Story of Army Education 1643–1963*.

In civilian life he was the Principal of the City Literary Institute between 1948 and 1953, a member of the Senate of the London University and appointed as a Fellow of King's College, London. Colonel White married Jean Will and they had three daughters, two of them twins. His wife died after a long and painful illness in 1960.

Colonel White died quietly at his home at Brucklay, Upper Park Road, Camberley, on 20 May 1971 aged eighty years. He was cremated at Brookwood Crematorium, Woking, and his ashes scattered in Tennyson Lake Garden. His VC and medals are on loan to the Green Howards Regimental Museum, Richmond.

WHITE, Jack [1917]

Rank/Service: Private (later Lance-Corporal); 6th Battalion, King's Own (Royal Lancaster) Regiment
VC Location: Private (Not on public display)
Date of Gazette: 27 June 1917
Place/Date of Birth: Leeds, Yorkshire; 23 December 1896
Place/Date of Death: Manchester, Lancashire; 27 November 1949
Grave: Jewish Cemetery, Blackley, Manchester
Memorial: The Priory, Lancaster
Town/County Connections: Leeds, Yorkshire; Manchester, Lancashire

Account of Deed: On 7/8 March 1917 on the Diyala River, Mesopotamia, signaller Private White, during an attempt to cross the river, saw the two pontoons ahead of him come under very heavy fire with disastrous results. By the time his own pontoon had reached mid-stream, every man except himself was either dead or wounded; unable to control the pontoon single-handed, he tied a telephone wire to it and then jumped overboard and towed it to the shore, thereby saving an officer's life and bringing to land the wounded and also the rifles and equipment of all the men in the boat.

Biographical Detail: Jack White was born Jacob Weiss in Leeds, Yorkshire, on 23 December 1896. After finishing his education, he joined the family business, a water-proofing company. When the First World War broke out, he returned home from a business trip and volunteered for active service with the King's Own Royal Regiment (Lancaster). He was originally assigned to a battalion destined for France, but he missed the battalion's deployment while home on compassionate leave to attend the death of his father. Instead, he was transferred to the 6th King's Own Royal Regiment (Lancaster), attached to the 13th (Western) Division. Originally ordered to Gallipoli, he remained with the battalion through the Gallipoli campaign. Eventually he and his unit were ordered to join the Tigris Corps, attempting to relieve the siege of Kut. After the failure of the relief effort, White's unit participated in the counter-offensive in 1917. It was during the 13th Division's crossing of the Diyala River that he earned the Victoria Cross.

Jack White later achieved the rank of lance-corporal. Ironically, although he was a Victoria Cross holder, he was not permitted to join the Home Guard during the Second World War because it was claimed that his parents had failed to be properly naturalised as British citizens, and despite the fact Jack himself was born in Yorkshire.

Upon his return to Manchester, Jack began an apprenticeship as a trainee pattern cutter and machinist at one of the many factories in the thriving Manchester raincoat industry of the early twentieth century. Having learnt his trade, he established his own manufactory and until his death in 1949 Jack White was general manager and owner of the factory which under his stewardship established itself as one of the most technically skilled and innovative factories in the region. The factory, now universally known as Cooper & Stollbrand, continues to manufacture and remains under the family's ownership. It is currently managed by Jack White's great-grandson.

A documentary about the clothing factory that he began, and which now manufactures clothes for companies such as Burberry and Paul Smith, was shown on 18 February 2011 on Channel 4. Not only is this factory one of the last remaining of its kind but it's also home to the 'Private White VC' menswear line, inspired by Private Jack himself and designed by Laura Ashley's son Nick. Each garment has a designer label showing a Victoria Cross emblem stitched on every piece.

Interestingly, Jack White's Victoria Cross exploits featured in the popular boys comic *Victor*, no. 1358, dated 28 February 1987.

WILKINSON, Thomas [1857]

Rank/Service: Bombardier (later Sergeant Instructor in Auxiliary Forces); Royal Marine Artillery

Other Decorations: French Legion of Honour, the Turkish Crimea Medal and the British Crimea Medal with clasps for Balaclava, Inkerman and Sebastopol

VC Location: Royal Marines Museum, Southsea

Date of Gazette: 24 February 1857

Place/Date of Birth: York; 1831

Place/Date of Death: York; 22 September 1887

Grave: York Cemetery

Town/County Connections: York

Account of Deed: On 7 June 1855 at Sebastopol in the Crimea Bombardier Wilkinson was especially recommended for gallant conduct with the advanced batteries. He worked at the task of placing sandbags to repair damage done to the defences under a most galling fire.

Biographical Detail: Following the battle of Sebastopol Bombardier Wilkinson was written up on the occasion as worthy of special notice by the Commanding Officer of the Artillery of the Right Attack. He later achieved the post of sergeant instructor for the Auxiliary Forces and was eventually invalided from the Royal Marines Artillery on 12 October 1859.

Wilkinson died in York on 22 September 1887, aged fifty-five, and was buried there. The memorial stone raised by his comrades reads: 'Honour the brave. To the memory of Thomas Wilkinson, pensioner RMA, who died in the City of York 22 September 1887 and was interred with full military honours.'

WOOD, Harry Blanshard [1918]

Rank/Service: 16444 Corporal (Lance-Sergeant); 2nd Battalion, Scots Guards

Other Decorations: MM

VC Location: York Castle Museum

Date of Gazette: 14 December 1918

Place/Date of Birth: Newton-on-Derwent, Yorkshire; 21 June 1882
Place/Date of Death: Bristol; 15 August 1924
Grave: Arnos Vale Cemetery, Bristol
Town/County Connections: Newton-on-Derwent, Yorkshire; Bristol, Avon

Account of Deed: During operations at the village of St Python, France, on 13 October 1918 the advance was desperately opposed by machine guns and the streets were raked by fire. Wood's platoon sergeant was killed and command of the leading platoon fell to him. The task of the company was to clear the western side of the village and secure the crossing of the River Selle. Command of the ruined bridge had to be gained, though the space in front of it was covered by snipers. Corporal Wood boldly carried a large brick out into the open space, lay down behind it, and fired continually at these snipers, ordering his men to work across while he covered them by his fire. This he continued to do under heavy and well-aimed fire until the whole of his party had reached the objective point. He showed complete disregard for his personal safety, and his leadership throughout the day was of the highest order. Later, he drove off repeated enemy counter-attacks against his position. His gallant conduct and initiative contributed largely to the success of the day's operations.*

Biographical Detail: Harry Blanshard Wood was born on 21 June 1882 in the village of Newton-on-Derwent near Pocklington, North Yorkshire, and joined the Scots Guards on 3 February 1903. After the outbreak of the First World War in August 1914, Harry Wood was sent to France with the 2nd Battalion, Scots Guards, in October 1914 and was later awarded the Military Medal for gallantry.

On leaving the army, Wood's nerves were badly affected by his experiences in the war. While on holiday he was walking along a street with his wife when a car mounted the pavement and hurtled towards them. His wife pushed him out of the way, but she became pinned against a wall. Although she suffered only minor injuries, her husband was so shocked that he collapsed and fell into a deep coma, from which he never recovered. He died several days later in hospital.

On 27 October 2001 a ceremony took place in Arnos Vale Cemetery, Bristol, to erect a replacement headstone over the grave of Corporal Harry Wood VC, MM. Organised by the South Western Branch of the Scots Guards Association, the ceremony was attended by relatives and friends; the Royal British Legion, Bristol; the Regimental Adjutant, Scots Guards; and a party representing the regiment from Headquarters Scots Guards.

* *London Gazette*, 14 December 1918.

WYATT, George Harry [1915]

Rank/Service: Lance-Corporal (later Lance Sergeant); 3rd Battalion, Coldstream Guards

Other Decorations: 1914 Star and Bar; British War Medal; Victory Medal; 1937 and 1953 Coronation Medal; Russian Order of St George (3rd Class)

VC Location: Private (Not on public display)

Date of Gazette: 18 November 1915

Place/Date of Birth: Worcester; 5 September 1886

Place/Date of Death: Doncaster, Yorkshire; 22 January 1964

Grave: Cadeby Churchyard, near Doncaster, South Yorkshire. 'In loving memory of George Henry Wyatt, 'won the VC 25th August 1915' who died 22nd January 1964 aged 77 years. Also his beloved wife Ellen who died 20th August 1972 aged 81 years. At rest'

Town/County Connections: Worcester; Doncaster, Yorkshire

Account of Deed: On 25/26 August 1914 at Landrecies, France, part of Lance-Corporal Wyatt's battalion was hotly engaged close to some farm buildings, when the enemy set alight some straw sacks in the farmyard. The lance corporal twice dashed out under very heavy fire from the enemy, only 25 yards away, to extinguish the burning straw, thus making it possible to hold the position. Later, although wounded in the head, he continued firing until he could no longer see owing to the blood pouring down his face. The medical officer bound up his wound and ordered him to the rear, but he returned to the firing line and continued fighting.

Biographical Detail: George Henry Wyatt, the son of a groom, was born in Worcester on 5 September 1886. After attending Holloway School at Droitwich, he enlisted in the Coldstream Guards at Birmingham on 23 November 1904. He served with the 2nd Battalion at home and with the 3rd Battalion in Egypt. After serving in Egypt for two and a half years, he left the British Army in November 1904.

Wyatt joined the Barnsley Police Force and later transferred to the Doncaster Borough Police. He was recalled to the colours on the outbreak of the First World War as a reservist. He rejoined the 3rd Battalion, Coldstream Guards, and as a member of the British Expeditionary Force left for France on 14 August 1914. Soon after arriving on the Western Front, Wyatt took part in the battle of Mons. On two occasions he displayed outstanding bravery and was awarded the Victoria Cross. It was presented to him at Buckingham Palace on 4 March 1916. Wyatt returned to France and on 28 February was promoted to lance sergeant. He was wounded on two occasions.

Wyatt returned to the Doncaster constabulary in 1919 and in June 1924 bravely stopped a runaway horse. He retired from the police in February 1934 and took up farming. He died on 22 January 1964 and was buried at Cadeby Cemetery near Doncaster.

After the war George Wyatt was interviewed about winning the Victoria Cross:

> Well, there's not much for me to say about it. I just did as I was told. During the retirement from Mons the 3rd Coldstream Guards reached Landrecies. It was dark at the time, and there we were attacked by a large number of Germans who must have been rushed up in motor lorries. We lost our machine-gun, and had to rely solely upon rifle and bayonet. Suddenly something flared up between us and the enemy, and Major Matheson shouted, 'Put out that light'. So I did it. I never thought it would bring me the Victoria Cross. How did I put the fire out? Oh, I jumped on it and dragged some equipment over it. After a while it burst out again, and I ran back and extinguished it. Yes, there was heavy fire from the Germans when I first obeyed the order. At that affair at Villers Cotterets, I got hit on the head and went on firing. That's all.

Appendix

The *London Gazette* and Victoria Cross Recipients

In different publications about the Victoria Cross and its recipients, discrepancies may occur in the date on which an award was announced in the *London Gazette*. This is because awards were published in either the first issue of a particular *London Gazette* or in a subsequent supplement (or supplements). Many authors and publishers quote the original date of the *London Gazette*, even though the actual award of the VC was not published until a later supplement. Up to twelve supplements are known for some issues of the *London Gazette*.

In the following list the *London Gazette* and its supplements have been checked and the particular issue in which an award was first announced, whether it is an original *London Gazette* or its supplement, has been noted. *London Gazette* 31259, 31 March 1919, pp. 4153–4163 (4th Supplement to the *London Gazette* 31255, 28 March 1919) contains a consolidated list of action dates and locations for 346 VC recipients, this information not having been announced with the original citations for security reasons. However, many of these entries contained errors, which were corrected by *London Gazette* 31340, 15 May 1919, pp. 6084–6085 (4th Supplement to *London Gazette* 31336, 13 May 1919).

Abbreviations Used

Adm. – Admiralty Office
Air Min. – Air Ministry
LG – *London Gazette*
WO – War Office

Name	London Gazette	Date	Page No.	Supplement [if any]	Release Date
Aaron, AL	36235	05/11/1943	4859	4 Supp. *LG 36231 · 02/11/1943*	Air Min. 26/10/1943
Allen, WB	29802	26/10/1916	10394	4 Supp. *LG 29798 · 24/10/1916*	WO 26/10/1916
Anderson, E	36110	29/07/1943	3421	Supp. *LG 36109 · 27/07/1943*	WO 29/07/1943
Atkinson, A	34928	08/08/1902	5086	*London Gazette*	W/O 08/08/1902
Bell, DS	29740	09/09/1916	3041	5 Supp. *LG 36579 · 23/06/1944*	Air Min. 27/06/1944
Best-Dunkley, B	30272	06/09/1917	9259	5 Supp. *LG 30267 · 04/09/1917*	W/O 06/09/1917
Bryan, T	30122	08/06/1917	5705	2 Supp. *LG 30120 · 08/06/1917*	W/O 08/06/1917
Butler, WB	30338	17/10/1917	10678	2 Supp. *LG 30336 · 16/10/1917*	WO 17/10/1917
Calvert, L	31012	15/11/1918	13472	7 Supp. *LG 31005 · 12/11/1918*	WO 15/11/1918
Chafer, GW	29695	05/08/1916	7744	Supp. *LG 29694 · 04/08/1916*	W/O 05/08/1916
Cooper, E	30284	14/09/1917	9532	2 Supp. *LG 30282 · 14/09/1917*	W/O 14/09/1917
Coverdale, CH	30433	18/12/1917	13222	5 Supp. *LG 30428 · 14/12/1917*	WO 18/12/1917
Cunningham, J (Pte)	29901	13/01/1917	559	Supp. *LG 2990 · 12/01/1917*	WO 13/01/1917
Daniels, H	29146	28/04/1915	4143	Supp. *LG 29145 · 27/04/1915*	WO 28/04/1915
Dresser, T	30154	27/06/1917	6382	4 Supp. *LG 30150 · 26/06/1917*	WO 27/06/1917
Edwards, W	30284	14/09/1917	9533	2 Supp. *LG 30282 · 14/09/1917*	WO 14/09/1917
Esmonde, EK	35474	03/03/1942	1007	3 Supp. *LG 35471 · 27/02/1942*	Wh. 03/03/1942
Firth, J	27322	11/06/1901	3933	*London Gazette*	WO 11/06/1901
Grant, R	22396	19/06/1860	2316	*London Gazette* (as EWART)	WO 19/06/1860
Hackett, W	29695	05/08/1916	7744	Supp. *LG 29694 · 04/08/1916*	WO 05/08/1916
Harper, JW	36870	02/01/1945	139/40	5 Supp. *LG 36865 · 29/12/1944*	WO 02/01/1945
Harrison, J	30130	14/06/1917	5866	4 Supp. *LG 30126 · 12/06/1917*	WO 14/06/1917
Hedges, FW	31155	31/01/1919	1503	8 Supp. *LG 31147 · 28/01/1919*	WO 31/01/1919
Hill-Walker, AR	25084	14/03/1882	1130	*London Gazette*	WO 13/03/1882

Hirsch, DP	30130	14/06/1917	5865/6	4 Supp. *LG 30126 • 12/06/1917*	WO 14/06/1917
Hollis, SE	36658	17/08/1944	3807/8	Supp. *LG 36657 • 15/08/1944*	WO 17/08/1944
Holmes, J	22154	18/06/1858	2958	*London Gazette*	WO 18/06/1858
Hughes, M	21971	24/02/1857	658	Supp. *LG 21970 • 24/02/1857*	WO 24/02/1857
Hull, C	29496	03/03/1916	2349	*London Gazette*	WO 03/03/1916
Insall, GSM	29414	23/12/1915	12797/8	5 Supp. *LG 29409 • 21/12/1915*	WSO 23/12/1915
Jackson, TN	31034	27/11/1918	14040	2 Supp. *LG 1032 • 26/11/1918*	WO 27/11/1918
Lambert, G	22154	18/06/1858	2957	*London Gazette*	WO 18/06/1858
Loosemore, A	30284	14/09/1917	9533	2 Supp. *LG 30282 • 14/09/1917*	WO 14/09/1917
McKay, IJ	49134	11/10/1982	12831/2	Supp. *LG 49133 • 08/10/1982*	MOD (Army) 11/10/1982
McKenna, E	22809	19/01/1864	261	*London Gazette*	WO 16/01/1864
McNess, F	29802	26/10/1916	10395	4 Supp. *LG 29798 • 24/10/1916*	WO 26/10/1916
Magennis, JJ	37346	13/11/1945	5529/30	3 Supp. *LG 37343 • 09/11/1945*	Adm. 13/11/1945
Maufe, THB	30215	02/08/1917	7906	4 Supp. *LG 30211 • 31/07/1917*	WO 02/08/1917
Meekosha, S	29447	22/01/1916	946	2 Supp. *LG 29445 • 21/01/1916*	WO 22/01/1916
Mountain, A	30733	07/06/1918	6776	6 Supp. *LG 30727 • 04/06/1918*	WO 07/06/1918
Moynihan, A	21971	24/02/1857	658	Supp. *LG 21970 • 24/02/1857*	WO 24/02/1857
Napier, W	22212	24/12/1858	5517	*London Gazette*	WO 24/12/1858
Nicholls, H	34909	30/07/1940	4659/60	3 Supp. *LG 34906 • 26/07/1940*	WO 30/07/1940
Ormsby, JW	30122	08/06/1917	5704	2 Supp. *LG 30120 • 08/06/1917*	WO 08/06/1917
Pearson, J	22233	28/01/1859	294	*London Gazette*	WO 26/01/1859
Poulter, A	30770	28/06/1918	7620	6 Supp. *LG 30764 • 25/06/1918*	WO 28/06/1918
Proctor, AH	29695	05/08/1916	7744	Suppl *LG 29694 • 04/08/1916*	WO 05/08/1916
Raynes, JC	29371	18/11/1915	11449	3 Supp. *LG 29368 • 16/11/1915*	WO 18/11/1915
Ridgeway, RK	24843	11/05/1880	2968	*London Gazette*	WO 08/05/1880

Sanders, G	29740	09/09/1916	8870	Supp. LG 29739 • 08/09/1916	WO 09/09/1916
Sandford, RD	30807	23/07/1918	8586/6	4 Supp. LG 30803 • 19/07/1918	Adm.23/07/1918
Shepherd, AE	30523	13/02/1918	2005	Supp. LG 30522 • 12/02/1918	WO 13/02/1918
Shepherd, J	21971	24/02/1857	652/3	Supp. LG 21970 • 24/02/1857	WO 24/02/1857
Short, WH	29740	09/09/1916	8871	Supp. LG 29739 • 08/09/1916	WO 09/09/1916
Smith, JAG	29074	18/02/1915	1700	4 Supp LG 29070 • 16/02/1915	WO 18/02/1915
Sykes, E	30122	08/06/1917	5705/6	2 Supp. LG 30120 • 08/06/1917	WO 08/06/1917
Symons, G	22065	20/11/1857	3920	London Gazette	WO 18/11/1857
Traynor, WB	27356	17/09/1901	6101	London Gazette	WO 17/09/1901
Waller, H	30122	08/06/1917	5706	2 Supp. LG 30120 • 08/06/1917	WO 08/06/1917
Ward, CB	27233	28/09/1900	5966	London Gazette	WO 28/09/1900
White, ACT	29802	26/10/1916	10394	4 Supp. LG 29798 • 24/10/1916	WO 26/10/1916
White, J	30154	27/06/1917	6382	4 Supp. LG 30150 • 26/06/1917	WO 27/06/1917
Wilkinson, T	21971	24/02/1857	654	Supp. LG 21970 • 24/02/1857	WO 24/02/1857
Wood, HB	31067	14/12/1918	14777	2 Supp. LG 31065 • 13/12/1918	WO 14/12/1918
Wyatt, GH	29371	18/11/1915	11449	3 Supp. LG 29368 • 16/11/1915	WO 18/11/1915

Concise Glossary

Orders and Decorations

AFC – Air Force Cross.

AK – Knight of the Order of Australia.

BEM – British Empire Medal.

CB – Companion of the Most Honourable Order of the Bath.

CBE – Companion of the Order of the British Empire.

CD – Canadian Forces Decoration.

CGM – Conspicuous Gallantry Medal.

CIE – Companion of the Most Eminent Order of the Indian Empire.

CMG – Companion of the Most Distinguished Order of St Michael and St George.

CSI – Companion of the Most Exalted Order of the Star of India.

CVO – Companion of the Royal Victorian Order.

DCM – Distinguished Conduct Medal.

DFC – Distinguished Flying Cross.

DFM – Distinguished Flying Medal.

DSC – Distinguished Service Cross.

DSM – Distinguished Service Medal.

DSO – Distinguished Service Order.

ED – Efficiency Decoration.

GCB – Knight Grand Cross of the Most Honourable Order of the Bath.

GCMG – Knight Grand Cross of the Most Distinguished Order of St Michael and St George.

GCVO – Knight Grand Cross of the Royal Victorian Order.

IOM – Indian Order of Merit.

ISM – Indian Service Medal.

KBE – Knight Commander of the Order of the British Empire.

KCB – Knight Commander of the Most Honourable Order of the Bath.

KCIE – Knight Commander of the Most Eminent Order of the Indian Empire.

KCMG – Knight Commander of the Most Distinguished Order of St Michael and St George.

KCSI – Knight Commander of the Most Exalted Order of the Star of India.
KCVO – Knight Commander of the Royal Victorian Order.
MBE – Member of the British Empire.
MC – Military Cross.
MM – Military Medal.
MSM – – Meritorious Service Medal.
MVA – Maha Vir Chakra.
MVO – Member of the Royal Victorian Order.
OBE – Order of the British Empire.
OBI – Order of British India.
OM – Order of Merit.
PVSM – Pararn Vishishe Seva Medal (India).
RD – Reserve Decoration.
RVM – Royal Victorian Medal.
SGM – Sea Gallantry Medal.
TD – Territorial Decoration.
VD – Volunteer Decoration.

Acronyms and Specialist Terms

A tk Tp Cmd – Anti-tank Troop Commander.
AA/Ack-Ack – Anti-aircraft – slang from the phonetic alphabet in which 'Ack' stood for 'A'. By 1943 replaced by 'Able', and now 'Alpha'.
ADC – Aide-de-Camp, a general officer's personal assistant; civilian equivalent PA.
Adjutant – the CO's personal staff officer in a battalion or regiment in the British and Indian armies. In the Second World War, and for several years thereafter, there was no operations officer at this level, so the adjutant was responsible for all operational staff work as well as discipline and all other personnel matters.
ADS – Advanced Dressing Station.
AIF – Australian Imperial Forces.
Aldis Lamp – a hand-held lamp used for flashing Morse Code signals.
ALO – Army Liaison Officer.
AMF – Australian Military Forces.
AP – Armour-piercing (ammunition) – see **HE**.
ARP – Air Raid Precautions.
AWOL – Absent Without Leave.
'Ayo Gurkhali' – 'the Ghurkhas are coming', battle cry of Ghurkha troops.
Bde – Brigade.

BEF – British Expeditionary Force.

Besa – a machine-gun, originally Czech, used in British armoured cars and tanks in the Second World War in 7.92mm and 15mm forms.

BGS – Brigadier General Staff.

Blue – the name for the desert.

BM – Brigade Major, the senior operations officer of a brigade, *de facto* chief of staff.

Bn – Battalion.

Bofors – a quick-firing 40-mm anti-aircraft gun of Swedish design.

Bren – the British light machine-gun of the Second World War and until the late-1950s. Fired a standard .303-inch round from a thirty-round magazine (usually loaded with twenty-eight rounds).

Brevet – until the Second World War an officer could have a rank in the army separate from his rank in his regiment. The officer took his army (or brevet) rank when he served outside his regiment or when his unit was brigaded with another.

Brigade – a formation of two or more infantry battalions or armoured regiments, commanded by a brigadier.

BSM – Battery Sergeant Major.

Bty – Battery.

Carrier – a lightly armoured tracked vehicle, often called a Bren-gun carrier, although it was also used to carry the Vickers medium machine-gun, and for many other tasks.

CDL – Canal Defence Light, searchlight tank.

CEF – Canadian Expeditionary Force.

CF – Chaplain to the Forces.

CGS – Chief of the General Staff.

chagal leather or **skin** – water bottle.

chaung – Burmese for watercourse or minor river; could be as narrow as a ditch or wide enough for small craft, particularly near the coast.

C-in-C – Commander-in-Chief.

Colour Sergeant – the senior sergeant of an infantry company (cf. **Staff Sergeant**).

Commando – can refer to an individual commando soldier or marine, or to his unit. A commando unit was around 450 strong, divided into five rifle troops each of about sixty men, a support troop of Vickers medium machine-guns and 3-inch mortars and a headquarters troop. The 3rd Commando Brigade, which served in Burma, consisted of two army commandos, Nos 1 and 5 Commandos, and two Royal Marine commandos, 42 (RM) and 44 (RM) Commandos.

Coolies – slang for foreign manual labourers (usually Chinese).

Corps – a formation of at least two divisions commanded by a lieutenant general. Also a generic term for arms and services except armour, artillery and infantry, hence Corps of Royal Engineers, Royal Signals Corps, Royal Army Service Corps, Indian Army Service Corps, Royal Army Medical Corps, Indian Army Medical Corps and so on.

COS – Chief of Staff.

CP – Command Post.

CSM – Company Sergeant Major.

DCGS – Deputy Chief of the General Staff.

DCM – Distinguished Conduct Medal.

DD – Duplex Drive, amphibious tank.

DF – Defensive Fire.

Dhoolie – 'rudimentary litter or palanquin used by lower classes in India, and as an army ambulance' (*OED*).

Division – a formation of two or more brigades commanded by a major general.

dorp – village.

DS – Director Station.

Duck/DUKW – American six-wheeled amphibious truck (pronounced 'duck').

DY – dockyard.

DZ – Drop Zone.

EA – Enemy Aircraft.

Echelon – the troops who man the rear, with supply dumps, cooks, etc..

(ER) – Extra Reserve.

FAA – Fleet Air Arm.

Flak – anti-aircraft fire, derived from the German *fliegerabwehrkanone*, later adopted universally by all sides.

F/O – Flying Officer.

gabion – a basket or container filled with stones, rubble, etc.

Ghazis – 'Muslim fanatics who have devoted themselves to the destruction of infidels' (*OED*).

GHQ – General Headquarters.

GOP – General Officer Commanding.

GP – General Purpose.

griff – rumour.

GRO – General Routine Order.

GSO – General Staff Officer, a staff officer who dealt with general (G) staff matters (operations, intelligence, planning and staff duties), as opposed to personnel (A) or logistic matters (Q). The grades were GSO1 (lieutenant colonel), GSO2 (major) and GSO3 (captain). The GSO1 in a division was the senior operations staff officer, effectively the chief of staff. The AAG, or Assistant Adjutant General, was the senior personnel staff officer in a division, and the AQMG, or Assistant Quartermaster General, was the senior logistics staff officer in a division.

HA – High Angle.

HE – High Explosive.

IFF – Identification Friend or Foe.

IO – Intelligence Officer.

Japs – derogatory term used during the period to describe the Japanese.

Jerry – derogatory term used during the period to describe Germans.

Jocks – slang for soldiers in Scottish regiments.

kop, kopje – small isolated hill.

KOYLI – King's Own Yorkshire Light Infantry.

KRRC – King's Royal Rifle Corps.

LAA – Light anti-aircraft, gun or regiment.

LCA – Landing Craft Assault.

LCG – Landing Craft Gun.

LCVP – Landing Craft Vehicle Personnel.

LMG – Light Machine-Gun.

LO – Liaison Officer.

LSI – Landing Ship Infantry.

LST – Landing Ship Tank.

Martial Class – the British Indian Army was mainly recruited from what were known as the martial classes (sometimes known as martial races), such as Sikhs, Jats, Rajputs, Ghurkas, Garwhalis, Dogras, Kumaonis, Punjabi-Mussulman (Punjab Muslims) and Pathans.

MDS – Main Dressing Station.

MO – Medical Officer.

MT – Motor Transport.

MTB – Motor Torpedo Boat.

Naga – Burmese hill tribe who worked as scouts.

NCO – Non-Commissioned Officer, lance corporal to colour sergeant.

nek – a pass in mountainous territory.

nullah – steep, narrow valley.

NZEF – New Zealand Expeditionary Force.

Oerlikon – 20 mm Swiss-made anti-aircraft gun.

PIAT – Projectile Infantry Anti-Tank. British shoulder-fired weapon issued from mid-1942, consisting of a tube containing a powerful spring that threw a hollow-charge projectile, effective up to 100 yards.

Pick-a-Back – air-launched V1 missile.

P/O – Pilot Officer.

Python Scheme – Scheme for repatriation to the UK of long-serving British troops.

Pz Lehr Division – Panzer Demonstration Division.

OC – Officer Commanding.

OP – Observation Post.

Pugree, puggaree – turban.

QGO – Queen's Ghurkha Officer.

QMG – Quartermaster General.

(R) – Regular battalion. See also **(S)** and **(T)**.

RA – Royal Artillery.

RAAF – Royal Australian Air Force.

RAF – Royal Air Force.

RAMC – Royal Army Medical Corps.

RAOC – Royal Army Ordnance Corps.

RASC – Royal Army Service Corps.

RCAF – Royal Canadian Air Force.

RE – Royal Engineers.

Regiment – (British and Indian Army) originally of horse, dragoons or foot, raised by command of monarch, and later Parliament, and named after its colonel, originally a royal appointee. The regiment became the basic unit of organisation of the British and Indian Army, for armour, artillery, engineers, signals, and logistic units equivalent to battalions of those arms in other armies. In the case of the infantry, the British or Indian Army battalion belongs to a regiment, of which there may be one or more battalions, which may not serve together in the same area, or even in the same theatre of operations. The Indian Army reorganisation of 1922 formed infantry regiments of up to British Army Equivalent six battalions each, and, on the outbreak of war, many more battalions.

Regt – Regiment.

RHA – Royal Horse Artillery.

RN – Royal Navy.

RSM – Regimental Sergeant Major.

(S) – Service battalion, e.g. a battalion of new army volunteers. See also **(R)** and **(T)**.

SAMC – South African Medical Corps.

Sangar – breastwork of stone.

sap – a trench or tunnel that conceals an approach to a defended position.

Sapper – Royal Engineers' equivalent to private, often used as a term for all engineers.

SEAC – South East Asia Command. The Supreme Allied Commander SEAC, Admiral Mountbatten, was responsible directly to the British Chiefs of Staff in London, and through them to the Combined British and US Chiefs of Staff for all operations by land, sea and air in Burma, Malaya and Sumatra, and for clandestine operations in Thailand and French Indo-China.

Sowar – 'a native horseman or mounted orderly, policeman, etc; a native trooper, esp. one belonging to the irregular cavalry' (*OED*).

Spandau – Allied name for the German MG34 and MG42 infantry machine-guns, and by extension any machine-gun.

spruit – stream or watercourse.

SR – Special Reserve.

Staff Sergeant – the senior sergeant of a non-infantry company (cf. **Colour Sergeant**).

Sten – gun a cheap, mass-produced submachine-gun of British design. It fired 9mm ammunition, and had a thirty-two-round magazine. Ineffective except at close quarters, it was inaccurate and the round had poor penetrating power. Its propensity to fire by mistake could make it more dangerous to its owner and those standing around than to the enemy.

(T) – Territorial battalion. See also **(R)** and **(S)**.

TBD – Torpedo Boat Destroyer.

TCP – Traffic Control Person.

TI – Torpedo Instructor.

TM – trench mortar.

Traverse – 'a pair of right-angled bends incorporated in a trench to avoid enfilading fire' (*COD*).

tulwar – Indian sabre.

UNRRA – United Nations Relief and Rehabilitation Administration.

veldt – open country.

Very – a smooth-bore pistol for firing green, white or red signal cartridges.

Vickers – slang for a specific medium machine-gun; belt fed, water-cooled, with a firing rate of 500 rounds per minute. Last fired in action in 1962.

Wadi – Arabic for valley.

wallah – an Anglo-Indian civilian and army slang expression mean 'chap' or 'fellow'. Often associated with a profession, or someone in charge of a particular activity; for example, the 'amen wallah' is the chaplain, the 'ghorry wallah' is the driver, and the 'box wallah' is a businessman.

Wop(s)/Ities – derogatory term used during the period to describe Italians.

WRNS – Women's Royal Naval Service.

Bibliography

Since 1855 many books have been published about the Victoria Cross and about individual winners of the award. Listed here are some of those books, together with general histories that deal with the background to the campaigns and battles, in which these awards were won. Three books deserve special mention: Chaz Bowyer, *For Valour: The Air VCs* (Kimber, London, 1978; Grub Street, 1992 edn); John Winton, *The Victoria Cross at Sea* (Michael Joseph, London, 1978); and *The Register of the Victoria Cross*, compiled and researched by Nora Buzzell for the quarterly magazine *This England* (Cheltenham, 1981 and 1988).

Bowyer's book, which covers all air VCs from 1914, is the result of exemplary and painstaking research. Delving beyond the citations, Bowyer interviewed VC winners, their comrades, friends and families. In this way he was able to prove, for instance, that Flight Sergeant Arthur Aaron was not shot down and killed by an enemy fighter but by the gunner of another British aircraft. For this revelation he was vilified by the head of the Air Historical Branch, who considered that citations were sacrosanct. He was mistaken; it is an historian's responsibility to find out and tell the truth, and this Bowyer does in *The Air VCs*.

Winton does a similar service for the Royal Navy, describing in detail the sea actions in which Victoria Crosses were won. This England's *Register of the Victoria Cross* presents a condensed version of every VC citation published between 1855 and 1982, with a small photograph of virtually every Victoria Cross winner. For VC holders after this date there are now a number of excellent works, many coming after the interest aroused by the 150th anniversary of the instigation of the Victoria Cross.

Arthur, Max (2004), *Symbol of Courage* (Sidgwick & Jackson).
—— (2002), *Forgotten Voices of the Great War* (Imperial War Museum).
Ashcroft, Lord Michael (2006; pb 2007), *Victoria Cross Heroes* (Headline Books).
Bancroft, James W. (1989), *The Victoria Cross Roll of Honour* (Aim High Productions).

—— (1994), *Deeds of Valour: A Victorian Military and Naval History Trilogy* (House of Heroes).

—— (2003), *Local Heroes: Boer War VCs* (House of Heroes).

—— (2004), *Zulu War Heroes: The Defence of Rorke's Drift* (James W. Bancroft).

Batchelor, Peter F. and Matson, Christopher (1999), *VCs of the First World War: The Western Front 1915* (Wrens Park Publishing).

Bond, Brian (ed.) (1967), *Victorian Military Campaigns* (Hutchinson).

Braddon, Russell (1954), *Cheshire VC* (Evans Brothers).

Cooksley, Peter G. (1999), *VCs of the First World War: The Air VCs* (Wrens Park Publishing).

Cowper, Marcus (2010), *The Words of War: British Forces' Personal Letters and Diaries During WW2* (Mainstream Publishing/Imperial War Museum).

Crawthorne, Nigel (2007), *The True Story behind every VC Winner since WW2* (John Blake).

Creagh, Sir O'Moore and Humphris, E.M. (eds), *The V.C. and D.S.O. Book: The Victoria Cross 1856–1920* (Naval & Military Press).

Crook, M.J. (1975), *The Evolution of the Victorian Cross* (Midas Books).

Doherty, Richard and Truesdale, David (2000), *Irish Winners of the Victoria Cross* (Four Courts Press).

Farwell, Byron (1999), *Queen Victoria's Little Wars* (Allen Lane, 1973; repr., Wordsworth).

Featherstone, Donald (1989), *Victoria's Enemies: A–Z of British Colonial Warfare* (Blandford).

Feilding, Rowland (1929), *War Letters to a Wife* (Medici Society, London).

Fraser, George MacDonald (1992), *Quartered Safe Out Here: A Recollection of the War in Burma* (HarperCollins, London).

Fraser, Ian (1957), *Frogman VC* (Angus & Robertson, London).

Giddings, Robert (1996), *Imperial Echoes: Eye-Witness Accounts of Victoria's Little Wars* (Leo Cooper).

Gilbert, Martin (1989), *The Second World War* (Weidenfeld & Nicolson).

Glanfield, John (2005), *Bravest of the Brave: The Story of the Victoria Cross* (Sutton Publishing, Stroud).

Gliddon, Gerald (1997), *VCs of the First World War: The Somme* (Budding Books).

—— (1997), *VCs of the First World War: 1914* (Budding Books).

—— (1997), *VCs of the First World War: Spring Offensive 1918* (Sutton Publishing).

—— (2000), *VCs of the First World War: Arras and Messines 1917* (Wrens Park Publishing).

—— (2000), *VCs of the First World War: The Final Days 1918* (Sutton Publishing).

—— (2000), *VCs of the First World War: The Road to Victory 1918* (Sutton Publishing).

Gordon, Lawrence and Joslin, Edward (eds) (1971), *British Battles and Medals* (Spink & Son).

Gurney, Major Gene, USAF (1962), *The War in the Air* (New York).

Harris, Barry (1985), *Black Country VCs* (The Black Country Society).

Harris, C. and Whippy, J. (2000), *The Greater Game – Sporting Icons who fell in the Great War* (Pen & Sword).

Hart, Sydney (1966), *Submarine Upholder (Wanklyn VC)* (Melrose, London).

Harvey, David (1999), *Monuments to Courage: Victoria Cross Headstones and Memorials Vols. 1 and 2* (Kevin & Kay Patience, 1999; repr., Naval & Military Press).

Hastings, Macdonald (1959), *More Men of Glory* (Hulton Press, London).

Haydon, A.L. (1906), *The Book of the VC* (Andrew Melrose).

Haythornthwaite, Philip J. (1997), *The Colonial Wars Source Book* (Arms & Armour Press).

HMSO, *Victoria Cross Centenary Exhibition 1856–1956* (HMSO, London).

Holmes, Richard (2006), *The First World War in Photographs* (Carlton Books/ IWM).

Jameson, William S. (1962), *Submariners VC* (Peter Davies, London).

Keegan, John (1989), *The Second World War* (Hutchinson, London).

Kirby, H.L. and Walsh, R.R. (1987), *Seven VCs of Stonyhurst College* (THCL Books, Blackburn).

Kitson, Lt-Col. J.A. (1949), *Story of the 4th Battalion 2nd King Edward VII's Own Ghurkha Rifles* (Gale & Polden).

Laffin, John (2000), *British VCs of World War 2: A Study in Heroism* (Budding Books).

Lassen, Suzanne (1965), *Anders Lassen VC: Story of a Courageous Dane* (Muller, London).

Liddle, Peter (2004) *D-Day by those Who Were There* (Pen & Sword Books).

Macdonald, W. James (1995), *A Bibliography of the Victoria Cross* (Privately published by author, Beddeck, Nova Scotia).

Macmillan, Norman (1944), *The Royal Air Force in the Second World War*, vol. 2, *1940–1941* (Harrap, London).

Magor, R.B (1993), *African General Service Medals* (R.B. Magor, 1979; repr., Naval & Military Press).

Massie, Alastair (2004), *The National Army Museum Book of the Crimean War: The Untold Stories* (Sidgwick & Jackson).

Masters, John (1961), *The Road Past Mandalay* (Michael Joseph, London).

Ministry of Information (1943), *Victoria Cross: Stories of VC Awards during the Second World War Up to June 1943* (London, 1943).

Morgan, M. (2004), *D-Day Hero: CSM Stanley Hollis VC* (Sutton Publishing).

Mulholland, John and Jordan, Alan (eds), (1999), *Victoria Cross Bibliography* (Victoria Cross Research Group, Spink & Son).

Owen, Frank (1946), *The Campaign in Burma* (The HMSO Official Report).

Pakenham, Thomas (1979), *The Boer War* (Weidenfeld & Nicolson, 1979; Avon Books).

—— (2002), *The Scramble for Africa* (Weidenfeld & Nicolson, 1991; Abacus).

Parrish, Thomas (ed.) (1978), *The Simon and Schuster Encyclopaedia of World War 2* (New York).

Pemberton, W. Baring (1969), *Battles of the Boer War* (Batsford, 1964; Pan Books).

Phillips, C.E. Lucas (1973), *Victoria Cross Battles of the Second World War* (Heinemann).

Ralph, Wayne (1997), *Barker VC: The Life, Death and Legend of Canada's Most Decorated War Hero* (Grub Street).

Richards, D.S. (2003), *The Savage Frontier: A History of the Anglo-Afghan Wars* (Macmillan, 1990; Pan Books).

Roe, F. Gordon (1945), *The Bronze Cross: Tribute to those who won the Supreme Award for Valour in the Years 1940–45* (P.R. Gawthorn).

Sandford, Kenneth (1962), *Mark of the Lion: The Story of Capt. Charles Upham, VC & Bar* (Hutchinson).

Scott, Kenneth Hare (1949), *For Valour* (Garnett, London).

Sims, Edward H. (1967), *The Fighter Pilots* (Cassell, London).

Smyth, Sir John (1963), *The Story of the Victoria Cross 1856–1963* (Muller, London).

Snelling, Stephen (1999), *VCs of the First World War: Gallipoli* (Wrens Park Publishing).

—— (1998), *VCs of the First World War: Passchendaele 1917* (Sutton Publishing).

Sowards, Stuart E. (1987), *A Formidable Hero: R.H. Gray VC* (Canav Books, Toronto).

Stevens, Lt-Col. G.R. (1952), *History of the 2nd King Edward VII's Own Ghurka Rifles*, Vol. 3 (Aldershot).

Thompson, Julian (2009), *Forgotten Voices of Burma* (Ebury Press/Imperial War Museum).

Turner, John Frayn (1960), *VCs of the Air* (Harrap, London).

—— (1956), *VCs of the Army, 1939–1951* (Harrap, London).

—— (1956), *VCs of the Royal Navy* (Harrap, London).
Whitman, J.E.A. (1941), *Gallant Deeds of the War* (OUP).

Journals and Magazines

Frost, Richard (ed.) (2001), *Journal of the King's Royal Rifle Corps Association* (The King's Royal Rifle Corps Association).
Best, Brian (ed.) (2004) *Journal of the Victoria Cross Society*, editions 1–4 (The Victoria Cross Society).
The Regiment of Fusiliers (1999, English Life Publications).
The Register of the Victoria Cross (1988, This England Books).

Websites

National Archives – www.nationalarchives.gov.uk/documentsonline
National Archives Library – www.library.nationalarchives.gov.uk/library
London Gazette newspaper – www.gazette-online.co.uk
Oxford Dictionary of Biography – www.oxforddnb.com
Grave sites – www.findagrave.com
Imperial War Museum – www.iwm.org
Ministry of Defence Records – www.mod.uk/defencenews
Rorke's Drift – www.rorkesdrift.com
Green Howards Regiment – www.greenhowards.org.uk
Australian VC holders – www.diggerhistory.info
Victoria Cross – www.victoriacross.org.uk
Victoria Cross Society – www.victoriacrosssociety.com

Index